Praise for *Blockchain* ~~Success Stories~~

I don't think I've ever had as much fun learning about a technology protocol as I had while reading *Blockchain Success Stories*. The authors use characters and stories masterfully to entertain while delivering a huge payload of knowledge. As I read the book, I couldn't help but get nostalgic about the early days of the web, when only the most technically savvy among us could figure out how to produce and consume content in a browser. The following 20 years brought us YouTube, Facebook, Twitter, Snapchat, TikTok, and countless other society-changing platforms. It's inspiring to think about the opportunities the blockchain may offer to create value and transform lives over the next 20 years!

—*Gregg Spiridellis,*
Founder of JibJab, Storybots, and HiHo Video

I was most impressed with the case studies in which blockchain technology addresses real-world problems like voting, supply chain, and especially credentialing. In today's world, it is preposterous that we still email around PDFs with sensitive financial information or protect a file cabinet or hidden drawer with our sacred documents (birth certificate, marriage license, immunization records, etc.) like it was 1950. If Apple Pay can eliminate the need to carry around a wallet full of credit cards, then blockchain can create an accurate, validated, securely accepted version of those closely guarded sacred paper relics. After reading this book, I can think of 50 credentialing/validation applications for the securities and banking industry.

—*Stephen D. Sautel,*
Former COO and cofounder of Guggenheim Investments'
Corporate Credit Group

Finally, a book that goes beyond the hype and explains how entrepreneurs are making blockchain technology work in the real world. *Blockchain Success Stories* provides an easy-to-understand, highly engaging, and eminently readable primer on how blockchain works and what you can do with it. The detailed case studies the authors develop and lessons they distill offer practical insights and actionable ideas for newcomers and experienced blockchain entrepreneurs alike.

—*Brian Ray,*
Leon M. and Gloria Plevin Professor of Law,
Director, Center for Cybersecurity and Privacy Protection,
Cleveland-Marshall College of Law

"The most successful blockchain professors are also blockchain students." As a professor of management, I love this quote. Hargrave and Karnoupakis lay a solid foundation for blockchain fundamentals and share real-world cases to highlight the current state. They also create a space to imagine the future which is a wonderful gift for me as an educator. This is essential reading for educators *and* their students.

—*Scott J. Allen, Ph.D.,*
Standard Products—Dr. James S. Reid Chair in Management,
John Carroll University

Hargrave and Karnoupakis possess a unique ability to take complex subject matter and then use analogies and stories to explain both its intricacies and relevance to any audience. I now see the potential for blockchain technology and how it would impact my industry. This is the team that I would want to write my story!

—*Michael Rinzler,*
Founder of Wicked Cool Toys and
EVP/Partner, Jazwares

Blockchain Success Stories

Case Studies from the Leading Edge of Business

Sir John Hargrave and Evan Karnoupakis

Beijing · Boston · Farnham · Sebastopol · Tokyo

Blockchain Success Stories

by Sir John Hargrave and Evan Karnoupakis

Copyright © 2021 Sir John Hargrave and Evan Karnoupakis. All rights reserved.

Published by O'Reilly Media, Inc., 1005 Gravenstein Highway North, Sebastopol, CA 95472.

O'Reilly books may be purchased for educational, business, or sales promotional use. Online editions are also available for most titles (*http://oreilly.com*). For more information, contact our corporate/institutional sales department: 800-998-9938 or *corporate@oreilly.com*.

Acquisitions Editor: Michelle Smith

Development Editor: Amelia Blevins

Production Editor: Kristen Brown

Copyeditor: Sharon Wilkey

Proofreader: Piper Editorial, LLC

Indexer: Ellen Troutman-Zaig

Interior Designer: Monica Kamsvaag

Cover Designer: Randy Comer

Illustrator: Rob Romano

November 2020:   First Edition

Revision History for the First Edition

2020-10-19:   First Release

See *http://oreilly.com/catalog/errata.csp?isbn=9781098114824* for release details.

The O'Reilly logo is a registered trademark of O'Reilly Media, Inc. *Blockchain Success Stories*, the cover image, and related trade dress are trademarks of O'Reilly Media, Inc.

978-1-098-11482-4

[LSI]

Contents

Introduction: Start with a Story

The opportunity of a technology like blockchain isn't to free us from trust in our institutions; it should be described as an experiment in building new kinds of collective institutions that we can trust. Trust is the currency of civilization.[1]

—Tim O'Reilly, founder and CEO, O'Reilly Media

Stories matter.

The human brain is hardwired for stories. Our earliest lessons come from children's stories—fairy tales and fables—always with a great lesson, a moral to the story. From the story of Cinderella, we learn *Beauty is skin deep*. From the myth of Icarus, we learn *Don't fly too close to the sun*. From practically every movie ever made, we learn *Good will triumph over evil*.

Stories are how we make meaning out of this funhouse ride called life. Stories are how we package up great human truths, then share them with future generations. Stories are how we get important concepts to latch on to the brain. Stories are sticky.

When your two authors were in business school, one of the most helpful methods of learning was the *case study*, which is a type of business story. In a case study, you're dropped into a real-world scenario—maybe you're the *New York Times* trying to go digital, or the CEO of Disney deciding whether to acquire

---

1 Tim O'Reilly, "Why America Slept," Medium, From the WTF? Economy to the Next Economy, Mar. 17, 2018, wtfeconomy.com/why-america-slept-cbd403810add.

Pixar. The case study ends at a point in time—like the end of a chapter—and you have to figure out what to do next. *You have to continue the story.*

Case studies are fun to read because they're real-world stories. They're interesting to analyze because, like business itself, there's no right or wrong answer. They're easier to remember because, instead of memorizing facts, you have a real-world example that will stick on to your brain like Velcro.

This is a book of stories.

They're not just any stories; they're stories of *people who built successful blockchain projects.* By reading these stories, you'll learn how to build successful blockchain projects yourself. This is not a blockchain programming book—there are plenty of those—but a book on *how to actually build billion-dollar blockchains.*

If you're new to blockchain, don't worry. We'll teach you the basics of this fascinating technology, using stories of the mysterious misfits who built the earliest blockchain projects. (Truth, you will see, is stranger than fiction.)

You'll also hear firsthand from the entrepreneurs and dreamers who successfully built billion-dollar blockchains, from their first shaky steps to their glorious victory laps. We'll bring their stories to life, from the roller-coaster highs to the death-valley lows. You'll breathe the stories through their lungs: the opportunities and the mistakes, the heart-wrenching challenges and the adrenaline-fueled triumphs.

Everywhere we'll tell you the moral of the story, in the form of *best practices* that you can take to your own technology project. These stories will stick.

Our audience for this book is the business leader of tomorrow. Whether you're a young entrepreneur or a seasoned technology manager, whether you're a student reading one of these stories in the classroom or a forward-thinking executive, we've written this as your reference guide. It's the bible of business blockchain.

What You'll Learn in This Book

We're not academics; we're entrepreneurs.

That means we're down in the trenches of building our own blockchain business. This is the book that we wish we'd had when we started. It's not just theory; it's a practical, real-world view of how to build blockchains.

We do blockchain consulting work for businesses and governments (see Chapter 13), which puts us in close proximity to the executives, entrepreneurs, and investors who are driving the blockchain ecosystem. We are always on the lookout for successful blockchain projects—not just blue-sky ideas but real projects with real users. (Generating ideas is easy; generating users is hard.)

Typically, business technology leaders—our clients—will get excited about blockchain, then try to explain it to their colleagues. Forty-five minutes later, their coworkers will be fast asleep, while they keep excitedly chattering away about "Merkle trees" and "zero-knowledge proofs."

Blockchain *is* exciting (if you're not already excited, get ready), but we wanted to help business leaders convey their excitement without getting mired in the excrement. In these stories, you'll get the broad strokes of the technology (enough to be dangerous), but more important, you'll learn practical applications (enough to stay safe).

We carefully selected our stories to represent these different applications of blockchain: from reimagining the global economy (Chapter 5), to reinventing government (Chapter 7), to rebuilding developing nations (Chapter 8). These are big ideas, dreamed up by larger-than-life characters, from a viral hitmaker (Chapter 6), to a government power player (Chapter 10), to the cofounder of Napster (Chapter 4).

These stories were also infused with hard-won lessons from writing our bestselling guide, *Blockchain for Everyone* (Gallery Books, 2019); the businessperson's guide, *What Is Blockchain?* (O'Reilly, 2019); and our industry overview, *State of Blockchain* (O'Reilly, 2020).

If you're new to blockchain, get ready for a wild ride. And it all starts with the amazing origin story that you'll read in the very first chapter.

How This Book Is Organized

In part 1 (Chapters 1–3), you'll learn the story of blockchain as we explain the technology by using real-world examples of the people and projects who have built the industry today. They're colorful characters, and you'll enjoy reading about their brilliant ideas and innovations.

In part 2 (Chapters 4–13), we'll cover real-world examples of blockchain being used in real-world businesses. You'll learn how these businesses overcame obstacles, and how they reaped rewards from this new technology, with battletested principles that you can immediately put into action.

In part 3 (Chapter 14), we'll lock in this learning with a set of blockchain best practices that will get you started on building your own blockchain success story.

After reading this book, you'll be able to discuss blockchain confidently with your colleagues and not just keep them awake but keep them *excited*. You'll understand how blockchain is fundamentally rewiring the world, and how to reposition yourself in this new world order. Finally, you'll unlock a wealth of new ideas for how to generate new wealth.

Because this is a collection of stories, you can dip into the chapters that seem most relevant to you and your industry. However, because we build on key blockchain principles as we go along, you'll get the most out of this book if you read (then reread) it from cover to cover.

If you want to learn about blockchain, then let us tell you a story...

—Sir John Hargrave and Evan Karnoupakis
July 2020

O'Reilly Online Learning

 For more than 40 years, *O'Reilly Media* has provided technology and business training, knowledge, and insight to help companies succeed.

Our unique network of experts and innovators share their knowledge and expertise through books, articles, and our online learning platform. O'Reilly's online learning platform gives you on-demand access to live training courses, in-depth learning paths, interactive coding environments, and a vast collection of text and video from O'Reilly and 200+ other publishers. For more information, visit *http://oreilly.com*.

How to Contact Us

Please address comments and questions concerning this book to the publisher:

O'Reilly Media, Inc.

1005 Gravenstein Highway North

Sebastopol, CA 95472

800-998-9938 (in the United States or Canada)

707-829-0515 (international or local)

707-829-0104 (fax)

We have a web page for this book, where we list errata, examples, and any additional information. You can access this page at *https://oreil.ly/blockchain-success-stories*.

Email *bookquestions@oreilly.com* to comment or ask technical questions about this book.

Visit *http://oreilly.com* for news and information about our books and courses.

Find us on Facebook: *http://facebook.com/oreilly*

Follow us on Twitter: *http://twitter.com/oreillymedia*

Watch us on YouTube: *http://www.youtube.com/oreillymedia*

What Is Blockchain?

What is blockchain?

Ask 50 technology leaders this question, and you'll probably get 50 different answers. Most business leaders know that blockchain is an important technology that's changing the world, but they struggle to simply explain it. They grasp the main concepts, but when they try to put them into plain language, everyone ends up more confused.

Most blockchain experts, on the other hand, struggle to explain it simply. It's as if you asked them to explain a car, and they launched into a 10-minute monologue about the physics of internal combustion engines. Meanwhile, you're thinking, *I really just wanted to know what makes a car go vroom.*

Simplifying is difficult, so we'll work hard to make things simple.

In this chapter, we'll explain what blockchain is, with easy-to-understand examples and diagrams. Through our writing, speaking, and consulting work, we've tested these examples with thousands of people worldwide, so we know they're useful, understandable, and (most important) memorable.

So even if you're an expert, this section is worth reading. You'll benefit from having a common language with which to talk about blockchain, using words that will resonate, making your voice echo in distant lands.

If you're a beginner, you're in for a treat. These are the stories of the great blockchain pioneers, the visionary geniuses who built this technology that we love so much.

But first, we need to answer that simple question: what is blockchain?

Blockchain: The Simple Definition

Blockchain is the Internet of Value.

Think about something that holds value for you. You might say your relationships, your pets, or your treasured diary from fourth grade. But for this discussion, let's focus on things that are a *store of value*, meaning things we generally *trust* and *agree* will hold their value.

Money is an obvious store of value: if someone gives you a dollar, it will generally be worth a dollar in the future. Lots of agreement, plenty of trust. But many other types of value exist: stocks and bonds, gold and silver, frequent-flier miles and Starbucks rewards points.

Blockchain is like a new kind of internet that lets us send and receive this value to each other. Just as today's internet lets us share *information*, blockchain lets us share *value*.

Think back to the olden days of yore, before the internet. If you had a question, you went to the library. There you located an encyclopedia, looked up the appropriate fact, and then discovered the encyclopedia was 10 years old and offered no help.

Today, of course, information is available in real time on the internet. Wikipedia contains the sum total of human knowledge, accessible from a device that fits in your pocket. When a new movie or product is announced, fan pages and blog posts instantly appear. Social media is like a real-time feed into human brains.

Before the internet, information had to be hand-pumped out of schools and libraries. Today we have a firehose of facts. *Any* information is available at *any* time, *any* place in the world. We live in the Information Age, an explosion of knowledge that will out-Renaissance the Renaissance.

But the internet was only act 1. Blockchain is act 2, allowing *value* to be shared as easily as information.

For example, today it's still kind of hard to send money. Sure, we have Venmo, Alipay, Google Pay, Apple Pay, and PayPal, but that's five competing standards (and there are many more). There's no all-in-one global payment app, except cash. But cash has plenty of other problems: every country has its own, it's easy to lose, and (since it's anonymous) criminals love it.

When it comes to sharing value, it's like we're still looking up facts in library encyclopedias.

As an analogy, imagine you could send money as easily as sending email: just type in the recipient address, the amount, and hit Send. That's the kind of easy, trusted, friction-free experience made possible by blockchain.

Just as Wikipedia made encyclopedias obsolete, and email made paper mail obsolete, blockchain is making the cash in your wallet obsolete, replacing it with something that's way faster and way more convenient (Figure 1-1).

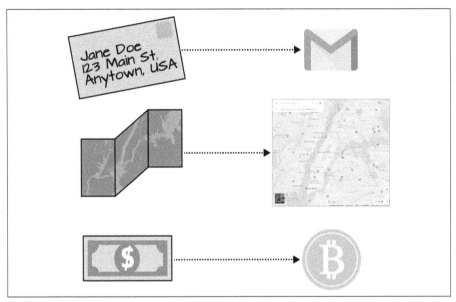

Figure 1-1. The evolution of paper to digital

Digital delivery is faster and cheaper than pushing paper. It's trackable and auditable. It also generates data, which can be fed back into computers for analysis and improvements, making transactions faster and cheaper still.

That's why most of the enterprise technology projects of the past 50 years have been focused on moving business systems from *paper* to *digital*: email, websites, cloud computing, big data, and analytics. Indeed, the trend is called *digital transformation*—and the trend is not only accelerating but also reshaping the global economy.[1]

---

1 "IDC Sees the Dawn of the DX Economy and the Rise of the Digital-Native Enterprise," *Business Wire*, November 1, 2016, *https://www.businesswire.com/news/home/20161101005193/en/IDC-Sees-Dawn-DX-Economy-Rise-Digital-Native*.

Blockchain technology plays an important role in this digital transformation —this shift from paper to digital—by making it easier to send and receive value.

Let's say, for example, that we're tracking the flow of a dollar. Each time a dollar changes hands—going from Alice to Bob, then Bob to Carol, then Carol to Devansh—we write that transaction to a *block* of data, and then we add that block to a *chain* of other blocks, as illustrated in Figure 1-2.

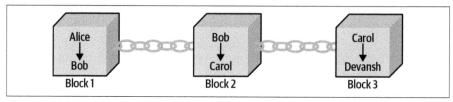

Figure 1-2. How to diagram a blockchain: blocks represent transactions and chains show the sequence of transactions

To understand how these blocks and chains work in real life, let's look at the first successful use case of blockchain: the digital currency called **bitcoin**.

Definition

Bitcoin: The first successful (and most successful) blockchain project, launched in 2008 by the mysterious Satoshi Nakamoto.

Bitcoin: The Blockchain Origin Story

It's one of the great mysteries of history: who invented bitcoin?

On Halloween 2008, a costumed character going by the name of Satoshi Nakamoto released a world-changing document called "Bitcoin: A Peer-to-Peer Electronic Cash System."[2] Published to an early message board for cryptography enthusiasts, it was part technical whitepaper, part political manifesto.

In the paper, the anonymous author painted a vision for a new kind of "e-cash" that could be sent worldwide as easily as sending an email: in short, moving from paper money to digital money. In the process, bitcoin would rewrite the rules of the global financial system, which was still in the throes of the 2008 financial crisis.

---

2 Satoshi Nakamoto, "Bitcoin: A Peer-to-Peer Electronic Cash System," Bitcoin.org, October 31, 2008, *https://bitcoin.org/bitcoin.pdf.*

For blockchain enthusiasts, the bitcoin whitepaper has since taken on the quality of holy scripture, with each section meticulously numbered and laboriously discussed. In just a few elegant pages, Satoshi springs a new financial universe into being, governed not by the laws of humans but the laws of mathematics.

The Satoshi whitepaper was the Big Bang of blockchain.

Like the main characters in all the success stories you'll read in this book, Satoshi was not satisfied with the theory; the challenge was in building it. Over the following years, Satoshi drew a small band of developers and enthusiasts who were attracted to both the technical challenge and the political ramifications of a money developed "by the people, for the people."

This early community—a motley assortment of cryptography geeks, cypherpunks, devout libertarians, and digital currency programmers—helped develop and test the bitcoin software, set up the first bitcoin network, and create (or **mine**) the first bitcoin.

Definition

Mine: To earn bitcoin by contributing computing power to the network.

At this point, bitcoin had no real value. For most of the early enthusiasts, it was a hobby, an interesting experiment. But as the size of the community and the codebase grew larger, those early pioneers began to excitedly whisper: *what if this bitcoin actually became valuable?* What if this was not just a geeky technolibertarian project, but, like, *real money?*

The First Bitcoin Purchase

In 2010, one of these early community members, a programmer named Laszlo Hanyecz, conducted a landmark experiment. To prove bitcoin had real-world value, he suggested using bitcoin to make a real-world purchase: a couple of pizzas.

Hanyecz found another early bitcoin enthusiast, Jeremy Sturdivant, who was willing to help. To pay for the pizzas, Hanyecz sent bitcoin to Sturdivant, who then called up a local pizza shop and arranged to have two pizzas delivered to Hanyecz (Figure 1-3). In exchange for Sturdivant's service as a "pizza broker," the two settled on the somewhat arbitrary number of 10,000 bitcoin.

Seven years later, those pizzas would be worth $100 million.

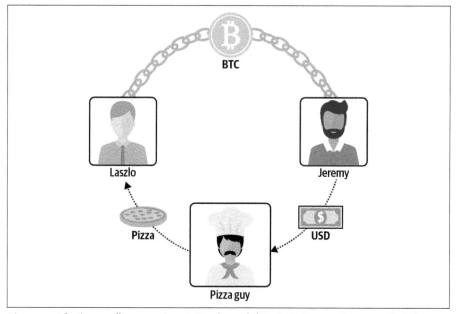

Figure 1-3. The $100 million experiment: Laszlo sends bitcoin to Jeremy. Jeremy sends dollars to the pizza guy. Pizza guy sends pizza to Laszlo's house.

The experiment proved that bitcoin had real-world value: that is, people would accept bitcoin as payment and assign a value to this payment in United States dollars. *Bitcoin was being used as money.* The post-pizza price of bitcoin began to take off: within 10 days, users were willing to buy and sell a single bitcoin for 8 cents each.[3]

Satoshi's dream of digital money was coming true! The reclusive programmer continued to work tirelessly behind the scenes, suggesting changes, making improvements, and managing the scrappy team of volunteer developers. Mysteriously, Satoshi communicated only via email or message boards; no one ever met the creator of bitcoin face to face.

Then something weird happened. Satoshi began handing over all the source code for bitcoin to the top developers...then vanished.

Satoshi left behind accounts worth some 1 million bitcoin (BTC), which seven years later would be worth nearly *$20 billion*. To this day, no one knows the identity of Satoshi, or even whether Satoshi really exists. Some think Satoshi is a

---

3 "Bitcoin History," BitcoinWiki, June 27, 2019, *https://en.bitcoinwiki.org/wiki/Bitcoin_history*.

woman. Some think Satoshi is a group or even a government. Some think Satoshi is an alien.

It's a remarkable origin story because it's absolutely true. And it teaches us one of our first lessons about successful blockchain projects: *have a good origin story*.

The story of your blockchain project is the way you get people interested in joining your blockchain. And getting people to join your blockchain, as you shall shortly see, is the primary challenge facing blockchain leaders.

Blockchain begins with bitcoin. If blockchain is the Internet of Value, bitcoin was the first *unit of value* to start flowing on it.

Within your enterprise, you also have units of value. Perhaps they're customer reward points. Or data shared between vendors in your supply chain. Or maybe the unit of value is just plain old money, flowing between international offices or through a global network of customers. Wherever value is flowing, there is a potential opportunity for blockchain.

Blockchain begins with bitcoin, not just because it's still the most successful blockchain project, but because it provides excellent lessons on how to build your own successful blockchain project.

One lesson is *you can't always predict where a blockchain project will go*. Satoshi, for example, could not have envisioned the long, strange trip that the bitcoin project would take. To understand this unusual journey, let's review what bitcoin was designed to do.

How Bitcoin Works

It's easiest to think of bitcoin as **peer-to-peer money**.

Definition

Peer-to-peer (P2P) money: Money that can be sent between users, without having to go through a central bank.

If you've never used bitcoin, the best way to understand it is to buy a little bit. (It's a business expense.) Even if you invest only $100, you'll learn a great deal just from the process of buying it. You can purchase any amount of bitcoin through a service like Coinbase, which will convert your plain old money into bitcoin, depositing the bitcoin in a digital wallet (like an online banking account).

From there, you can send bitcoin anywhere around the globe, as easily as sending email. Your digital wallet comes with a public key (like an email address) and a private key (like a password). To send bitcoin to someone else, you enter their public key, confirm the transaction with your private key, and the money is transferred.

No banks. Peer-to-peer money.

Peer-to-peer money has the potential to radically disrupt the world economy. Think back to how P2P file-sharing services like Napster changed the game for music and software companies: no longer was Sony or Disney the single point of distribution. Now anyone could (illegally) download their latest album or video game by simply connecting to the Napster network, which was run by millions of users running the Napster software. Anyone running Napster became a **node** in the global file-sharing network.

Definition

Node: Broadly speaking, a single computer within a blockchain network.

If you wanted to download from Napster, in other words, you also became a Napster node. (Read that sentence again.) This meant that when you started up the software, you weren't just a "taker," you were also a "giver." Suppose that you downloaded the latest Metallica album. As long as you kept Napster running, other people could start downloading from *you*.

Napster solved the user adoption problem by making every user a contributor: as you were downloading an album, you were also sharing that album with anyone else who wanted it. By making every user a node, the Napster network exploded like a wildly contagious virus.

Similarly, Satoshi's whitepaper outlined a plan for P2P money: anyone running the bitcoin software would become a node in the network, effectively **decentralizing** the network and protecting it from interference by centralized governments or banks. No one would "own" the network, so no one could shut it down. Figure 1-4 shows the difference.

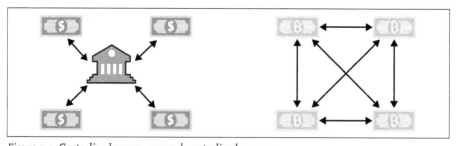

Figure 1-4. Centralized money versus decentralized money

Definition

Decentralized: Shared among nodes, with no central authority. Think peer-to-peer software, rumors, potluck dinners, memes, or a catchy song.

This was not just a political statement. Earlier experiments with digital money had failed, either through lack of user adoption (DigiCash in 1998)[4] or through legal battles with the US government (e-gold in 2006).[5] What made Satoshi's vision different was this idea of peer-to-peer money. It would spread naturally across the planet, and no government would be able to shut it down. Bitcoin would be decentralized.

The Decentralized Ledger

But here we run into a problem: money has value, and that value needs to be recorded somewhere. We want to know where the money is and where it's been. If I pay you a million dollars, I want a receipt. And you want to know that the money landed in your bank account.

Broadly speaking, this is the practice of *accounting*—and traditionally, we keep track of money in **accounting ledgers**. Anywhere we keep track of money— Microsoft Excel files, Intuit QuickBooks, even an old-school checkbook—is an accounting ledger.

Definition

Accounting ledger: A central repository for all accounting data (the inflows and outflows of money). Blockchain uses decentralized accounting ledgers, which have both advantages (more trustworthy) and disadvantages (lots of coordination).

Traditionally, these accounting ledgers have been centralized, meaning they're held by one central party: you, your accountant, or your bank. They all work on the basic accounting principle of credits and debits, or inflows and outflows of money.

For example, let's imagine that Alice transfers $1 million to Bob, who transfers it to Carol, who transfers it to Devansh (Figure 1-5).

---

4 "DigiCash," Wikipedia, August 6, 2019, *https://en.wikipedia.org/wiki/DigiCash*.

5 "E-Gold," Wikipedia, December 17, 2018, *https://en.wikipedia.org/wiki/E-gold*.

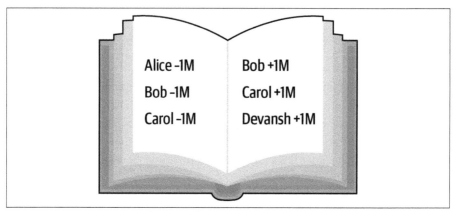

Figure 1-5. Alice, Bob, Carol, and Devansh as we'd represent them in an accounting ledger

With blockchain, we are dealing with a *decentralized ledger*; it's not kept on a single computer or bank account. So where do we record that transfer? There is no QuickBooks file to record the transaction, just a massive shared database spread across hundreds of nodes. How does the blockchain system "know" who now owns the bitcoin?

Here's where we make the mental shift to blockchain, to go from paper to digital. Blockchain is a different method of accounting: we write each transaction to a block of data and then *chain* those blocks together, as shown in Figure 1-6.

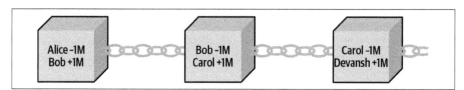

Figure 1-6. Alice, Bob, Carol, and Devansh as we'd represent them on a blockchain

Imagine a long line of wooden blocks connected sequentially by chains. Each time a bitcoin is transferred, we engrave this transaction in a new block and then chain this block to the end of the line. This digital system has benefits over paper:

- Unlike in an old-fashioned paper checkbook, we can't go back and erase an entry.
- Unlike in QuickBooks, we can't overwrite the file.
- Unlike an accounting firm, we can't convince anyone to "cook the books."

With blockchain technology, we have a permanent—or **immutable**—record of Alice's transfer to Bob.

Definition

Immutable: Permanent.

But how does this information make it back to the nodes? Through a process called **consensus**. Think of the way a domain name is gradually replicated to domain name servers around the world. Within 24 hours, a website can be up and running at a new address, thanks to the cooperation among thousands of independent domain name servers, functioning like internet nodes that check and agree with one another, as demonstrated in Figure 1-7.

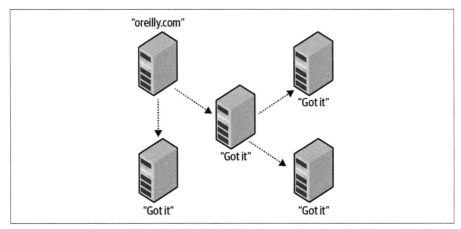

Figure 1-7. A new website domain replicating to domain name servers around the world

Definition

Consensus: The way nodes come to "agree" on who paid what to whom (more on this later).

Consensus is why, far from being sketchy or dangerous, blockchain-based money is *more* trustworthy than traditional money. As we all know from spy movies, paper money can be stuffed into duffel bags and exchanged in the lower levels of parking garages. With blockchain, we can trust the transaction (there's a permanent record of it), and we even know who made it (their digital address).

There's one more piece of the puzzle: good money should also have **scarcity**: we shouldn't be able to produce it out of thin air. When we download a PDF file from the internet, we are essentially creating another copy of the document; that won't work for money. People should work hard for their money, which keeps the wheels of society turning.

Definition

Scarcity: A fixed or limited supply (as opposed to digital assets that can be infinitely copied).

Satoshi's masterstroke was to combine *P2P file sharing* (which allowed the network to spread rapidly) with *decentralized ledger technology* (which allowed money transfers to stay safe, secure, and scarce—more on this in Chapter 2). By mashing up these two technologies, Satoshi provided an incentive for users to build the network, by rewarding them with small amounts of bitcoin (which they now trusted) for hosting a node in the network (which was now exploding).

And as the size of the network grew, so did the price of a single bitcoin: from $0.08 in 2010, to $800 in 2014, to $8,000 in 2017. This created a virtuous circle: as bitcoin soared in price, the bitcoin network soared in size and power.

Satoshi's blockchain experiment was working. More important, it was about to give birth to the next big innovation in blockchain: an explosion of baby bitcoins.

Blockchain Is a Platform

As the price of bitcoin began to rise, developers realized bitcoin was just a starting point. Because bitcoin was open source, developers rushed to build their own spin-off projects, essentially "minting their own money."

Some of these alternatives to bitcoin (or **altcoins**) began to build their own passionate communities. And because the value of a blockchain is directly correlated with the number of people using it,[6] some of these altcoins are today worth billions of dollars.

Definition

Altcoins: Alternatives to bitcoin, also called *cryptocurrencies*. (Since *crypto* sounds mysterious and scary, we prefer *altcoins* or, more broadly, *digital assets*.) Top altcoins include Ethereum, Ripple, and Litecoin. (See *CoinMarketCap.com*.)

---

6 Sir John Hargrave, *Blockchain for Everyone* (New York: Gallery Books, 2019), 321–328.

An ecosystem of digital exchanges quickly emerged, allowing users to buy and sell these new digital assets. While skeptics scoffed that these assets had any value, a new class of digital traders started trading them anyway. As the industry matured, the market capitalization (or total value) of these digital assets swelled and today stands at about $300 billion.

These units of value are variously called *coins* or *tokens*, but it doesn't matter what you call them; what matters is how users perceive them. What the first explosion of digital assets taught us is that blockchain projects will have the best chance of user adoption if *users perceive they are receiving something of value.*

In other words, even if you don't call them money, think about these digital assets as money.

The creation of any type of money involves many players besides the "buyer" and the "seller": you'll need banks, payment rails, accounting systems, and so on. Similarly, the creation of digital money (or digital value) on the blockchain platform typically involves an ecosystem of players. We'll explore these in Chapter 2.

Key Takeaways

- Blockchain is the Internet of Value, a new platform for sharing value.

- Bitcoin was the first—and remains the most successful—project built on blockchain.

- Altcoins (alternatives to bitcoin) quickly followed, sometimes called *cryptocurrencies, coins,* or *tokens.*

- These new types of "money," or value, are typically shared peer to peer, without a central bank.

- Likewise, we keep track of these digital assets by using decentralized ledgers: an accounting system spread across a worldwide network of computers.

- Technology leaders have two challenges: getting people to understand blockchain (building awareness), and getting people to use their blockchain (building users).

- Creating a blockchain is like creating a mini-economy. Mastering the building blocks of blockchain is what you'll learn next.

2

Blockchain Building Blocks

Vitalik Buterin was only 19 years old when he changed the world.

Vitalik was born in Russia, and his parents emigrated to Canada when he was six. It was clear that Vitalik was a child prodigy: educators quickly recognized his remarkable talents and moved him into a class for gifted children, where he excelled in math, programming, and economics.

As a teen, the young Vitalik was introduced to bitcoin by his father, a computer programmer. While Vitalik was fascinated by the technology, he saw bitcoin not as an end in itself but as a means to an end. What if you could develop applications on top of bitcoin—essentially turning bitcoin itself into a platform?

Vitalik proposed a new kind of scripting language that could be built on top of bitcoin. (As an analogy, think of this like Android scripting languages, which make it easier for developers to create Android apps.) He was young and inexperienced, so his idea didn't get much traction among bitcoin's core developers, who were now the "old guard." So Vitalik built the project himself.

Like Satoshi before him, the young developer described his idea in a whitepaper.[1] He described his project, announced in 2013, as a general blockchain platform with a simple scripting language that would allow developers to rapidly create new blockchain apps. The platform would come with its own built-in units of value, its own *digital currency*.

---

1 Vitalik Buterin, "Ethereum White Paper: A Next Generation Smart Contract and Decentralized Application Platform," Ethereum.org, 2013, *http://blockchainlab.com/pdf/Ethereum_white_paper-a_next_generation_smart_contract_and_decentralized_application_platform-vitalik-buterin.pdf.*

Also like Satoshi, Vitalik attracted a small team of developers around his idea, and they helped him prototype and launch the platform. The project quickly attracted a network of volunteers who were willing to build the network because (as with bitcoin) they were rewarded with small units of value for hosting nodes.

Vitalik called the project *Ethereum*, named after ether, the hypothetical invisible substance that permeates the universe.[2] The unit of value—the "money" that developers paid to use the network—was called *Ether*. (These terms would quickly become confused, and today *Ethereum* is commonly used for both the network and the unit of value.)

Ethereum was a big step forward for blockchain, because it allowed for a common set of development standards, which meant a faster time to market. It was almost *too* successful because it made it easy for anyone to create blockchain-based units of value that could be bought and sold by digital traders.

Just as the internet made it easy for anyone to publish information (whether true or not), this new invention made it easy for anyone to create new units of value (whether valuable or not). In a sense, it allowed people to "print money." As you shall see, this was both a blessing and a curse.

History will remember Vitalik, along with Satoshi, as one of the founders of blockchain. Today, Ethereum is the second-largest blockchain project behind bitcoin, and it serves as a terrific case study for the building blocks of a successful blockchain project.

But like Satoshi before him, Vitalik could not have foreseen how his blockchain project would change the world. (You can't always predict where a blockchain project will go.) To understand the next part of our story, let's see how blockchain pumps blood into the body.

---

2 Rugbyowl, "So Where Did the Name Ethereum Come From?" Ethereum Community Forum, March 20, 2014, *https://forum.ethereum.org/discussion/655/so-where-did-the-name-ethereum-come-from*.

Decentralized Ledger Technology: The Beating Heart of Blockchain

Let's return to our accounting ledger, in which Alice has now transferred one unit of Ethereum to Bob, who transfers it to Carol, who transfers it to Devansh (Figure 2-1).

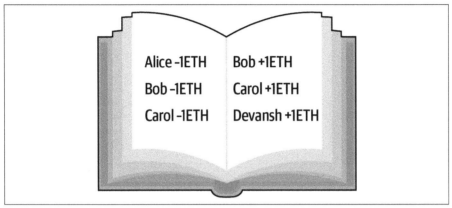

Alice -1ETH   Bob +1ETH

Bob -1ETH   Carol +1ETH

Carol -1ETH   Devansh +1ETH

Figure 2-1. Alice, Bob, Carol, and Devansh as we'd represent them in an accounting ledger

First imagine that we record this information into a local Excel spreadsheet. It's now stored on one copy, one computer, as illustrated in Figure 2-2.

	A	B	C
1	Alice	-1	ETH
2	Bob	+1	ETH
3			

Figure 2-2. A sequence of ETH transactions, as recorded in an Excel sheet

Next, imagine that we copy the information out of Excel and into a Google Sheet: it's now shared across hundreds of network nodes, across a cloud computing cluster, as shown in Figure 2-3. Compare the Excel file (one copy, one computer) to the Google Sheet (one copy, many computers).

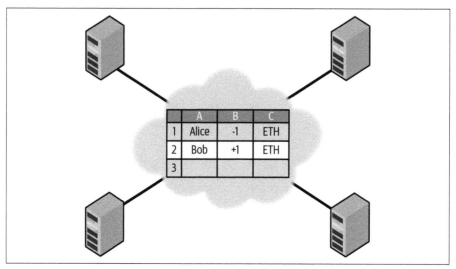

Figure 2-3. Alice transfers one ETH to Bob, as recorded in a Google sheet

Blockchain takes it one step further: many copies, many computers, as demonstrated in Figure 2-4.

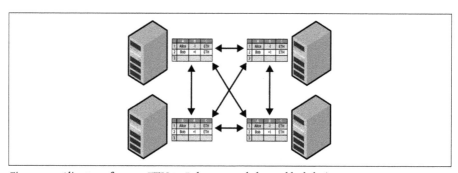

Figure 2-4. Alice transfers one ETH to Bob, as recorded on a blockchain

Look again at Figures 2-3 and 2-4 to engrave in your mind how **decentralized ledger technology** (DLT) is different from cloud computing. Even though a Google Sheet is spread across multiple servers, it's still centralized, since Google owns the servers. Blockchain is decentralized, meaning the users run the servers.

Definition

Decentralized ledger technology: The beating heart of blockchain. It allows us to keep all the transactions synchronized, across a distributed network of computers.

To be clear: there's only one ledger, but that ledger is not stored in any one central location. Rather, identical copies exist on every node—a copy on every computer.

Compare again Figures 2-3 and 2-4 to lock this model in your mind. It's a big deal. DLT is the beating heart of blockchain.

Note

DLT is often defined as *distributed* ledger technology, and sometimes confused with blockchain itself. *Distributed*, however, refers only to copies of the same ledger being stored on different computers (like cloud computing).

We define DLT as *decentralized* ledger technology to show that the ledger is not only distributed, but also isn't bound by any central authority. The power to *maintain* the ledger is decentralized across nodes. This definition of DLT more accurately describes the "beating heart of blockchain."

The remarkable thing about DLT is that we can keep all these distributed copies *synchronized*, anywhere in the world, while making multiple transactions per second. (Think about how difficult it is to just schedule lunch with friends.)

What's more, we synchronize all of these copies in a way that is trusted, timestamped, and auditable. Let's unpack each of these terms:

- The decentralized ledger is *trusted* because it was arrived at through consensus (more on this shortly), with no central party being able to alter the data. A centralized Google Sheet could be altered by Google, but a decentralized ledger can't be altered by a central company or institution. (Like the internet, no single organization "owns" it.)

- The decentralized ledger is *timestamped* by creating *blocks*—a single record of data, like an entry on our accounting ledger—that ensures the proper sequence of transactions. Noting the time a transaction was made keeps the system safe and secure: when we pay someone in Ethereum at 12:02, we know when that Ethereum landed in the recipient's wallet.

- The decentralized ledger is *auditable* because it's transparent: as with a Google Sheet, we can all look back in time and see the complete sequence of transactions. Unlike cash, which is truly anonymous, a digital ledger leaves a trail whenever we make a transaction. The parties can still be anonymous, but their transaction is broadcast in broad daylight.[3]

That said, is DLT right for you? For most enterprise technology managers, a shared centralized database is a better solution: it's faster, cheaper, and easier to deploy. Blockchain technology is better when you need to share "money" (or units of value) across a global network of participants: in other words, when you need to *share the wealth.*

DLT is how we circulate value into the Internet of Value, in the same way that the heart pumps blood into the body. It's the technology behind blockchain, the organ that keeps the ecosystem vibrant and healthy.

Over the next four years after Ethereum was launched, that heart began to beat faster and faster. Then things exploded.

Nodes and Miners

Ethereum—like the entire blockchain market—was going insane.

Because people could create their own tokens on top of Ethereum (the platform), the price of Ethereum (the asset) began to skyrocket. At the beginning of 2017, a single ETH was $10; a year later, that same ETH was $1,000.

As the price shot into the ether, so did the number of *miners* (people contributing their computers to the network). This, in turn, grew network capacity, so even more projects could launch on Ethereum, making even more money for the Ethereum ecosystem. More people meant more decentralization, which meant more security (fewer points of failure), which made the network even more valuable. It was the same virtuous circle that powered the early growth of bitcoin.

The increasing price radically increased the number of nodes, as more people joined their computers to the network. These nodes served a few key roles:

Maintaining copies of the ledger
Like teens sharing an NSYNC album on Napster, many nodes host the ledger, constantly staying in sync. Because the ledger can become quite large over time, some nodes host only a part of the ledger.

---

3 "Is Cryptocurrency Money Laundering a Real Threat?" AML RightSource, January 15, 2019, *https:// www.amlrightsource.com/news/posts/cryptocurrency-money-laundering-red-flags.*

Validating transactions

Through the process of consensus (coming up next), the nodes are constantly coming to "agreement" on which transaction blocks are valid, and then recording valid blocks on the blockchain (i.e., writing a timestamped block of data to the distributed ledger).

Mining

Broadly speaking, miners are dedicated computers that use specialized hardware and software to run a blockchain network, receiving a reward in the form of bitcoin or other digital assets for generating new transaction blocks. Users set up a *mining rig*—a custom-built computer—and earn rewards for hosting a node in the network.[4]

This concept of *nodes* and *miners* is critical. At their outset, all blockchains face a "chicken-or-egg problem": without users, you don't have a blockchain, but without a blockchain, you can't attract users. The blockchain isn't centralized: you can't just spin up a cluster of servers. It's decentralized: you have to convince users to build the network.

So how do you kickstart a blockchain? You mine it.

Definition

Mining: Let's expand our definition from Chapter 1 to include the process of earning rewards (usually in the form of coins or tokens) by contributing computing power to the network.

Users want a reward for participating in your blockchain: again, the perception of value. The term **mining** is now used generically to mean any reward for hosting a node in the network.

This is another reason we think of blockchain as the Internet of Value: your value (your digital assets, commonly called *coins* or *tokens*) is typically used to reward your miners for participating in the network.

This is how we solve the chicken-or-egg problem: we pay off the chickens.

---

4 This further illustrates why we define DLT as decentralized ledger technology. *Distributed* refers only to the nodes that maintain identical copies of the same ledger. *Decentralized* refers to the nodes that also perform mining and validate transactions.

The Consensus Algorithm

We reject: kings, presidents, and voting. We believe in: rough consensus and running code.[5]

—Dave Clark, Internet Engineering Task Force

Now you understand that blockchain uses a distributed ledger (a massive shared database), which is maintained through nodes and miners (a global network), who are rewarded with tokens (your custom currency, or units of value). This is how blockchains are built in real life.

But with transactions simultaneously happening all over the globe, how do we keep all this synchronized? We call this *consensus.*

Consensus (also called the **consensus algorithm**, or **consensus protocol**) is the process through which all the nodes reach agreement on a transaction. *We don't mean that humans are manually agreeing on each transaction.* Quite the opposite: as Dave Clark points out, consensus is not voting. Consensus is happening behind the scenes, in code: machines agreeing with machines.

Consensus currently comes in several flavors, which we cover next. (If this section gets too technical for your taste, you can skim the sentences in italics and skip ahead to Chapter 3.)

Definition

Consensus protocol: The algorithm that computers use to automatically "agree" with one another.

PROOF OF WORK

Proof of Work (PoW) is the original consensus protocol used by bitcoin. In this method, computer nodes solve increasingly complex mathematical problems for the right to validate transactions (i.e., approve them to be written as a new block of data). As the complexity increases, so does the processing power required to solve those problems.

The computers providing that processing power are not only increasingly expensive to build but increasingly expensive to run: computing power requires electrical power. The idea is that this challenging mathematical "work" further

---

5 A. L. Russell, "'Rough Consensus and Running Code' and the Internet-OSI Standards War," *IEEE Annals of the History of Computing* 28, no. 3 (2006): 48–61, *https://doi.org/10.1109/mahc.2006.42.*

justifies the value of the bitcoin, because it uses real processing power and real electricity.

In fact, a common criticism is that bitcoin uses *too much* electricity. According to *The Economist*, the total energy consumption used by the bitcoin network alone could power Ireland![6] This massive energy draw is the reason that blockchain developers are experimenting with alternative consensus mechanisms.

In the early days, anyone with a home computer could mine bitcoin. Then it specialized into custom mining rigs, then warehouses of mining rigs, then enormous server farms located near cheap energy sources. As it became more competitive for individual miners to make any money, they began joining together in huge profit-sharing collectives, or *mining pools*. Many of these pools further consolidated into companies that now control large chunks of the bitcoin network.

Consensus is a funny thing. As power consolidates among competing mining companies, we end up with something like an oligopoly, with a handful of enormous players controlling most of the mining power: exactly the problem that a decentralized network is trying to solve.

We call this problem the **Consensus Paradox**: a decentralized consensus algorithm tends to become more centralized as it becomes more widely adopted.

Definition

Consensus Paradox: As a decentralized consensus mechanism becomes more widely adopted, it tends to become more centralized.

PROOF OF STAKE

The most common alternative to Proof of Work is *Proof of Stake* (*PoS*), in which nodes have mining power proportional to the number of tokens they own. For example, in Ethereum 2.0,[7] which is built on PoS, someone who owned 1% of all the Ethereum could validate (or approve) a maximum of 1% of all the transactions.

Definition

Proof of Stake (PoS): A consensus mechanism, whereby users have to prove their stake in the network in order to validate (or *mine*) new tokens.

---

6 "Why Bitcoin Uses so Much Energy," *The Economist*, July 9, 2018, *https://www.economist.com/the-economist-explains/2018/07/09/why-bitcoin-uses-so-much-energy*.

7 "Ethereum 2.0 Specs," GitHub, Sept. 3, 2019, *https://github.com/ethereum/eth2.0-specs*.

Proof of Stake's huge advantage is that it uses far less electricity: rather than everyone "competing" for rewards, we just distribute the rewards proportionally to who owns the tokens.

But here again we run into the Consensus Paradox: under this scheme, the rich get richer, while the poor get poorer. Like the Monopoly player who's developed hotels on the most valuable properties, the wealthiest token holders get proportionally more of the benefits.

PoS does, however, create an enormous incentive for players to ensure the integrity of the system: the more blockchain tokens you own in a PoS system, the more you want that blockchain to succeed. Nobody wants the Monopoly game to end early if they're winning.

EXPERIMENTAL CONSENSUS ALGORITHMS

The Consensus Paradox is one of the most interesting problems in blockchain, so a host of new consensus algorithms are in the works, such as Delegated Proof of Stake, Tangle, and Hashgraph. It's a difficult problem: how do you get thousands of independent nodes to continually stay in agreement? Each solution has its own strengths and weaknesses.

As you can see, blockchain presents challenges that are both technical and financial. Ethereum got it right on both fronts: a good consensus protocol (technical), with built-in incentives for nodes and miners (financial).

We're seeing that blockchain—the Internet of Value—has many moving parts. When we build a blockchain, we're not just building a technological system; we're building an economic system (Figure 2-5).

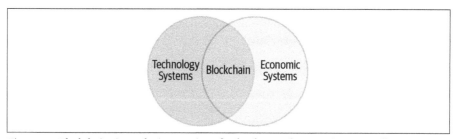

Figure 2-5. Blockchain sits at the intersection of technology and economics. Let's call it "techonomics."

Indeed, it's helpful to think of blockchain as a new discipline that sits at the intersection of money and technology. This requires new skills. A traditional network admin will not understand how to create economic incentives, just as a traditional economist will not be able to understand consensus protocols.

Instead, we encourage enterprise blockchain leaders to begin training in "tokenomics": the art/science of designing tokenized digital assets. This will lead to a new job position, the **tokenomist**, who understands economic principles as well as blockchain technology. In the job market of the future, tokenomists— both literally and figuratively—are going to mint money.

Definition

Tokenomist: Part economist, part blockchain guru—starting salary is $200,000 annually (but you can pay it in tokens).

Key Takeaways

- Decentralized ledger technology allows us to keep all our blockchain transactions synchronized, across a distributed network of computers.

- This technology is run on a network of computers called nodes, usually for the right to mine (or earn) tokens.

- The consensus algorithm is how all these computers stay synchronized. Proof of Work and Proof of Stake are the two most common algorithms, though many more are being tried.

- Blockchains are a mashup of technology and economics: you have to think about both the code and the coins. (We call this *techonomics*.)

- Understanding some of the deeper ideas—the principles—behind blockchain will help you get the techonomics right. Let's cover those next.

How to Build a Successful Blockchain

Changpeng Zhao became a blockchain billionaire in less than a year.

CZ, as he is known, was born in China, where both his parents were educators. His father, however, was a strong-minded intellectual who was exiled from the country for his "pro-bourgeois" ideas, and the family moved to Canada, like the Buterins.[1]

After studying computer science at McGill University in Montreal, CZ quickly developed a reputation for building high-speed financial trading systems for companies like Bloomberg and the Tokyo Stock Exchange. Then, he was bitten by the bitcoin bug.

When he was introduced to blockchain in his late 20s, he quickly saw the potential of the new Internet of Value and left his day job to join several early projects. He was one of the first employees of digital wallet provider Blockchain.info, followed by a stint at OKCoin, a platform for trading between traditional and digital currencies.

CZ saw two problems with the emerging world of digital trading:

- The first problem was *technical*. When traders wanted to sell bitcoin and buy Ethereum, for example, the technology wasn't ready for prime time. The early days of blockchain, like the early days of the internet, were

---

1 Pamela Ambler, "From Zero to Crypto Billionaire in Under a Year: Meet The Founder of Binance," *Forbes*, February 10, 2018, *https://www.forbes.com/sites/pamelaambler/2018/02/07/changpeng-zhao-binance-exchange-crypto-cryptocurrency/#4d946d31eee8*.

plagued by frequent site outages, confusing user interfaces, and a lack of scalability.

- The second problem was *legal*. The moment you accepted **fiat currency**, you were considered a money transmitter, which required expensive licenses and lawyers. Also, these new digital assets had not been legally defined: they were kind of like stocks, kind of like currencies, but they were really something new. These new exchanges were operating in new territory.

Definition

Fiat currency: Traditional currency, such as dollars, euros, or yuan.

CZ outlined his idea for a new digital exchange called *Binance*, whereby traders could buy and sell digital assets, like a stock exchange for blockchain. Binance would cleverly work around these two problems:[2]

- To solve the *technical* problem, CZ would build a best-in-class tech stack that would rapidly allow new digital assets to be added to the platform. He would build in scalability from the beginning, concealed behind an easy-to-use interface.

- To solve the *legal* problem, Binance would simply not accept fiat currencies. Traders would need to buy bitcoin or tokens somewhere else, and then transfer them over to Binance to start trading. This allowed CZ to bypass traditional regulation altogether.

CZ launched his new exchange in mid-2017, and his timing was perfect. The great Crypto Boom of 2017 was in full swing, hundreds of new projects were being launched each month, and Binance could easily add new digital assets as they showed market demand.

To fund the new exchange, CZ launched an altcoin of his own, Binance Coin (BNB). Again, the timing was perfect, as the price of a single BNB rocketed from about 10 cents to more than $30. Within a year, CZ was one of the richest figures in the blockchain industry.

---

2 Pete Rizzo, "The Unbelievable Brilliance of Binance," CoinDesk, April 19, 2019, *https://www.coindesk.com/the-unbelievable-brilliance-of-binance*.

The story of Binance is an excellent case study for some of the principles behind successful blockchain projects, which we explore in this chapter. These principles will serve as your introduction to the stories ahead, and valuable lessons on how to create your own blockchain success story. (If this gets too technical for your tastes, feel free to skip ahead to the stories, which begin in Chapter 4.)

Open It Up

Blockchains are networks. Like all networks, their value comes from people using the network.

Today's most powerful companies—Facebook, Tencent, Apple—are network companies. Even Tesla, an auto company, is really a network company (Elon Musk calls Tesla's cars "sophisticated computers on wheels"[3]). Networks are valuable because of **network effects**: for every user that joins a network, the network becomes more valuable for all users, as shown in Figure 3-1.

Definition

Network effects: As every new user joins a network, the network becomes more valuable for all users.

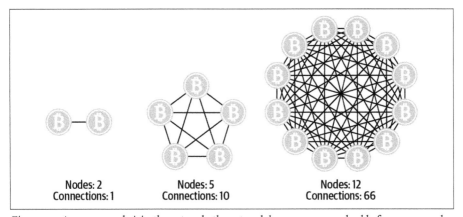

| Nodes: 2 | Nodes: 5 | Nodes: 12 |
| Connections: 1 | Connections: 10 | Connections: 66 |

Figure 3-1. As more people join the network, the network becomes more valuable for everyone who joins

---

3 Jerry Hirsch, "Elon Musk: Model S Not a Car but a 'Sophisticated Computer on Wheels,'" *Los Angeles Times*, March 19, 2015, *https://www.latimes.com/business/autos/la-fi-hy-musk-computer-on-wheels-20150319-story.html*.

Imagine a world in which only 12 people use Twitter: not very useful. Now imagine a world in which all of your friends are on Twitter: extremely useful. Now imagine a world in which all of your friends, plus celebrities, politicians, and you are on Twitter: most useful.

Successful networks build their own momentum, generating a kind of magnetic force that attracts even more users, making the network grow even bigger and more useful. Like a growing snowball, the more people who join, the more people who want to join.

Put simply, the more people who use a blockchain, the more powerful that blockchain becomes. We call this the **blockchain network effect**, and wise technology leaders will write this rule on a sticky note and keep it on their desk.

Definition

Blockchain network effect: For every user who joins a blockchain, the more valuable that blockchain becomes.

So the critical question becomes, how will you get people to join your blockchain?

CZ saw that the technology for Binance was important to get right, but he saw that user adoption was even more important. He had to get users buying and selling on his platform.

One way he rapidly attracted new users was to quickly offer many assets on the Binance exchange, attracting a new community of users with each one. Competitor exchanges were slow to add new tokens; consequently, they were slow to add new users.

Thanks to network effects, networks that are more open are generally more successful. Note that more open does not mean completely open: Apple allows developers to create apps for the iPhone, but it famously protects the quality of those apps through extensive review. The sweet spot is somewhere between wide open and invite only, as shown in Figure 3-2.

Figure 3-2. The sweet spot between permissioned and permissionless

This decision about open versus closed is an important one for building blockchains. We call open blockchains permissionless (you don't need permission to join) and closed blockchains permissioned (invite only):

- In a public or *permissionless* blockchain, as envisioned by Satoshi Nakamoto, there is no central authority controlling or restricting access to the system. Anyone is free to participate in the system, even anonymously. But users have no authority in the governance or decision-making of the system because those rules were "hardcoded" into the system in the beginning.

- In a private or *permissioned* blockchain, a central authority figure—usually the owner or company—controls or restricts access to the system. Therefore, we generally know the identities of the people using the blockchain. And although the blockchain is still trusted, it may not be transparent to those on the "outside."

This is not just a blue-sky argument. Let's imagine we're creating a blockchain for the airline industry, through which users can buy and sell frequent-flier reward points with each other. At the beginning, we're simply trying to convince airlines to join our blockchain. Table 3-1 shows two possible pitches: which approach is more likely to succeed *for the industry as a whole*?

Table 3-1. More openness leads to more adoption

Type	Pitch	Likely result
Permissioned (private)	"Only the Big Three airlines will be invited. Their miles will be compatible."	More likely to end up with a handful of incompatible blockchains. Consumers are likely to have a mishmash of blockchain-based rewards points, many of which go unredeemed (in other words, like frequent-flier systems today).
Permissionless (public)	"Any airline can join. All airline miles will be compatible."	More likely to lead to a single frequent-flier standard, as airline miles become interoperable (like the one-stop listings of Google Flights today). Consumers will save and spend frequent-flier miles more, well, *frequently*, buying companion tickets and flying more often.

Assuming that the pricing mechanics are designed correctly (so that airlines aren't losing money), the permissionless approach—a public blockchain—benefits the industry as a whole. More openness leads to more adoption.

But *open* can be a hard sell for a private company. Indeed, research from the International Finance Corporation (IFC) shows that most enterprises are currently choosing permissioned (private) blockchains.[4] However, the more permissioned (or closed) a blockchain becomes, the more it opens itself up to threats of disruption from a permissionless (or open) alternative.

An analogy may help. Consider the "closed" network of taxi companies, with their regulatory protection, medallion system, and specialized networks of drivers and dispatchers. Taxis were disrupted by the "open" networks of ride-sharing companies like Uber and Lyft, which allowed anyone to drive after passing a background check.

Uber is still a centralized company, not a blockchain. But Uber is more permissionless when compared with the taxi industry's permissioned system. (We mean this literally, given that Uber usually did not ask for permission before taking over a new market.)

In the chapters ahead, you'll see how open standards win the day, again and again. You'll read about Helium (Chapter 4), a blockchain networking company that went radically open source, even giving away the plans to its hardware, so that electronics manufacturers could make them as cheaply as possible. You'll read about the Chamber of Digital Commerce (Chapter 10), a blockchain industry association that makes its publications open source, so that lawmakers can copy and paste language to create new blockchain legislation.

When considering where your blockchain project falls on the continuum, push for permissionless. That's how you attract the most users and become an industry standard. Open it up.

Eliminate the Intermediaries

Imagine that you're biting into a sweet, juicy Fuji apple. Now, take a moment to trace that apple backward in time, like watching a movie in reverse, all the way to the tree. Before your teeth sank into that crisp deliciousness, you bought the apple at a store. Before that, it was delivered on a truck from a warehouse. Before

---

4 "Blockchain in Financial Services in Emerging Markets Part 1: Current Trends," EMCompass, August 2017, *https://www.ifc.org/wps/wcm/connect/a3559b7c-19b7-4f8d-94be-30d1cf7e172b/EMCompass +Note+43+FINAL+8-21.pdf?MOD=AJPERES&CVID=lU51Cxz.*

that, a distribution center. Before that, it was put into a box, harvested, and picked from a tree in a farmer's sunny orchard.

Of course, you could have just driven to the farm and picked the apple yourself. But few of us have time to drive around to a dozen farms to pick up the week's groceries. We've developed these complex delivery and distribution networks—these **supply chains**—to make life easier.

Definition

Supply chain: The complex network of people, processes, and technology that gets the goods from producer to consumer (in this example, getting your apple from farm to table).

The downside to this convenience is that each person who handles our apple drives up the cost. The driver, the distributor, the delivery person: each adds on a few cents. You and I get squeezed—and so does the farmer. And so do the apples, to make juice.

Now compare your store-bought Fuji with a community supported agriculture (CSA) share, where local residents each buy a share of the farm's harvest. Throughout the summer and fall, you get a big delivery of whatever is in season: apples, corn, and usually kale. Lots and lots of kale. Seriously, you will run out of uses for kale.

What you give up in control over your kale supply, you gain in variety (you get to try a lot more things) and savings (it's a lot cheaper). By eliminating the "go betweens" that go between the farm and the store, you get cheaper, fresher food.

The second principle of blockchain, then, is *eliminate the intermediaries*. The network of middlemen, middlewomen, managers, agents, resellers, jobbers, brokers, dealers, and broker-dealers—with all the accompanying paperwork and markup—drive up costs and drag down efficiency. Blockchain can help eliminate these "in-betweeners."

Ask yourself: where do we have inefficient intermediaries? Who can we eliminate from our supply chain? "Going direct to the customer" has always been a way to save money for both producers and consumers. With blockchain, this can be done with code, resulting in improved performance and lower costs. We call this process **disintermediation**.

Definition

Disintermediation: Elimination of an intermediary, someone who drives up cost while not adding much value.

For example, by issuing its own BNB token, Binance raised initial funds directly from users, disintermediating the usual Silicon Valley VC network. By offering a Binance Coin that investors could buy and sell on the Binance exchange, CZ created his own "digital money" that other entrepreneurs can now use to launch their own projects on Binance: in essence, a mini-economy that disintermediates dollars.

Ask yourself: where can we eliminate steps in our supply chain? Where can we replace a centralized record keeper with a decentralized ledger? Where can we eliminate an intermediary? That's where a blockchain solution is often hiding.

In the stories ahead, you'll read about Voatz (Chapter 7), a blockchain-based voting platform that lets citizens vote directly from their smartphones—with arguably more security than traditional in-person voting. And you'll read about Binance's own charitable foundation (Chapter 8), which is revolutionizing charitable giving by letting people donate bitcoin and then see where their money is going, by recording their transactions on a public blockchain.

Automate Transactions

Think back to the sweet crunch of that Fuji apple. Again, follow that apple backward in time: from your hand back to the grocery store, the warehouse, the distribution center, and finally back to a tree in a sun-dappled orchard.

At every step of that journey was *paperwork*: invoices, receipts, bills of lading, and so on. Even though much of the paperwork is computerized, a surprising amount is still done using physical paper (just check your grocery store receipt, which is probably the length of a small child).

This paperwork—whether it's literally paper or not—is what we might call a **contract**. You buy the apple from the store, and you get a receipt verifying the transaction: a mini-contract of your transaction. As you follow the apple through its journey from farm to food, visualize every step involving a contract: a buyer, a seller, and a signature.

Definition

Contract: Any record of a transaction between two or more parties.

Any business traveler knows the hassle of managing a mountain of receipts: they're often misplaced, miscategorized, or missing. Now multiply that times millions of apples, millions of shipments, millions of buyers and sellers, and you see the magnitude of the mountain.

This is where blockchain comes in. A **smart contract** is computer code that establishes agreements between parties and then executes the transaction when certain conditions are met, without the need for a third party. The contract is maintained on the distributed ledger (our massive P2P Google Sheet), which is automatically "signed" when both parties have fulfilled their end of the bargain.

Definition

Smart contract: Computer code that establishes an agreement between two or more parties, without the need for a third party.

As an example, Alice wants to pay one unit of Ethereum to Farmer Bob in exchange for a bushel of apples (Figure 3-3).

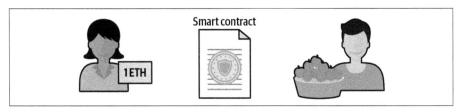

Figure 3-3. The smart contract

She sends one ETH to a smart contract that "holds" the ETH until Bob has delivered the apples. This smart contract functions like an escrow account, except it doesn't require a third-party escrow company; it's all handled through code, as demonstrated in Figure 3-4.

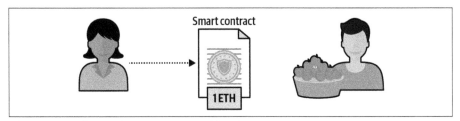

Figure 3-4. Loading up the smart contract with ETH

When Bob delivers the apples, he holds out a QR code, which Alice scans on her phone. This clears the one ETH to be delivered to Bob's account, as shown in Figure 3-5.

Figure 3-5. Everybody's happy

As Figure 3-6 makes clear, if Bob doesn't deliver the apples, Alice can just "withdraw" the money back into her account.

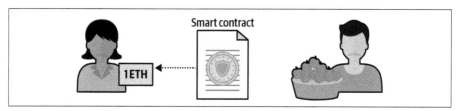

Figure 3-6. Stupid contract

Smart contracts are potentially more efficient than paper contracts because they can be used to coordinate transactions among multiple parties. Imagine, for example, the entire life cycle of your Fuji apple being tracked on a smart contract. Talk about farm-to-table: blockchain will let us see the entire journey from farm to table, as depicted in Figure 3-7.

Figure 3-7. From farm to warehouse to delivery to Alice's restaurant

Today, the international shipping giant Maersk has partnered with IBM to create a global shipping blockchain called TradeLens.[5] In keeping track of items as they move through ports from their source to their destination, Maersk saves money anytime shipments need to be screened or checked. Instead of keeping track of all the "receipts," Maersk has only one record for each item, stored on blockchain.

Smart contracts automate routine transactions. This is what blockchain does really well. Maersk now has code-based smart contracts, not paper-based contracts issued by third parties. CZ's Binance exchange operates exclusively on smart contracts—not on the old-fashioned paper contracts of a traditional exchange.

In the chapters that follow, you'll read about companies like Circle (Chapter 5), which are creating new types of payment systems that automate transactions between traditional money and digital assets like bitcoin. When creating your own blockchain success story, look for opportunities to automate.

Follow the Three C's: Collaborate, Communities, Consortia

In 1517, a German academic professor wrote a paper that would change the course of history. According to legend, he dramatically nailed his paper to the door of a local church—which may or may not be true, but definitely makes for a better story.

That professor was Martin Luther, and his paper, *Ninety-five Theses*, is generally recognized as the start of the Reformation. His paper outlined a different vision for the way the Catholic church should be run, and that vision eventually became a division: the Protestant church.

In blockchain terms, we call this a **fork**: a new project splitting off from the primary project, like a fork in the road. Forks come about when developers have fundamental disagreements on how to move forward: because most blockchain projects are open source (Catholics), it's easy for a subgroup of developers to start their own competing project (Protestants).

Definition

Fork: A new blockchain project splitting off from an existing project.

---

5 Michael del Castillo, "Blockchain 50: Billion Dollar Babies," *Forbes*, July 28, 2019. *https://www.forbes.com/sites/michaeldelcastillo/2019/04/16/blockchain-50-billion-dollar-babies/#545250d57ccb.*

Forks are abundant in the blockchain world: bitcoin itself has been forked over a dozen times,[6] creating altcoins like Bitcoin Cash (faster transactions), Bitcoin Gold (easier to mine), and Bitcoin Private (better privacy).

To be clear, a fork is not creating a brand-new digital asset, as in the early days of bitcoin. A fork makes a copy of an existing blockchain—like copying an accounting ledger—and then goes its own way with a new blockchain, as shown in Figure 3-8.

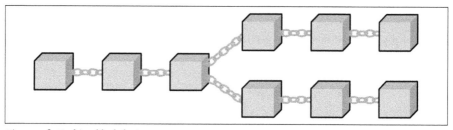

Figure 3-8. Forking blockchain

Forks are generally undesirable, for two reasons:

You lose users
> As we've seen, the value of a blockchain relies on the number of people who use it. When you split a project, you reduce your user base significantly because users and developers generally must choose between one project or the other.

You are more likely to fork again
> Just as Martin Luther's Protestant church would eventually splinter into hundreds of denominations, blockchain forks often fragment into smaller and smaller projects. Once you've forked, you tend to keep forking.

This is not to say all forks are doomed to fail. Two famous forks—Bitcoin Cash (BCH) and Ethereum Classic (ETC)—have each prospered, while

---

6 Alex Lielacher, "A History of Bitcoin Forks: Top 5 Bitcoin Forks, Rated and Reviewed," *Bitcoin Market Journal*, September 19, 2018, *https://www.bitcoinmarketjournal.com/bitcoin-forks*.

maintaining a separate vision from the "one true faith" of bitcoin and Ethereum, respectively. In 2019, in fact, Bitcoin Cash returns doubled those of bitcoin.[7]

Even though a fork demolishes your user base and sets a dangerous precedent, you have a chance of survival if you're really able to build a better blockchain. (Just accept that your bitcoin spin-off will never be considered the "real" bitcoin.)

Forks come about when each side is convinced it holds the one true solution to a problem, usually with a kind of fervent zeal. Because the industry is young and immature, blockchain developers typically hash out these hashing debates on message boards and Twitter.

So how do you build an enduring blockchain project, one that doesn't end in forks?

Most successful blockchain projects start with a culture of collaboration. You'll read several excellent examples in the stories ahead, such as CryptoKitties (Chapter 6), which collaborated with industry leaders to create a new type of blockchain "collectible"—then called on their help again when the demand for those collectibles began to spiral out of control.

You'll also see the power of *consortia*, or groups of related companies, in building some of the most enduring blockchain projects. Many of these success stories involve the **Enterprise Ethereum Alliance** or the **Hyperledger project**, both professional organizations in which competing companies set aside their differences to achieve a common technology goal.

Like executives who serve on the board of a nonprofit, member companies volunteer time and resources to help the industry move forward. In return, they are rewarded with a seat at the table of governance: a say in *how* the industry moves forward.

Definition

Enterprise Ethereum Alliance and the **Hyperledger project**: Two industry groups that help guide the corporate development of the Ethereum and Hyperledger blockchain platforms, respectively.

---

7 Charles Bovaird, "Bitcoin Cash 2019 Returns Double Those of Bitcoin," *Forbes*, April 9, 2019, *https://www.forbes.com/sites/cbovaird/2019/04/09/bitcoin-cash-2019-returns-double-those-of-bitcoin/#59db3e5231f1*.

The best way to secure a seat at the table is to pull up a chair now, while some are still left. If joining a consortium is too much of a commitment, attend local blockchain meetups. Introduce yourself. Form friendships.

This idea of collaboration—even with competitors!—can be difficult for technology managers to take seriously. (Take it seriously.) Collaboration provides the foundation for achieving the network effects to make your blockchain project unstoppable.

To be sure, collaboration is difficult. Building communities is messy. (You'll see plenty of digital drama in the chapters ahead.) But collaboration isn't just a feel-good suggestion: without it, your blockchain project may end in forks. Collaboration lets you work it out, not fork it out.

Invest in Good Governance

One of the earliest political cartoons, the *Unite or Die* graphic shown in Figure 3-9, offered a powerful message to the early American settlers: this disunited collection of colonies, all looking out for their own self-interest, needed to pull it together in order to survive as the United States of America.

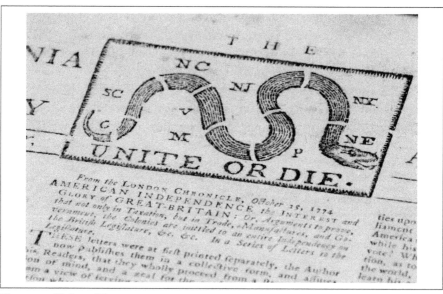

Figure 3-9. Unite or Die

But there were problems with working together. The states were independent and free; why should they subject themselves to a powerful national government? In other words, how could this collection of states come together as a centralized nation, while still maintaining a measure of decentralized control?

These are the same problems playing out in the blockchain industry today. As we've seen, it's difficult enough for a group of independent developers to agree without forking. So how do we possibly balance the needs of all these other players: nodes, miners, investors...not to mention your boss? Just as government is a system for organizing human effort, **governance** is the system for organizing blockchain effort.

Definition

Governance: The system for organizing blockchain efforts, made up of code (like laws) and code developers (like lawmakers). Although blockchain (the technology) is decentralized, governance (like government) is more centralized.

Just as we can break government into two broad categories of laws and lawmakers, we can break governance into two broad categories of code and codemakers:

- The codemakers (developers) make decisions by coming to consensus or compromise, and then building those decisions into code.

- The code itself—in the form of smart contracts—then carries out those decisions, effectively "enforcing the law."

Here's a real-world example. Miners who maintain the Ethereum blockchain need to be paid for running this global network of computers, so developers decided to charge a little Ethereum—a service fee, or **gas**—for each Ethereum transaction.[8] They wrote this "law" into code, in the form of a smart contract that sits on top of our initial contract (Figure 3-10).

---

8 For a list of the transaction fees for other altcoins, see Sean Williams, "Which Cryptocurrencies Have the Lowest Transaction Fees?" *The Motley Fool*, Mar. 30, 2018, *https://www.fool.com/investing/2018/03/30/which-cryptocurrencies-have-the-lowest-transaction.aspx*.

Definition

Gas: A transaction fee on Ethereum.

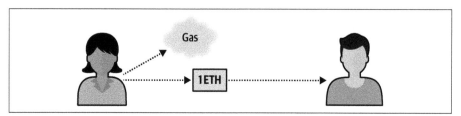

Figure 3-10. Think of gas as a service fee for Ethereum transactions

Code is now law: you can't send Ethereum without paying for gas. If Ethereum users complain loudly enough, developers need to get involved again, figuring out a way to make everyone happy. Like the process of government, this governance process never ends.

The challenges posed by blockchain are not so much technological as political. Large alliances quickly form, and smaller players can find themselves excluded from the governance process. This is why forming these alliances is so critical in the early stages—getting involved, meeting people, and contributing where you can.

In the chapters that follow, you'll see how successful blockchain leaders have tackled the tricky problem of governance. You'll read about Cardano (Chapter 9), which has created a "balance of powers" similar to a national government, while still allowing its users—the "citizens" of that government—to exercise their influence.

Invest in good governance. *Unite or die.*

Build a Great Product

Even Satoshi Nakamoto, that mysterious genius behind bitcoin, could have benefited from a better product team.

Satoshi's vision was digital money that could be sent as quickly and easily as email. Instead, sending bitcoin is expensive (we'll call it $1 per transaction),[9] slow

---

9 Alyssa Hertig, "Bitcoin Fees Jump to Nearly 1-Year Highs—But Why?" CoinDesk, April 18, 2019, *https://www.coindesk.com/bitcoin-fees-jump-to-nearly-1-year-highs-but-why*.

(we'll call it an hour),[10] and not scalable (we'll call it 10 transactions per second, compared to the Visa network, which handles up to 24,000 transactions per second).[11] If this is money, it's not very good.

Yet the early web was also not very good. It was slow and clunky. Browsers weren't compatible. The default color of web pages was dirty-laundry gray. But it got better, cheaper, faster. Today the internet is how we consume information. For all practical purposes, Wikipedia has replaced encyclopedias, and email has replaced paper mail. Follow the trend line.

In order for the Internet of Value to go mainstream, however, it needs to be a better product. Just as the seeds of the web blossomed into rich media, streaming video, and browser-based applications, the bare-bones blockchains of today must evolve into beautiful applications—*products*—that people want to use.

For the technology leader, this means the following:

Build great product teams

You'll need great blockchain developers, of course, but you'll also need talented people to design the interface, write the messaging, and manage the marketing. Our CryptoKitties case study (Chapter 6) diagrams a blockchain team structure that created a wildly successful product—almost *too* successful.

Hide the complexity

Consumers don't care whether blockchain is the technology; they care about what it can do for them. Just as billionaire investor Warren Buffett was famously skeptical of computers until someone showed him he could play online bridge with his friend Bill Gates,[12] we must package blockchain benefits into fun, interesting, and useful products.

Speed it up

In an age when it still takes three days to clear an international bank transfer, blockchain-based money already offers a superior alternative. But consumers demand the instant gratification of email and texts. Just as Jeff

---

10 Hertig, "Bitcoin Fees Jump."

11 Trey Popp, "Blockchain Fever," *The Pennsylvania Gazette*, University of Pennsylvania, July 2018, *https://thepenngazette.com/blockchain-fever*.

12 Alice Schroeder, *The Snowball: Warren Buffett and the Business of Life* (New York: Bantam Books, 2008), 649.

Bezos relentlessly focused on removing friction from the online shopping experience, which ultimately resulted in Amazon 1-Click, blockchain projects must strive for instant.[13]

Plan for scale

Like a plumber planning ahead, think carefully about the size of your "pipes"—your infrastructure—because bigger is usually better. CZ wisely built scalability into his Binance platform from the beginning, which let it grow without crashing. Like Binance, strive for scalability.

Stick to the vision

Most products are not great out of the gate. Similarly, none of the projects in the following chapters were overnight successes: all were fraught with failed experiments. All traveled the "long and lonely road" of learning by doing, where success was uncertain and failure looked more likely. Those who stayed true to the vision—the "germ of the idea"—were more likely to succeed.

In our concluding case study (Chapter 13), you'll see how we used many of these principles to propose a new set of simple, scalable "products" for dealing with the crisis that smashed the globe as we finished writing this book.

Anticipate the Future

We'll wrap up this history of blockchain by walking you through three seasons we'll call Crypto Summer (2017–2018), Crypto Winter (2018–2019), and Crypto Spring (2019–2020).

At the beginning of 2017, the price of bitcoin was about $1,000; by the end of the year, the same bitcoin was worth $20,000. Like the Summer of Love, *Crypto Summer* was a blockchain hugfest, with starry-eyed dreamers raising buckets of money for any blockchain project, no matter how far-fetched.

Almost overnight, blockchain birthed a $250 billion asset class, with new tokens being launched and traded globally, 24 hours a day. Exchanges like Binance quickly rose up to handle the demand, creating a newer kind of New York Stock Exchange.

---

13 Brad Stone, *The Everything Store: Jeff Bezos and the Age of Amazon* (New York: Little, Brown & Company, 2014), 76–77.

Then governments started asking, *What are these things? Are they securities? Currencies? Something else?* In the US, the Securities and Exchange Commission, which is charged with protecting investors, decided to proceed slowly. *Wait and see.*

Then the lawyers began to get involved. And the lawyers, who urged timidity and caution, and who were also not well educated on this new technology, mostly advised new blockchain projects to hold off. *Wait and see.*

And so this torrent of innovation slowed to a trickle, and that trickle began to freeze. Thus began the *Crypto Winter* of 2018–2019, as the price of bitcoin crashed from $20,000 down to $5,000, taking the entire digital asset market with it. These were dark days.

There was a great shakeout, not unlike the collapse of the dot-com bubble in 2000, when only the strong survived. But the companies that made it through Crypto Winter—like the internet companies that survived the early 2000s—grew even stronger. They survived to see the spring.

At the time of this writing, a new *Crypto Spring* is emerging, and the first buds of blockchain are bursting forth. Facebook is launching its own digital asset, called Libra. Countries like Switzerland and Malta are prospering, thanks to blockchain-friendly legislation. Central banks are even talking about launching their own digital currencies, called **CBDCs**.

Definition

Central bank digital currencies (CBDCs): A digital currency (like bitcoin) that is issued by a central bank (unlike bitcoin). Think of CBDCs as a "walled garden" (like Apple), compared to the open ecosystems of other digital currencies and digital assets (like Android).

The takeaway is that successful technology leaders must *anticipate the future*. It is not enough to see things *how they are*; we must peer into the future to see *how they will likely be*.

For government leaders, anticipating the future means creating fertile soil so this new technology can blossom. We don't want to smother seedlings with heavy-handed regulation; the growth will just flourish elsewhere. Instead, we want a friendly regulatory "garden" where we can plant and nourish blockchain projects, allowing a thousand flowers to bloom.

For blockchain builders, understand that you're planting a garden on a wild frontier. Proceed carefully—but do proceed. You can't wait for everything to be finalized. Listen to your lawyer, but take legal advice with a grain of salt, because after reading this book you may understand more about enterprise blockchain than your attorney does.

Blockchain presents an entirely different framework. In a sense, it sits outside the jurisdiction of any one government, so no government can adequately regulate it. We're building one money for one world, a global currency for a global economy, shared ledgers that transcend both companies and countries.

Just as business technology leaders must begin collaborating with other companies—grabbing a seat at the table—government leaders must begin collaborating with other countries. We encourage the creation of an international consortium to create global regulations for this new Internet of Value. Call it the *United Nations of Blockchain*.

Don't fight the future. Anticipate it.

The World of Tomorrow

In these first three chapters, you've learned how to explain blockchain with a clear and simple definition (the Internet of Value), real-life use cases (bitcoin, Ethereum, and Binance), and easy-to-remember principles (like the three C's of collaboration, communities, and consortia).

Now it's time to see these ideas come to life.

The Internet of Value is springing to life all around us—and for our money, blockchain is the most exciting field today. We're not just building value; we're building the rails to deliver *all kinds of value* for decades to come.

With blockchain, we're building the world we'll be living in tomorrow. We must ask ourselves: what kind of world do we want? Do we want a world filled with get-rich-quick schemes and quick-payout unicorns, a world where 1% control 99% of the world's wealth?

Or do we want a future that is smarter, greener, and fairer? A world where we can send value where it's most needed, where the pie is sliced more evenly, where everyone has access to the Internet of Value—and the power to use it?

We've come full circle. We began by talking about the things you value: your relationships, your pets, your fourth-grade diary. These things *are* valuable, because they are what make us human.

Humans, in the end, are what matter. (Technology serves us, not the other way around.) The stories ahead are human stories, with dizzying highs and gut-wrenching lows. They are stories of vision, courage, and resiliency: our best human qualities.

At the same time, our heroes are only human. They make mistakes, go down blind alleyways, and get frustrated and discouraged. While we admire their success, they're not superhumans: they're just regular humans, like all of us.

Get ready for their stories.

4

Helium: A Blockchain-Based Wireless Network

The first major [blockchain] breakthrough was bitcoin, which invented digital gold. The second was Ethereum, which introduced general-purpose smart contracts. Helium presents the most ambitious new use case for blockchains we've seen since Ethereum.[1]

—Kyle Samani, managing partner, Multicoin Capital

Helium was no longer just hot air.

As CEO Amir Haleem looked over the crowd of several hundred people who had filled Austin's trendy La Condesa restaurant for the August 2019 Helium launch party, he was overwhelmed by the enthusiastic response of all these early users who were eager to build *The People's Network*. After months of marketing and promotion, participants had come from all over Texas to pick up their Helium Hotspots. Helium was now a real shipping product, not just vaporware.

As Amir conversed with members of the crowd, he noted some were blockchain enthusiasts, some were Internet of Things (IoT) experts, and some were just geeks who wanted to be part of this groundbreaking experiment. These early users would be building a massive wireless network not on phone company towers, but on small wireless devices located in their offices and bedrooms. In return, they'd be paid in blockchain-based Helium tokens.

---

1 Guillermo Jimenez, "Helium's Trial Balloon: A New Peer-to-Peer Wireless Network Goes Live in Austin," Decrypt, August 1, 2019, *https://decrypt.co/8179/helium-trial-balloon-a-new-peer-to-peer-wireless-network-goes-live-in-austin.*

These little Hotspots, in other words, would be minting money.

Knowing that the strength of any blockchain project is user adoption—getting people to join your blockchain—Amir understood that this small but committed tribe of early adopters would be key to kickstarting the initial wireless coverage for the Helium network. This was a critical time to achieve critical mass, and Helium tokens were the hook.

As the party attendees returned home and began to plug in their Hotspots, Amir monitored the growth of the network over the next several days. As he saw each Hotspot blip to life on his digital map of Austin, each widening the circle of coverage, he felt a mixture of pride and relief that the dream he and his team had envisioned six years ago was finally becoming a reality.

One side of his marketplace—the network—was lighting up, but the other side was still shrouded in darkness. It was a classic technology problem: they were building supply, but would there be enough demand? Would the company be able to find customers who wanted to use this new low-cost, lower-power wireless network, or would Helium ultimately tank?

The Helium Origin Story

Founded in 2013 by Amir Haleem, a championship video gamer, and Shawn Fanning of Napster fame, Helium's original business idea was to create a giant wireless network, like a cellular network, but for the low-cost, low-power, low-bandwidth world of sensors. Before the Internet of Things was even a thing, the two entrepreneurs saw that tiny sensors would soon be embedded in millions of devices: thermostats, fire alarms, kitchen appliances, inventory trackers, and maybe eventually your dog.

All these devices had one thing in common: they would need a low-cost, low-power wireless connection to the internet (Figure 4-1).

By 2014, Amir and Shawn's idea had evolved into creating a wireless network out of millions of *hotspots*. These hotspots would connect with hotspots around them, like repeaters that boost a wireless signal within your home, creating a kind of decentralized mesh network. Instead of the cell towers of centralized phone companies (large and expensive), a network of volunteers would host mini cell towers that connected to each other (small and inexpensive).

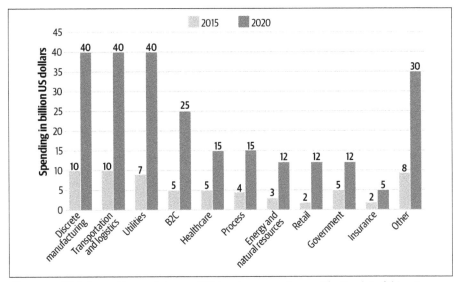

Figure 4-1. Global spending on Internet of Things in 2015 and 2020 (that's a lot of things)

The idea of a *decentralized network* was taking hold in Cuba, where citizens were fed up with the slow and expensive internet service provided by the state-owned telecommunications company. With a do-it-yourself work ethic, citizens formed a grassroots Street Network, eventually known as SNET, hosted by a huge network of volunteers who set up and maintained wireless stations from their homes and apartments across the island.[2]

But that was Cuba; this was the US, where internet service was already cheap and fast. If Helium wanted to blanket the country with its own wireless network —a US version of SNET—how could the team convince people to set up hotspots, much less install them in high windows or rooftops where they would get maximum coverage?

The Helium founders had a few other false starts, but the extra time worked in their favor. By 2016, their prediction had come true: an ecosystem of small devices needed to connect to the internet. Scooters. E-bikes. Lawn sprinklers. And yes, even your dog (or at least your dog collar). The Internet of Things was officially a thing.

---

2 Antonio García Martínez, "Inside Cuba's DIY Internet Revolution," *Wired*, July 16, 2017, *https://www.wired.com/2017/07/inside-cubas-diy-internet-revolution.*

They saw that the millions (soon to be billions) of tiny sensors had specific needs that were much different from a those of a cell phone:

Battery life
Measured in years, not hours

Size
Small enough to fit on many devices (scooters, dog leashes, etc.)

Location tracking
Without needing an expensive cellular connection

Long range
The ability to connect over entire cities

Encryption
Secure enough to transfer sensitive personal data (the location of your pet or valuables)

The extra time worked in their favor in another way: as many television stations switched to digital, they were auctioning off their unused bandwidth spectrum. At the same time, the US Federal Communications Commission (FCC) was opening up new wireless frequencies that didn't require a license. As the entrepreneurs saw it, these devices would need only a slice of that spectrum, and there was plenty of it.

They had a model of what they wanted: a nationwide network of Helium Hotspots, which they came to call *The People's Network*. But how would they get the people to build the network? How could they get these Hotspots to sell like hotcakes?

It was Shawn, the Napster creator, who first said it as a joke: "What if we could get these things to mine bitcoin?"

Solving the Chicken-or-Egg Problem

By offering blockchain-based tokens, Helium incentivizes anyone to own a Hotspot and provide wireless coverage—so the network belongs to participants, not a single company. A network can be scaled much faster and more economically than if a single company tried to build out infrastructure.

—Dal Gemmell, Helium head of product marketing

In their simplest form, blockchains use a two-sided marketplace: bitcoin, for example, has buyers and sellers. But how do you build a two-sided marketplace? Buyers can't buy if there are no sellers, and vice versa. It is the classic **chicken-or-egg problem**: which comes first?

Definition

Chicken-or-egg problem: When building a two-sided blockchain marketplace (buyers and sellers, or buyers and miners), which comes first, the chicken (miners) or the egg (buyers)? One solution: pay off the chickens.

Bitcoin began by attracting enthusiasts who built the network, who were rewarded in turn with small amounts of bitcoin. At first, they bought and sold this bitcoin from each other for fractions of a penny—but as their numbers grew, so did the network, and so did their net worth. As the price of bitcoin grew, more buyers attracted more sellers, and vice versa (Figure 4-2).

Figure 4-2. Most blockchains are multisided marketplaces

The lesson: to kickstart its blockchain, Helium needed to *reward the Hotspot owners*. When users plugged in a Hotspot (i.e., when they created a new node on the network), they'd earn money. The company would create a blockchain-based token—the Helium token—to reward users for building the network, for holding their nodes.

They called this activity **mining**.

Definition

Mining: As we covered in Chapter 2, this is a powerful word that now means *paying users small rewards for supporting the network.* Like mining gold, mining requires "work" (like setting up and maintaining a Hotspot), and a reward is not always guaranteed (that reward may go to a nearby Hotspot instead of yours).

By framing Hotspot ownership as mining, Helium was creating a new mental model of money. Now it was in miners' best interest to not only install Hotspots but also configure them for optimal coverage, since they would also earn Helium tokens for the data that passed through each Hotspot. In fact, Helium Hotspots were an investment opportunity for landlords and businesses with multiple properties (Figure 4-3).

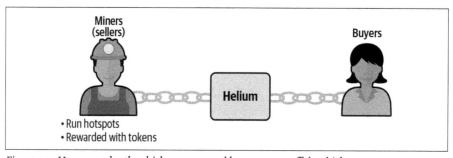

Figure 4-3. How you solve the chicken-or-egg problem: you pay off the chickens

Helium minted its own money—the Helium token—to motivate users to build out one side of the marketplace. The next problem was how to build the other side. Assuming these Helium tokens were worth real money, where would that money come from? In other words, who would pay to use this thing?

As it turned out, there were a lot of Things that would pay to use this thing.

An Internet for the Internet of Things

Package delivery. Rental returns. Supply chains. Energy metering. Temperature sensors. As the team envisioned from the beginning, all these internet-connected devices were potential use cases for the Helium network (Figure 4-4). For manufacturers of these connected devices, Helium had several advantages over existing solutions:

Operating cost

Whereas a sensor that connected to the 3G cellular network would cost a few dollars per month,[3] a sensor connected to the Helium network would cost a few pennies per month. For companies with millions of sensors, the cost savings were enormous.

Range

Bluetooth sensors worked at only short ranges, as anyone with a Bluetooth phone headset can attest. The Helium network could provide connectivity several miles away from the nearest Hotspot.

Power

Whereas cellular chips kill batteries (think about how often you charge your cell phone), the Helium sensors could last several years.

Encryption

All communications over the Helium network would have end-to-end encryption, meaning it was suitable for sensitive data. Even though ordinary users were funneling packets of data through their Hotspots, that data was scrambled so they couldn't read it.

Decentralization

With a traditional *centralized* telecom, your data plan gets more expensive every year (as users increase, the company has to invest in more infrastructure). With the Helium *decentralized* network, it grows organically as more Hotspots are added, driving costs down.

---

3 Brian Ray, "Examining Cellular IoT: Cost, Battery, & Data," Link Labs, August 28, 2015, *https://www.link-labs.com/blog/cellular-iot*.

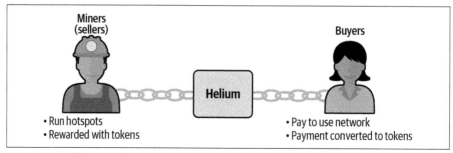

Figure 4-4. Building out the buyer side of the marketplace

After securing a $16 million round of funding, the entrepreneurs built a team of hardware, software, and blockchain experts, with a small business development team that began to search for prospective customers, including the following:

Bike and scooter rental companies

Rental apps for pedal bikes, electric bikes, and scooters were growing quickly. One of their challenges was the short lifespan of their vehicles, which were relatively expensive to maintain and replace. In some cities, users could drop off a scooter anywhere, leaving vehicles scattered across the city. Helium sensors could help rental companies keep track of inventory—as well as provide valuable usage data for peak rental times and neighborhoods.

Food and beverage delivery

Water delivery companies wanted monitoring devices on machines so they could quickly replenish water jugs and eliminate unneeded deliveries from their routes.[4] Any business operating vending machines or automated kiosks could use the same technology to notify the delivery company when an item was out of stock.

Smart trackers

Another emerging industry was smart pet collars, with a low-cost sensor that allowed owners to keep track of their pets and easily locate missing animals through a downloadable app. This was potentially a huge market,

---

4 Amir Haleem, "Entering the Next Phase of Helium," *The Helium Blog*, Medium, August 3, 2019, *https://blog.helium.com/entering-the-next-phase-of-helium-cfd7df3c6e3.*

since similar location trackers could be developed for children, the elderly, or those with special needs. Location trackers could also be used for package deliveries, rental cars, and anti-theft devices.

Wildfire detection

In places where it isn't fiscally feasible for traditional telecom providers to build infrastructure to reach remote wilderness areas, a Helium network could be created to cover vast areas of forest for just a few thousand dollars. Hotspots connecting to sensors that monitor temperature (heat) or air quality (smoke) could easily detect and notify firefighters and forest rangers before these fires got out of control.

Agriculture

Sensors could guide farmers on which crops to grow, at the optimal time of year, in order to maximize yields. Helium sensors could collect data from automated irrigation devices and transmit it back to cloud-based control centers.[5] Given the small profit margins generated by many farms, this data could be a matter of survival for family farms—and the future of agriculture.

With the growing list of use cases, the Helium team realized that a proprietary technology would probably get limited reception: customers would not want to be locked into a solution from a single company and would likely work toward a global standard (like 3G).

So Helium made a critical decision: it would *become* the global standard. The company made a bold move, in the spirit of the decentralized blockchain, by open sourcing the design of the Hotspot, the sensors, and the software. Other companies would be free to manufacture their own Hotspots; anyone could build on the Helium network. By opening up the technology to everyone, the company placed a big bet that Helium would take off (Figure 4-5).

But first, the technology had to actually work.

---

5 Haleem, "Entering the Next Phase of Helium."

Figure 4-5. The open source chip for the Helium Hotspot, free for any company to manufacture

The Hotspot Heats Up

At the heart of this decentralized network was the Helium Hotspot, a small hardware device about the size of a smartphone, using a new long-range, low-power wireless protocol. The result was a $500 consumer-focused network node that was easy to set up and configure through a user-friendly smartphone app.

The company hired product development experts who put a great deal of effort into the look and feel of the app. Helium wanted a seamless, user-friendly experience for configuring and maintaining Hotspots, so anyone could own one —not just hardware geeks and blockchain wonks. In addition to hiding the complexity of the network behind a simple interface, they designed the app (see Figure 4-6) to provide friendly, colorful, real-time stats on how much wireless traffic each Hotspot was routing.[6]

Maximizing range was critical for making the network usable, because Hotspot coverage could be dramatically impacted by location, building materials, and radio wave interference. A Hotspot in San Francisco, for example, might have a range of about two to three miles, meaning Helium would need about 150

6 Brady Dale, "Crypto-Powered IoT Networks Are on Their Way to Over 250 US Cities," Yahoo! Finance, September 24, 2019, *https://finance.yahoo.com/news/crypto-powered-iot-networks-way-120050824.html*.

Hotspots to cover the city. In rural areas, however, the range could extend out to ten miles.

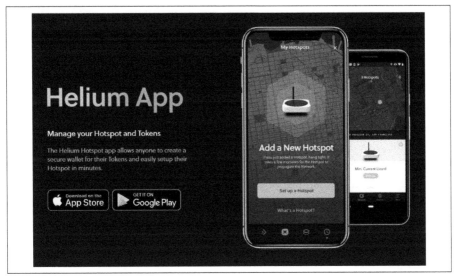

Figure 4-6. Easy to add, easy to monitor[7]

To achieve this range, the Helium team had to develop a new wireless protocol called LongFi, a kind of long-range WiFi. It allowed any IoT device to connect to any Hotspot—up to thousands of devices per Hotspot—and transmit data back and forth over long ranges while maximizing battery life.[8]

But that wasn't enough. The protocol also had to be *decentralized*, meaning it had to:

- Set up without third-party assistance or verification
- Connect and send data without centralized validation
- Send payment from devices to Hotspots without intermediaries

7 Helium, *http://www.helium.com*.

8 Dal Gemmell, "Learning about LongFi," *The Helium Blog*, Medium, August 28 10, 2019, *https://blog.helium.com/learning-about-longfi-4b7b36c9bf54*.

In typical networks, a centralized figure often provides access to the network (like your network admin). Helium's decentralized wireless protocol (LongFi) and its decentralized hardware (the Helium Hotspot) allowed for unlimited growth of the network, without a central authority.

Even the sensors were decentralized. Let's imagine a scooter rental company using the Helium network to track a fleet of scooters: it would receive a unique ID to be used across all its scooter sensors, with all Hotspots trusting that ID. This enabled sensors to "roam" without needing to reauthenticate. A rented scooter moving through a city, for example, would always stay logged into the network.

LongFi was built to transfer small packets of data, not for the high-bandwidth requirements of smartphones or computers. But LongFi, unlike WiFi, didn't require you to keep logging in. Any authenticated sensor on any Helium Hotspot could be trusted. As COO Frank Mong explained, the system is **permissionless**, meaning a username and password are not needed, as trust is stored on the decentralized blockchain.[9]

Definition

Permissionless: A confusing term that means *not requiring permission*. Permissionless systems do not require a username and password because the permission (i.e., the trust or authentication) has been stored on a blockchain.

The two-sided marketplace was coming together, with network "owners" on one side, and network "users" on the other. As Figure 4-7 shows, Helium was a set of open source hardware and software standards that sat in the middle.

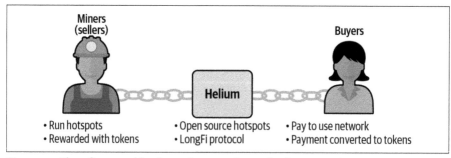

Figure 4-7. The software and hardware that runs the marketplace

---

9 Bill Guida, "Helium | Longfi | Peer-to-Peer Wireless Network | IoT | Helium Token |," Bull Flag Group, YouTube.com, August 13, 2019, *https://www.youtube.com/watch?v=IW866pj6yQQ*.

The team was building an entire ecosystem around the Helium token, the digital currency that would run this blockchain. But as with any economic system, there was quickly a lot of value at stake.

Helium Tokenomics

Miners hoped Helium tokens would rise in value, like an investment. But buyers wanted a fixed price. A scooter rental company, for example, wouldn't use a technology that cost 5 cents per device this year, and 10 cents per device next year.

The solution was to create two separate tokens: Helium Network Tokens (HNT) and Data Credits (DC). Whereas HNT could change in value (like an investment), DC would be a stable unit of purchasing power to use the network (like a currency). Think of these as *mining tokens* and *usage tokens* (Figure 4-8).

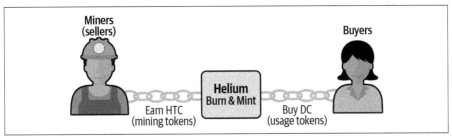

Figure 4-8. The tokenomics of Helium

Here the company made an important decision: HNT would be created only when users did real "work." Whereas most blockchain projects begin with a fixed amount of *pre-mined* tokens, HNT tokens would be created only when users set up Hotspots, validated other Hotspots, or had data transferred over their Hotspots.[10] We call this idea *token creation = value creation*, represented by the equation $T_c = V_c$.

10 Haleem, "Entering the Next Phase of Helium."

Tip

A best practice is to create new blockchain tokens only when a valuable unit of work has been performed (like validating a transaction on the blockchain). We generally do not recommend *pre-mining* tokens (creating a bank of tokens at the outset), or awarding tokens in *airdrops* (free giveaways), as these do not encourage building long-term value.

On the other side of the marketplace, companies could use the Helium network by purchasing DC tokens, which gave them predictable costs and avoided crypto concerns such as how the DC tokens would be classified by regulators. A Data Credit was true to its name: literally, a credit that allowed you to transfer 1 byte of data over the network, denominated in US dollars.

The Helium team made another critical decision: Data Credits could be acquired only by **burning**, or deleting, Helium Network Tokens. This process was managed through a burn-and-mint equilibrium developed by Multicoin Capital.[11] The fixed price of DC, based on market analysis, was set at $0.0001 per data fragment, or around 24 to 32 cents per megabyte.

Definition

Burning and **minting**: Two sides of the same virtual coin. *Minting* is creating a new token; *burning* is destroying it, or removing it from circulation. (Think of it like creating and deleting a file.)

As HNT was converted into DC through this burning process, those HNT were eliminated from circulation. Thus, Helium's monetary policy was market driven; that is, it was based on who was actually using the system. Theoretically, the more people who used the Helium network, the more tokens would be removed from the system, thus making the existing tokens more valuable—and providing an incentive for more Hotspots (Figure 4-9).

In theory, as the demand for HNT tokens increases, the price of HNT should also increase. However, because Data Credits can't be sold to other users, customers can be confident that DC will maintain their value.

In summary, Helium's tokenomics were designed to create price stability for customers through the DC *usage token*, while still allowing miners to make

---

11 Samani, Kyle, "New Models for Utility Tokens," Multicoin Capital, February 13, 2018, *https://multi-coin.capital/2018/02/13/new-models-utility-tokens*.

money with the HNT *mining token*. Whereas the DC was nontransferrable, the HNT could be bought and sold freely, and perhaps later even sold on digital exchanges at a profit. Miners, of course, were hoping that the price of HNT would slowly rise.

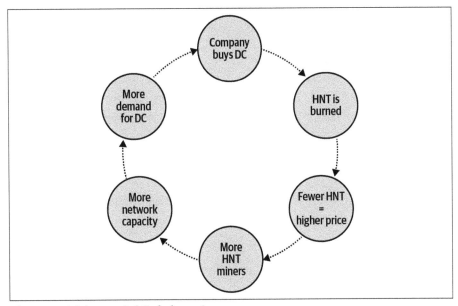

Figure 4-9. A "virtuous circle" of tokenomics

Funding and Team

Throughout this six-year journey, Helium pivoted several times but always tried to solve the same problem: simplifying the process of connecting small, low-bandwidth devices to the internet on batteries that will last for years, with sensors that connect over miles. The company completed three rounds of venture funding:

Series A funding
$16 million from Khosla Ventures, with participation from FirstMark Capital, Digital Garage, Marc Benioff, SV Angel, and Slow Ventures[12]

---

12 Ryan Lawler, "With $16M in Funding, Helium Wants to Provide the Connective Tissue for the Internet of Things," TechCrunch, December 10, 2014, *https://techcrunch.com/2014/12/09/helium*.

Series B funding

> $20 million from GV (formerly Google Ventures), with participation from Khosla Ventures, FirstMark, and Munich RE/Hartford Steam Boiler Ventures[13]

Series C funding

> $15 million from Union Square Ventures, Fred Wilson, and Multicoin Capital

One of the key takeaways from the Helium story is the importance of a consistent vision—both inside the company and with outside investors—even while the product pivots. This vision had to be both large and compelling enough to attract all the partners needed to build this massive ecosystem.

Internally, the company built small, agile teams around this vision in several key areas:

- Distributed Systems Blockchain Team (six to seven employees)
- Wireless Protocol Team (six to seven employees)
- Mobile App Team (two to three employees)
- Hardware Manufacturing (largely outsourced, with two employees managing the vendor)
- Business Development (four employees, each assigned a geographical region)

In summary, Helium's business model had two sides. On one side, Helium paid tokens to miners for helping build and maintain the network. On the other side, Helium provided services and support for companies that wanted to use that network (similar to Red Hat software, which offers services and support for the open source Linux). In this two-sided business model, Helium empowered the people to create a network that companies paid to use. Helium didn't own that network; the people who own the Hotspots do. The company was, in a sense, creating a network only to give it away.

---

13 "Helium Raises $20 Million Series B Funding Round to Accelerate Smart Sensing Solutions," Business Wire, April 25, 2016, *https://www.businesswire.com/news/home/20160425005330/en/Helium-Raises-20-Million-Series-Funding-Accelerate.*

But it all came down to getting network coverage: without a network of sufficient size, Helium would be nothing but vaporware.

The Launch

The company chose Austin, Texas, as the site for the initial launch. As a rising technology hub, Austin had plenty of wireless technology early adopters and blockchain enthusiasts. It was a prime location for innovators, startups, and investors. And Austin had local companies that were interested in piloting Helium (Lime, the scooter rental company, was already lined up).

Helium determined it would take about 100 to 150 Hotspots to provide full coverage for the city. Within a month, the company had exceeded that goal, with 200 Hotspots installed in Greater Austin—enough coverage for the entire city. By offering a user-friendly product with blockchain-based rewards, Helium doubled its minimum goal, convincing users to install enough $500 Hotspots to provide wireless coverage for the city of Austin.

As Amir eagerly checked and rechecked his map of Austin to watch new Hotspots coming online, he reflected on the company's success:

- Helium tokens were now being earned for real work.
- Data was being transmitted from sensors over the network.
- The burn-and-mint equilibrium was working properly.
- Hotspot owners were happy with the user-friendly apps and customer support.
- The solution was now stress-tested and ready to be rolled out to other cities.

Lessons Learned

Helium offers several best practices for technology leaders working on blockchain projects:

Stick to your knitting
> Even as the product pivots, keep to your overarching principles (decentralized, open source, permissionless networks) that are consistent with your vision for the project.

Focus on the frontend

While good backend blockchain developers are critical, be sure to hire a team capable of hiding the complexity of blockchain in a well-designed, user-friendly product.

Build open and scale quickly

As most blockchains will become a winner-takes-all or winner-takes-most scenario, lean toward making blockchain projects that are open and free. (Remember the principle of network effects from Chapter 3.)

Design tokenomics carefully

Be sure that tokens are created only when value is created, and think through the needs of both sides of your marketplace, the chicken and the egg.

Keep it simple

To reach the mass market, your blockchain ultimately needs to be easy to explain and understand. When it's not possible to keep it simple, hide the complexity (Figure 4-10).

Figure 4-10. Hide the complexity[14]

---

14 Helium. *http://www.helium.com.*

Next Steps

The larger the network, the more valuable it becomes.

—Amir Haleem, Helium CEO

The telecommunications industry was ripe for disruption. Amir knew that when The People's Network reached a critical mass, the blockchain-based network would become a powerful disruptive force, democratizing network access and distributing wealth to the masses. As Amir watched new Hotspots lighting up on his map of Austin, he pondered the company's next move (Figure 4-11).

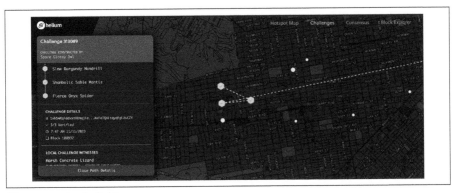

Figure 4-11. Austin lights up

How could the company rapidly scale The People's Network, making sure both sides of the marketplace stayed in sync?

- Should Helium *seek additional IoT applications*, including wearable technology and personal security? If so, on which of the many IoT applications should Helium's business development team focus its efforts?

- Should Helium *consider listing its token on digital exchanges*? This would increase demand for HNT, providing more liquidity for buyers and sellers. But listing on digital exchanges was expensive and time-consuming, and no one could predict how the market might price HNT.

- Should Helium even be in the hardware business, or should the company *partner with a manufacturer* to take its open source designs and produce Hotspots at scale, enabling Helium to focus on blockchain and software?

If you were the CEO of Helium, where would you float your next trial balloon?

5

Circle: Building a Blockchain Ecosystem

This is the moment that we have been waiting for. When we started our company, we thought it would take five to ten years to reach this point, but six and a half years later, we are now here.

—Jeremy Allaire, Circle cofounder and CEO, December 12, 2019

With its large open workspaces and kitchen stocked with free food, Circle had the feel of a hip technology company. Yet its sweeping panoramic views of the Boston skyline placed it squarely in the middle of the city's financial district, home to some of the world's largest financial institutions.

This combination—new tech meets old money—was perhaps a perfect way to describe the company. From its startup ambition of being a "blockchain bank" in 2013, Circle had quickly attracted venture capital from major financial players like Goldman Sachs, and five years later had a valuation of over $3 billion.[1]

As the company had grown, so had its vision. Circle had grown into a new kind of global financial services company—where individuals, entrepreneurs, and institutions come together to use, trade, invest, and raise capital with easy-to-use financial products and services.

But unlike traditional financial services companies, this one was built on blockchain.

---

1 Dan Frommer, "Circle Has Raised Another $110 Million—at a Nearly $3 Billion Valuation—in One of the Largest Rounds Yet for a Crypto Startup," Recode, Vox, May 15, 2018, *https://www.vox.com/2018/5/15/17356990/circle-bitmain-funding-round-jeremy-allaire-centre-bitcoin.*

It had been a long road for Jeremy Allaire, the cofounder and CEO of Circle. As he looked out the window of his office at Circle's HQ, his gaze fell once again on the fortress-like Federal Reserve building, the center of the US financial system. Both literally and figuratively, they were *so close.*

But like everything he had done before, there was no road map for where to go next. He had long believed open blockchain technologies would replace the world's closed, proprietary financial systems—but the two had to work together. Even a new highway had to have on-ramps and off-ramps into the old highway.

As Jeremy looked back on his experiences as a serial entrepreneur, and how Circle had reached this point, he realized that certain themes ran throughout his 30-plus year journey as a technology business leader. There were larger lessons from his story that he could apply to Circle's future.

It was a story in three acts.

Act 1: Allaire Corporation

Jeremy Allaire had three aha moments in his career.

The first was when he downloaded the Mosaic web browser in September 1993. Unlike the crude, early browsers, Mosaic was the first graphical browser that ran across multiple operating systems. It could render content more fully. It gave users the ability to input data. He immediately saw that this open platform —the World Wide Web, accessed through the web browser—was a game changer (Figure 5-1).

This insight resulted in Allaire Corporation, a company started by his brother and built with Jeremy and several close college friends. They had the belief that open standards built on HTTP and HTML would make content distribution, communication, and software all open and ubiquitous. This belief in open standards—rather than closed proprietary networks—was behind all the products Allaire Corporation would go on to create, including ColdFusion, the first internet programming language, and HomeSite, the popular HTML development tool that made it easy for anyone to create a website.

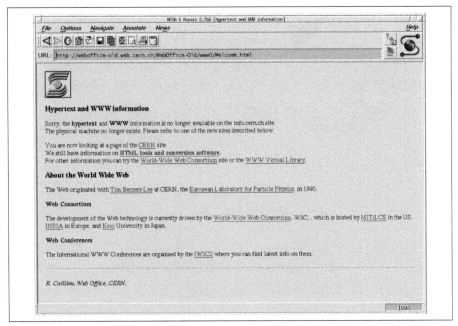

Figure 5-1. The browser that changed the world[2]

As the company grew, Allaire eventually merged with Macromedia. With the rollout of broadband, together they could combine Allaire's developer and programmer tools with Macromedia's Flash Player and content tools to make rich internet applications that would enhance the web-browsing experience further. Then, in March 2002, they introduced another game changer: the ability to embed video objects into Macromedia Flash (Figure 5-2).

---

2 NCSA Mosaic Browser Screenshot courtesy of Programm: National Center for Supercomputing Applications, CC0.

Figure 5-2. O'Reilly books on ActionScript, the language used to program Flash video objects

Given the simplicity of now having a programmable video object in 98% of web browsers, Jeremy realized that Flash plus broadband would make streaming video as ubiquitous as text on the web. Inspired by this second aha moment, Jeremy handed over the reins and left Macromedia to incubate his ideas for online video as an executive in residence at VC firm General Catalyst Partners—which resulted in his second company, Brightcove.

Act 2: Brightcove

Like Allaire Corporation, Brightcove was built on the principle of open standards. Whereas the existing media landscape was dominated by closed, proprietary networks (think broadcast and satellite TV), Jeremy believed the future of media would be open, permissionless, and built on the public internet. If TV were to become democratized, then anyone in the world could be a distributor, and content could go directly to consumers on any device.

In 2004, this was not an obvious prediction. This was before YouTube, smartphones, and the explosion of online video. Creating and distributing video was still expensive, which was why you needed a TV network. As broadband took hold and cameras proliferated, video became cheap and plentiful. How could traditional media companies adapt?

That became Brightcove's sweet spot. The firm partnered with a wide array of traditional media companies, including Reuters, Discovery Communications, and the New York Times, to help them launch online video portals. This experience of helping traditional media companies (closed networks) adapt to the new world of online video (open networks) would later be a parallel for Jeremy's work at Circle.

As Brightcove grew, the deals got bigger. The company began partnering with international media companies in Europe and Asia, then preparing for its own initial public offering. In his travels, Jeremy met many international investors and found his interest in the global economy reignited.

After the financial crisis of 2008, the heads of the Chinese central bank, the International Monetary Fund (IMF), the Bank of Japan, and the Bank of England came forward with proposals to replace the US dollar as the global reserve currency. This idea of a new currency—based on a *basket*, or mix, of global currencies—appealed to Allaire: it would eventually become open standards, applied to money.

He had long been interested in the global economy—his undergraduate work was concentrated in political science, economics, and philosophy—but now Jeremy began to read about the history of the banking system, with central banks and the international monetary system becoming a personal passion.

In 2012, as Brightcove went public, Jeremy learned about bitcoin. He read about the digital currency on a tech blog, and the idea instantly intrigued him. When he downloaded his first bitcoin, synchronized the blockchain to his computer, and conducted his first transaction, he had another aha moment.

Even though the process of buying bitcoin was cumbersome, the kernel was there. This was a kind of open money, like the open internet and the open video protocols that had enabled Jeremy's first two companies. The idea of *open financial protocols* completely captured his imagination.

He had a vision that in the next 10 to 20 years, he could help to rebuild the global financial system in the image of the internet. This new *Internet of Value* would be open and democratized, just like the web and online video had democratized information and communications. This open system would also naturally lead to a global currency, upon which he could build interesting financial services businesses.

So, despite now leading a public company, in early 2013 Jeremy made the decision to move on from Brightcove, promoting the existing leadership team to fill his shoes. He called up Sean Neville, his trusted technologist at both Allaire and Brightcove, to learn that Sean had also been bitten by the bitcoin bug.

Jeremy and Sean now saw an opportunity to build a new type of company around digital currency. As with Brightcove's vision for video content that could go to anyone, anywhere, on any device, they now saw a similar opportunity in the world of money.

Act 3: Circle

When Jeremy and Sean started Circle, the big challenge was just getting someone to take a meeting.

The vision of a blockchain bank seemed so simple. But they hadn't counted on the level of fear from the established players—regulators, bankers, and financial companies—that they would somehow get into trouble for getting involved with bitcoin.

As an entrepreneur, Jeremy was used to seeing opportunities that others did not, and then pursuing those ideas with tenacity. He was used to resistance from the establishment. But this time, he and Sean were surrounded by an almost impenetrable wall of skepticism.

People thought they were lunatics. First, they might go to jail (this was not far-fetched; early efforts to create new digital currencies had led to indictments and federal government crackdowns).[3] If that didn't happen, no government would allow something that cut so deeply against the state-controlled monetary system. Even if they cleared the legal hurdles, they'd have to create an entire financial ecosystem to support the vision. The big banks were a walled fortress, and they were two lonely troubadours.

The worst part was that Jeremy and Sean knew they were right: starting Circle would be a challenge unlike anything they had faced. They would have to create an entirely new banking infrastructure, built from scratch on software and open standards, and invent new forms of money that could be run across the internet—all while somehow winning the support of regulators on a state-by-state and country-by-country basis.

---

3 See, for example, Wikipedia's "E-gold" entry: *https://en.wikipedia.org/wiki/E-gold*.

One thing was clear: to build this system of new money, they'd need regular money, and a lot of it.

To Bet or Not to Bet (on Bitcoin): That Is the Question

Even though they first thought of Circle as a *bitcoin bank*, Jeremy and Sean didn't think bitcoin would become the world reserve currency. They went out of their way to position the company as something bigger than bitcoin (they didn't name it *BitCircle*); the company was offering a new global financial experience.

Instead of bitcoin, they talked about *digital currency*. They believed you could take existing currencies, convert them into cryptocurrencies, and have all the benefits of open protocols: global money, available on any device, cheaper and faster to send, and fully interoperable between any digital wallet.

For the first time, money would be *data*.

The entrepreneurs saw how web protocols like HTTP allowed siloed databases to talk to each other, so any device with a web browser could exchange content, anywhere in the world. They saw how email protocols like SMTP opened up the closed world of corporate email, allowing any device to exchange emails, anywhere in the world. Texting. GPS. WiFi. All built on open protocols. So why not money too?

Still, bitcoin was the dominant player in blockchain in the mid-2010s, so Jeremy and Sean thought it had potential as a protocol or base layer—the "rails" that might allow a global financial system to run. Their startup team began hacking together a hybrid system that would allow users to convert US dollars and euros into bitcoin, and then move that value by using the bitcoin blockchain.

They quickly found out that bitcoin didn't scale: it was slow and expensive, and it wasn't easy to program on top of it. Bitcoin was still the leading digital currency—but for a protocol, they'd have to look elsewhere.

The First BitLicense

Around the time that Circle began in March of 2013, the US Department of the Treasury issued its first guidance on digital currency. Any company that converted dollars to digital currencies was classified as a *money transmitter*, which meant they'd need a special license in each state: a difficult and expensive proposition, especially for startups.

This decision enraged many in the blockchain industry. *This is a new global technology*, they argued, *so the old rules shouldn't apply.*

Circle took a different approach: rather than fight the framework, they chose to work within it. Their vision was to sit at the intersection of the traditional financial system and this new financial system. In order to use US dollars over the bitcoin network, in other words, they'd have to work with the US government. Over the next few years, they went state to state and became the most licensed company in the industry.

New York, however, posed a special problem. Benjamin Lawsky, the first superintendent of its Department of Financial Services, saw an opportunity to put a stake in the ground around blockchain regulation and created a new licensing model called the **BitLicense**. Only in New York.

Definition

BitLicense: A license required for virtual currency businesses doing business in New York. The BitLicense stands as an example of regulators moving too quickly to put frameworks around new technologies, which can stifle innovation and paradoxically work against a regulator's goals.

The BitLicense applied to any company doing business in New York involving digital currencies. Applying for a BitLicense required a 30-page application, a $5,000 filing fee, and sizable legal costs. As blockchain businesses began leaving the state rather than submit to the lengthy licensing process, the press called it "The Great Bitcoin Exodus."[4]

Circle responded on two fronts: while publicly opposing the initial version of the BitLicense, it continued to work behind the scenes in closed-door meetings to make the license more acceptable. In a sense, the company became the poster child for working constructively with regulators to achieve a workable solution for both sides.

As a result, in 2015 Circle became the first company to receive a BitLicense from the State of New York, with BitLicense certificate number #000001 (Figure 5-3). The BitLicense was a very high standard, and it would be over a year until the state issued certificate #000002.

---

4 Michael del Castillo, "The 'Great Bitcoin Exodus' Has Totally Changed New York's Bitcoin Ecosystem," *New York Business Journal,* August 12, 2015, *https://www.bizjournals.com/newyork/news/2015/08/12/ the-great-bitcoin-exodus-has-totally-changed-new.html.*

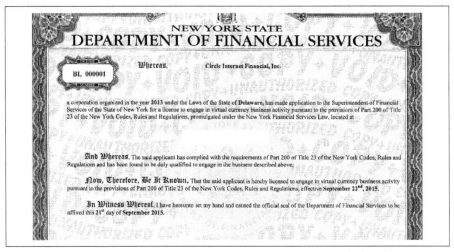

Figure 5-3. BitLicense #000001. Note the six digits, implying that New York thought up to a million might be issued. Five years later, they had granted fewer than 20.

As of this writing, New York is finally beginning to relax this standard. For years, Circle caught flack from many in the blockchain industry for working with the government, but the industry as a whole is now benefiting from Circle's collaborative efforts and long-term approach. Circle embraced evolution, not revolution.

But the permit was just one piece of the puzzle. Circle still needed a product. To be more precise, it needed an ecosystem of products.

Building the Ecosystem

New technology products often require new ecosystems.

As an example, consider that Thomas Edison didn't just invent the light bulb. He also developed the lighting fixtures, the electrical systems, and the modern electric company. The light bulb, in isolation, was of limited use: an entire **ecosystem** of electricity was needed to really make it useful (Figure 5-4).

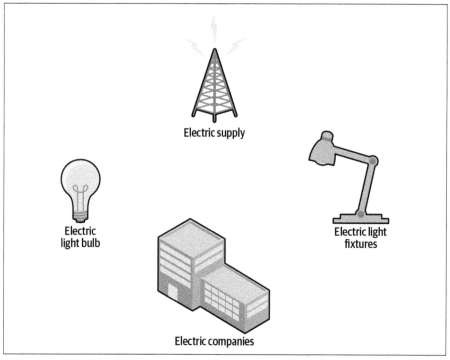

Figure 5-4. Edison's electric ecosystem

For a more recent example, consider Tesla, which does not just make electric cars. The company is also one of the largest producers of electric storage (batteries), electric networks (charging stations), and the world's largest electric production facility, Gigafactory 1 (Figure 5-5).

Jeremy, Sean, and the growing Circle team had a core competency in building open internet ecosystems (i.e., products, platforms, infrastructure). This would be the source of their sustainable competitive advantage in the emerging ecosystem of decentralized finance, or **DeFi**.

Definition

DeFi: The ecosystem of decentralized financial applications built on blockchain. This community of players includes banking services, lending and borrowing platforms, and digital exchanges.

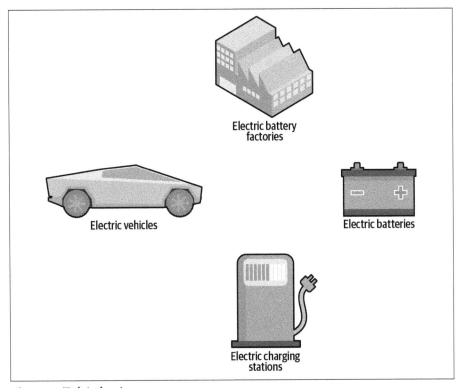

Figure 5-5. Tesla's electric ecosystem

To realize its vision, Circle would need to build four separate but interrelated systems (Figure 5-6):

- A *fiat-to-crypto system* for transferring traditional currency to digital currency
- A *payments system* for making it easy to send and receive digital currency
- A *risk and compliance system* for managing fraud and criminal risk
- A *custody system* for safely storing digital currencies, like a traditional bank

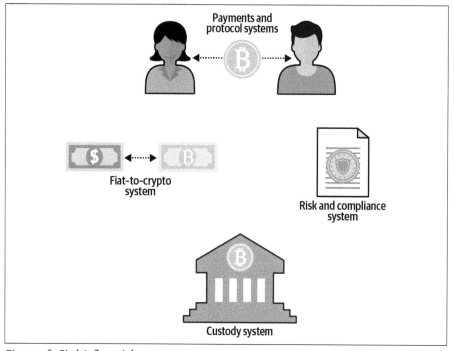

Figure 5-6. Circle's financial ecosystem

Flush with funding from top investors, Circle spent the next few years building each of these systems from scratch, packaging them into user-facing products:

Circle Invest

A fiat-to-crypto product to easily convert dollars into bitcoin or other digital assets

Circle Pay

A user-friendly app that sat on top of a new blockchain-based payment and settlement protocol

Circle Trade

A licensed, regulated service that allowed institutional-grade trading of digital assets, with full legal compliance

As blockchain technology evolved, Circle saw that it could now convert central bank money (like dollars) into digital currency units that could be easily used on the public internet. It was the best of both worlds: digital currency backed by stable currency.

Thus began the next phase of Circle's evolution: to create an industry-leading **stablecoin.**

Definition

Stablecoin: A digital currency that is designed to hold its value, without day-to-day price swings. Stablecoins are typically tied, or *pegged*, to a traditional currency such as the US dollar.

The Creation of Centre and USDC

Throughout this book, we've seen the power of the *consortium*: a group of industry partners that work together to achieve some common good. Often these companies are competitors, but they understand that achieving a common consensus around a project or protocol will be more successful than trying to go it alone. This is often referred to as *coopetition*, when competitors cooperate with each other.

The Centre Consortium was cofounded by Circle and Coinbase, two giants of the emerging decentralized finance space. Their first project was to define open standards for digital currencies, upon which the consortium launched its first stablecoin, US Dollar Coin (USDC).

The advantage to launching USDC as part of Centre was that the stablecoin could grow far beyond Circle. Coinbase had the largest digital asset exchange in the US; by making USDC available to traders and investors, it could quickly become a digital currency standard.

The disadvantage was that now Circle didn't own USDC; Centre did. Although Centre was spun out of Circle and Coinbase, it was now an independent entity that neither of them fully controlled. This trade-off—whether to centralize a project or form a consortium—is a classic blockchain dilemma. Table 5-1 details the contrast.

Table 5-1. Centralize versus consortium: the great blockchain dilemma

Centralize	Consortium
Go it alone	Partner with "frenemies"
Rapid, efficient decisions	Inclusive, effective decisions
Own a minority of the market, but it's yours	Own the majority of the market, but it's shared

Centralize	Consortium
Beat competitors to market	Share the market with competitors
Create your own standards	Create the industry standards
Inexpensive, incompatible infrastructures	Expensive, interoperable infrastructures
You own a small table	You have a seat at the big table

Launched in September 2018, USDC became the fastest-growing stablecoin in blockchain history (Figure 5-7). It was a fully collateralized stablecoin, meaning it was backed one to one with US dollars held in reserve by regulated financial institutions. At any time, in other words, users could redeem 1 USDC for 1 USD.

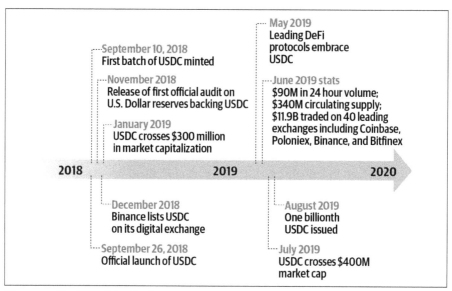

Figure 5-7. The USDC timeline[5]

You may be wondering, why go to all the trouble to create a USDC stablecoin? After all, if it has the same value as a dollar, why not just use dollars? There were two reasons.

---

5 Team Circle, "ICYMI: USDC Celebrates Its First Anniversary!" Circle, October 16, 2019, *https://blog.circle.com/2019/10/01/icymi-usdc-celebrates-its-first-anniversary*.

First, it was still slow and expensive to move from dollars to digital. Second, the value of these digital assets (like bitcoin) could swing wildly from one day to the next. To maintain the value of their "digital money" without constantly having to convert back to "traditional money," traders and investors could store them in stablecoins.

Once again, Circle was proving the value of open protocols: instead of moving value back and forth between traditional currencies and digital currencies (i.e., closed systems and open systems), it was easier to store value in the open system (USDC), with the peace of mind that it was still backed by the traditional system (USD). The government didn't own it; USDC holders owned it.

Here again the Centre collaboration paid off: instead of a "Circle cryptocurrency," USDC became an ecosystem in its own right. The more digital wallets supported USDC, the more money went into those wallets. The more digital exchanges that supported USDC, the more investors and traders who used it to store value (Figure 5-8).

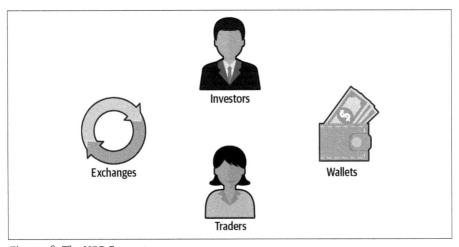

Figure 5-8. The USDC ecosystem

But USDC wasn't just a digital dollar. It was computer code.

Traditional currency is static, inert. Digital currency is alive. New features can be programmed into it and pushed out in automatic updates. In other words, digital currency is software. This new concept—digital currency built on blockchain technology—we'll call **programmable money**.

Definition

Programmable money: Digital currencies built on blockchain technology. Since they are software products, they can be constantly upgraded with new features; for example, built-in escrow, or the ability to automatically reconcile payments. This gives us the potential to completely reimagine traditional financial products—provided we have a price-stable currency.[6]

But programmable money wasn't enough: it also had to be global. Money should work like email: unencumbered by distance, borders, and service providers. As an example, a Gmail user can email a Yahoo! mail account because the two systems are interoperable, working with a shared email protocol. An Alipay user, by contrast, can't pay someone who is using PayPal, because their payment systems aren't interoperable. There's no shared protocol.

Thus, USDC was built on the ERC-20 open token standard on top of the open Ethereum blockchain so that it would be interoperable with any application that also adopts those standards and would no longer be confined to a user's choice of digital wallet.

The open source, open protocol strategy paid off. According to Forbes, upon reaching $335 million in market value, USDC not only was the fastest-growing stablecoin, but also had become one of the 20 most valuable cryptocurrencies worldwide.[7] Another reason for this rapid growth was that unlike other stablecoins, Circle was not the sole issuer: even the creation of USDC was open.

The Circle team realized that to build a stablecoin tied to the US dollar, many companies must be able to issue it. For a currency to thrive, it must become widely accepted, so people can use it in many places (widespread *agreement*), with a set of technical and governance standards protecting it (widespread *trust*).

If a digital currency has these two components—widespread agreement and widespread trust—then many companies can support it, and movement of value will become like the internet: ubiquitous, free-flowing connections between every wallet.

---

6 Team Circle, "A Deeper Look at Stablecoins and USDC," Circle, November 8, 2018, *https:// blog.circle.com/2018/11/07/a-deeper-look-at-stablecoins-and-usdc*.

7 "Circle," Forbes, February 4, 2019, *https://www.forbes.com/companies/circle/#2b3b54fddb35*.

Thus, the USDC ecosystem was built with the open frameworks that Jeremy had seen work in his first two companies.[8] But by opening USDC to the world, Circle had willingly given up key elements of its design and control. How could Circle continue to grow as a centralized company?

Next Steps

Over the past six years, Circle has built one of the broadest technology platforms in the crypto industry...and a custody solution that has helped secure billions of dollars in digital assets.[9]

—Sean Neville and Jeremy Allaire

Jeremy's first aha moment was when he discovered the web browser and saw the potential of decentralized information. That led to his first company, Allaire Corporation.

His next aha moment was when he first saw video hosted online and realized the potential of decentralized video. That led to his second company, Brightcove.

His final aha moment was when he discovered bitcoin and saw the potential of decentralized money. That led to his third company, Circle.

In each case, his aha moment came when he realized that open protocols lead to decentralized products, which lead to radically new business models. From their first vision of a bitcoin bank, Jeremy and Sean had a clear idea of what an open financial system would look like:

- Money and value would move around the world as easily as any other data on the internet.

- As on the internet, people would send and receive value to each other in a decentralized way, not through a single company or government.

---

8 "A Governed Network Powered by Price-Stable Crypto Assets," Centre, accessed January 8, 2020, *https://www.centre.io/index.html.*

9 Sean Neville and Jeremy Allaire, "Poloniex to Spin Out of Circle," Circle, November 1, 2019, *https://blog.circle.com/2019/10/18/poloniex-to-spin-out-of-circle.*

- Anyone with a mobile phone would have access to the same powerful financial services, anywhere in the world.[10]

It's been quite an adventure, Jeremy thought as he gazed at the Federal Reserve building. They had come a long way from not being able to get a meeting with banks. Jeremy had recently been called to testify on Capitol Hill, where he implored the Senate Committee on Banking, Housing, and Urban Affairs to allow blockchain innovators room to grow in the US and for Congress to adopt a national policy framework for digital assets with appropriate rules and exemptions.[11]

Change was coming. It was clear that the old guard would be replaced by fintech and blockchain startups. In China, it had already happened: the leading financial services companies were now Tencent and Ant Financial Services Group, both relatively young technology upstarts.

New tech was transforming old money. Digital currencies were improving on traditional currencies. USDC was being built on top of USD.

More than six years after its launch, Circle had evolved from a "bitcoin bank" into an open ecosystem of value exchange, enabling new financial products and services to be built on top of these open standards, resulting in a new type of global financial institution.

The company had become one of the rare "blockchain unicorns," with a multibillion-dollar valuation; indeed, its USDC traded nearly a billion dollars in value *each day.*[12] However, it needed to continue building products and services on top of USDC that were both meaningful and scalable.

If you were in Jeremy's shoes, where would you focus your efforts?

- What financial products and services would you support?

- Should you focus on partnering with other financial institutions? If so, which ones?

- Would you look for opportunities for additional acquisitions? What types of companies might you buy?

---

10 Neville and Allaire, "Poloniex to Spin Out of Circle."

11 "Circle CEO Jeremy Allaire—Opening Remarks to US Senate Banking Committee," Circle, YouTube, 2019, *https://youtu.be/aDubCR8xZF4.*

12 "USD Coin (USDC) Price, Charts, Market Cap, and Other Metrics," CoinMarketCap, accessed February 11, 2020, *https://coinmarketcap.com/currencies/usd-coin.*

- How would you deal with the challenge of losing control of USDC as more partners are added to the Centre Consortium?
- Should you look to collaborate with governments, and do these governments represent more of an opportunity or a threat?

Looking at the evolving financial landscape, where would you center your efforts?

6

CryptoKitties: Blockchain-Based Collectibles

Every new technology gets a game that helps bring it careening into the mainstream. Social networks had FarmVille. Mobile phones had Angry Birds. And, its investors hope, blockchain has CryptoKitties.[1]

—*Nellie Bowles*, The New York Times

"Oh, no."

Mack Flavelle, chief creative officer of Dapper Labs and cofounder of Crypto-Kitties, was walking up the basement stairs at his parents' house while glancing at his phone, when he got hit with a one-two punch.

First, he saw hundreds of messages from prospective kitten buyers asking him why the CryptoKitties network was moving so slowly: it was taking up to two hours for their transactions to process. Then his eyes were drawn to an email with the heading, "We just sold a kitten for $30,000."

When Mack reached the top of the stairs, his father saw the look of shock and surprise on his son's face. Stunned, the young entrepreneur turned to his father and said, "Everything is broken."

For most blockchain projects, the problem is getting enough participants to grow your blockchain. In less than a day, Mack had run into the opposite problem: there were so many users that CryptoKitties was slowing down the entire Ethereum network. Worse, the exorbitant prices that people were paying for

---

1 Nellie Bowles, "CryptoKitties, Explained...Mostly," *New York Times*, December 28, 2017, *https://www.nytimes.com/2017/12/28/style/cryptokitties-want-a-blockchain-snuggle.html.*

these virtual kittens was spiraling out of control: within 12 hours, one would sell for $100,000.

The blockchain community was livid that this silly game, with its colorful cartoon cats, was taking over its precious Ethereum network—and making so much money. The CryptoKitties hype cycle was matched only by the CryptoKitties hate cycle, as Twitter exploded with both fans and foes of the virtual cats. Overnight, CryptoKitties had become the first blockchain viral hit.

Mack felt a mix of euphoria and horror. As successful as CryptoKitties was, if it didn't become scalable fast, the network would grind to a complete stop, potentially taking Ethereum down with it. Further complicating matters, this was not a problem with a single point of failure: solving it would take the combined efforts of the entire CryptoKitties team, the digital wallet provider (MetaMask), and the underlying blockchain platform provider (Ethereum).

By a lucky coincidence, many of the key players from these groups would be getting together at a blockchain retreat in New York. But could they come together on a strategy to fix their scaling problems, and could they implement it in time? Or was the cat already out of the bag?

The CryptoKitties Story

Guys, we are going to put cats on the blockchain.

—Mack Flavelle, CryptoKitties cofounder

Launched in 2017 by the Vancouver-based venture studio Axiom Zen, CryptoKitties was a collectible trading game whose users could buy, sell, trade, and breed virtual kittens called *CryptoKitties*. Imagine a cross between a Beanie Babies collectible and a Tamagotchi digital pet, stored on a blockchain.

As a CryptoKitty collector, you were buying a one-of-a-kind virtual pet with its own genetic attributes like fur pattern and eye color. Your CryptoKitty could be bred with other CryptoKitties and would pass on some of these "cattributes" to its offspring. As when breeding physical cats, some of these offspring would be highly prized; others would be alley cats.

Your CryptoKitty was represented by an adorable cartoon illustration—but underneath this virtual character, you owned a real blockchain token, stored on the CryptoKitties blockchain, which was in turn built atop the Ethereum network. Each token was one of a kind, just like a physical cat (Figure 6-1).

Most prized of all were the Generation Zero CryptoKitties, which were the virgin cats created to seed the game. These cats were released every 15 minutes for the first year, in order to stimulate buying and breeding.

Figure 6-1. One cool cat

Mack Flavelle, Axiom Zen's chief creative officer, had tried for over a decade to build a breeding or gardening game in which a player experiences the delight and discovery of never knowing what exactly will sprout. After numerous failed attempts, he found that hatching the next FarmVille was harder than it looks.

He was also inspired by an early blockchain project called CryptoPunks, unique characters that looked like something out of an 8-bit Nintendo game for adults. Only 10,000 were created and sold to collectors, with the proof of ownership stored in a digital contract on the Ethereum blockchain.

It's been said that creativity is simply combining two existing things to make something new, and these two concepts—online breeding and digital collectibles—fused in Mack's mind as a new kind of collectible game. But what form should this game take?

To anyone who has spent time on the internet, the answer was obvious: cats.

As Mack later explained it, "If you're building consumer apps, you shouldn't have to explain why you are using cats; you should explain why you are *not* using cats. Everything that grows on the viral internet eventually has something to do with cats."

He gathered his team of designers and engineers and boldly proclaimed, "Guys, we are going to put cats on the blockchain. We are going to create a new category of gaming in which cats have sex on the blockchain and we are going to build a whole new company around this."

Critically, Mack had an outstanding product team already in place (Figure 6-2):

- *Graphic designers* to create the funny and cuddly appearance of the cats
- *User-interface designers* to make a user-friendly application and experience
- A *viral marketing team* that was well versed in helping ideas spread quickly
- A talented *development team* with a deep interest in blockchain

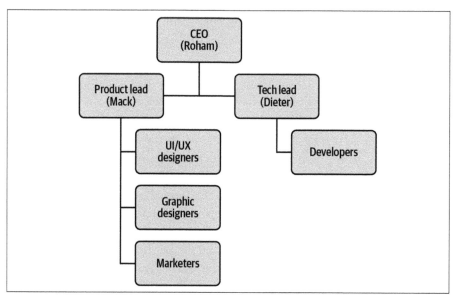

Figure 6-2. The Kitty Core team at Axiom Zen

This team structure can be seen as a best practice in creating an outstanding blockchain product, since it covered everything from the user experience to the tokenomics. Whereas most blockchain products were geeky and hard to use, this cross-functional team skillfully concealed the technology layer beneath an adorable design: art and science, head and heart.

Best of all, the team members hatched an innovative business model: they would also create an auction marketplace in which owners could buy and breed CryptoKitties, with the company earning a 3.75% commission on all transactions.[2] The more the ecosystem grew, the more money it would make. The more cats, the more cash.

The Technology

If you think about any modern game you download on your phone, you can buy things but you can never really sell them....Because of blockchain, when you buy a CryptoKitty, it is 100% yours.[3]

—Roham Gharegozlou, cofounder and CEO of CryptoKitties

Underneath the seemingly simple game of CryptoKitties was a real blockchain innovation: the **non-fungible token**, or **NFT**.

Definition

Non-fungible tokens (NFTs): While most blockchain tokens are fungible (interchangeable), NFTs are unique (like collectibles). Think of the difference between dollar bills (one dollar is equal to every other dollar) and baseball cards (rare cards are worth more money to collectors).

While it sounds like something you'd catch in a public shower, *fungible* means *interchangeable*. Most blockchain projects use fungible tokens: every bitcoin, for example, has the same value as every other bitcoin, regardless of when it was mined or who owned it.

CryptoKitties used non-fungible tokens; each token represented a unique digital object with a unique, market-driven value. Whereas two people who each owned five bitcoin would be holding the same value, two people who each owned five CryptoKitties could have vastly different values, depending on the rarity of the breed.[4]

If blockchain is the Internet of Value, this was a new kind of value. CryptoKitties were more like a collectible—like coins, stamps, or baseball cards. There were many low-value items, and a few hard-to-find items that were highly prized because of their scarcity. *Non-fungible tokens were a new unit of virtual value.*

---

2 Bowles, "CryptoKitties, Explained...Mostly."

3 "CryptoKitties and the Future of Crypto (with Roham Gharegozlou)," Real Vision Finance, YouTube, July 23, 2019, *https://www.youtube.com/watch?v=p3s05-rqCmM.*

4 Kevin Werbach, *The Blockchain and the New Architecture of Trust* (Cambridge, MA: The MIT Press, 2018), 66.

The use cases went far beyond CryptoKitties: anything that was both valuable and unique could be tracked using NFTs: diplomas, jewelry, fine art, cars, even real estate. There was only one problem: non-fungible tokens didn't exist.

Fortunately, Mack had a collaborator in Dieter Shirley, the chief technology officer of Axiom Zen. Dieter, who had configured his laptop to mine bitcoin back in 2010, had a long-standing interest in blockchain. "I was the Kitty guy, and Dieter was the crypto guy," Mack explained, highlighting the importance of their creative/technology partnership.

Like Vitalik Buterin and Satoshi Nakamoto before him, Dieter began with a **whitepaper**, a project proposal for a new kind of token, ERC-721. (The acronym stands for *Ethereum request for comments*, illustrating the open source model of getting community feedback from the beginning.)

Definition

Whitepaper: Most groundbreaking blockchain projects start with a paper that clearly explains the need and the technical solution, soliciting comments and feedback from the decentralized developer community. This open source approach helps build early community and consensus—as opposed to developing your technology behind closed doors.

"It was one of the most ridiculously well-written smart contracts in the industry at the time," recalled Mack. "The early comments were awe inspired by how rational it was. It was technically robust and sophisticated." If any blockchain project could scale, the team felt, this was the one.

As the NFT proposal made its way through the Ethereum developer community, Dieter began to consider how users could buy and sell CryptoKitties (which, remember, were essentially blockchain tokens). They needed an easy on-ramp to convert dollars to Ethereum, then Ethereum to the CryptoKitty token. In the end, the CryptoKitties team chose the digital wallet MetaMask, which could be installed into most web browsers as a user-friendly plugin.

Thus, the technology stack comprised Ethereum (the blockchain platform), with the user on-ramp of MetaMask (the digital wallet), running CryptoKitties (the blockchain application); see Figure 6-3. Bryce Bladon, another cofounder, stated that it was "very scary having two of those structures outside of our control —which is why cooperation was so important!"[5]

---

5 ConsenSys, "The Inside Story of the CryptoKitties Congestion Crisis," Medium, May 22, 2019, *https:// media.consensys.net/the-inside-story-of-the-cryptokitties-congestion-crisis-499b35d119cc.*

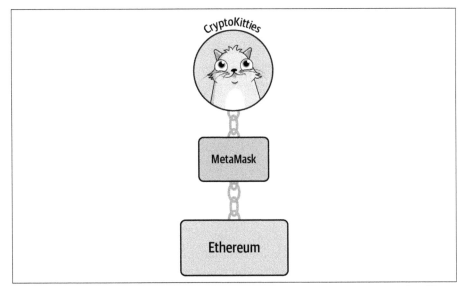

Figure 6-3. Crypt cat tech stack: Ethereum platform, MetaMask wallet, CryptoKitty collectible

Cooperation was also key to creating a seamless user experience. As Dan Finlay, the lead developer of MetaMask pointed out, "We come up with these cryptoeconomic games that are theoretically perfect, but if people don't know how to play them, then they're useless. MetaMask is in a funny position in that we don't work at the protocol layer, but we are totally responsible for how people *perceive* the protocol."[6]

In other words, the users didn't care about the technical underpinnings; they just wanted to be able to easily buy (at a reasonable price), breed (for desirable qualities), and sell (at a profit). That required radical cooperation and collaboration—not just within Axiom Zen but also with its technology partners. If people couldn't buy Ethereum, they couldn't buy a cat.

---

6 ConsenSys, "The Inside Story of the CryptoKitties Congestion Crisis."

Building a Blockchain Marketplace

Games are an amazing way to teach new behaviors. Rather than explain-
ing the values of a decentralized economy, let's have them experience it
and feel the values rather than hearing them.[7]

—Roham Gharegozlou

But buying cats was just the beginning. Any collectibles company is built on the concept of upselling: get customers to purchase low-priced, commonplace items, and then convince them to gradually purchase higher-priced, hard-to-find items.

Let's say a collectibles company has a license to sell products for a popular brand, like Harley-Davidson. The company runs an expensive newspaper ad for a $35 Harley pocket knife. Although the sales will not cover the ad spending, the real value is getting the contact information for Harley enthusiasts. Now, the company can inexpensively target these consumers with a Harley catalog that includes the following:

- Additional pocket knives in the series, each with a different motorcycle, also for $35

- Pewter mugs with the Harley logo for $75

- Die-cast 1:24 scale motorcycle replicas for $125

- Limited edition sculptures in 1:12 scale for $250

Thus, just like blockchain, the collectibles industry follows the business tactic of building a community and then finding creative ways to monetize it.

With CryptoKitties, Axiom Zen could do this at scale. Users would be acquired online, with built-in viral tactics like being able to share your Crypto-Kitty across your social media accounts. Users could browse the CryptoKitty marketplace (think eBay for virtual cats) to see how much the most valuable cats were earning. This would drive speculation on buying and breeding even more cats, fueling the furball.

In other words, by allowing users to easily buy inexpensive CryptoKitties (which tugged at the heartstrings), the team made it easy to upsell users into rare

---

7 "CryptoKitties and the Future of Crypto," YouTube.

and valuable CryptoKitties (which tugged at the purse strings). Fans would quickly become superfans. It was collectibles, on caffeine.

According to Mack, CryptoKitties was a first for the industry: the only project that, on day one of its brand-new collectibles market, already had speculators. That's because—depending on your perspective—the timing for the launch was either perfect or perfectly wrong: the height of the 2017 Blockchain Boom.

The Launch

We were expecting to have to deal with things like scaling at some point. We did not expect it to be in the first week.[8]

—Bryce Bladon, director of communications, CryptoKitties

On November 28, 2017, the online game made its debut. It quickly went viral; then it went *epidemic*.

In the first week of December, the Ethereum network experienced a sixfold increase in requests, and the number was growing (Figure 6-4). By December 4, 11% of the total Ethereum network traffic was CryptoKitties, making it the most popular **dapp** on the platform.[9]

Definition

Decentralized applications (dapps): While most applications are centralized (run from a central server or company), dapps are run by independent nodes on a network. Think of the way information on the internet is served not from a central "internet computer" but from millions of distributed servers.

While many industry commenters scoffed that CryptoKitties wasn't a "real" blockchain project, and others marveled at how they were able to grow so quickly, a community of "kittenvestors" sprang up almost overnight. Across social media and community forums, users began talking about how they were paying off their student loans by *flipping cats*—buying, breeding, and selling quickly for a profit (Figure 6-5).

---

8 ConsenSys, "The Inside Story of the CryptoKitties Congestion Crisis."

9 Olga Kharif, "CryptoKitties Mania Overwhelms Ethereum Network's Processing," *Bloomberg*, December 4, 2017, *https://www.bloomberg.com/news/articles/2017-12-04/cryptokitties-quickly-becomes-most-widely-used-ethereum-app.*

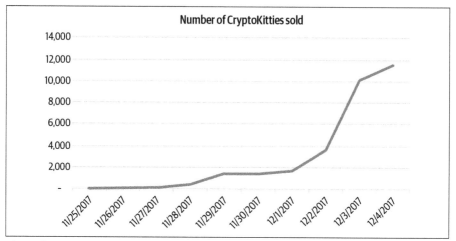

Figure 6-4. Cat-astrophic growth[10]

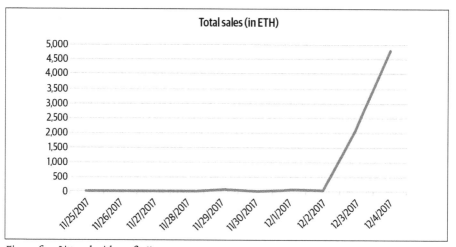

Figure 6-5. Littered with profits[11]

While the virtual cat market was heating up, the Ethereum network was melting down. It was the height of blockchain mania, with new tokens launching every day on the Ethereum network, "minting money" for prospective investors. However, those transactions weren't going through, thanks to the CryptoKitties

---

10 Kitty Explorer, *https://www.kittyexplorer.com/stats.*

11 Ibid.

congestion. This fueled the fire, as the crypto community vented its ire—which publicized the project further, attracting even more users to breed even more cats, making the problem both better and worse.

The situation recalled the early days of the internet, when the first viral websites began to attract the attention of the general public. The academics and researchers using the web were aghast: their precious technology was being used for singing hamsters and dancing babies? Or take the flash flood of users who discovered the internet when the America Online service—formerly a walled garden—suddenly opened itself to the web in the mid-1990s. It was a culture clash as the techno-savvy were suddenly confronted with the techno-silly.

But cat videos and easy on-ramps are what brought the internet to the masses. They're what made it accessible for people who didn't want to suffer through complex software installations or troubleshooting configuration files—which, it turns out, is most people.

Most people want applications that just work. They want them to be simple, intuitive, and even fun. CryptoKitties was all that and more: it was a way of making money.

The situation escalated quickly: on December 4, the network came to a grinding halt. The CryptoKitties network was no longer just running slowly; it stopped completely. The source of the problem wasn't immediately obvious, and with such a new technology, there was no precedent for tracking it down.

Although critics had written off CryptoKitties as a joke, it had quickly become one of the highest-profile applications in the history of blockchain. Its untimely demise—just as it was becoming a phenomenon—not only would mean the end of Axiom Zen but also could have repercussions for Ethereum and the entire digital asset market.

Amid this chaos, the team members realized that finding and fixing the CryptoKitties scalability problem was central to the network's survival. But to do that, they'd need to collaborate quickly across a wide array of stakeholders. It was time to herd the cats.

The Collaboration

Fortunately, many of the major players of blockchain were already scheduled to meet up at a conference in New York. They quickly created an impromptu task force of Ethereum developers, which worked late into the night with the Crypto-Kitties team to identify the immediate problem.

The problem was *gas*, a small service fee for making transactions on the Ethereum network. To buy or sell a CryptoKitty (i.e., a CryptoKitty Ethereum token), you had to pay this service fee. As the volume of requests grew, so did the gas fee. Quite simply, CryptoKitty users were running out of gas.

Ethereum was designed to balance the supply and demand of using the network. In a typical scenario, miners (the supply) would increase the cost per transaction—the gas fee—when network spikes occurred (the demand). Think of how Uber implements surge pricing during periods of heavy demand, like after a sports game.

But the continuous rise in the pending transaction queue meant the gas fees were growing higher and higher. It was as if everyone was trying to hail an Uber at once, and the surge pricing was spiraling out of control. For a low-priced CryptoKitty—which was most of them—the transaction fees exceeded the value of the cat, rendering the network unusable.

Worse, users did not understand what was happening: when they tried to buy a CryptoKitty, all they saw was an endlessly spinning progress bar, as pending transactions piled up. Miners were furiously processing transactions with the largest service fees, like Uber drivers picking off the most profitable fares. But from a user perspective, the network didn't work.

With a collaborative problem-solving approach, the ad hoc group of developers from Axiom Zen, MetaMask, and many other blockchain projects worked into the early morning, communicating with other developers worldwide through video chat, Twitter, and Slack.[12]

The nucleus of this team was the Axiom Zen *Kitty Core*, designed more like a game-oriented product design team rather than a typical tech team. These were people who had worked together for years and implicitly trusted each other. They understood the problem was not just technical; it was psychological. From the beginning, they had designed CryptoKitties with a user-friendly interface, which was a radical concept for blockchain. As a result, they had attracted many users who didn't understand digital assets; they just fell in love with the cute cat collectibles.

To address this issue, the team began with basic blockchain education to communicate to users the challenges they were facing. Across Twitter and Telegram, they explained that blockchain moves slowly—like the early internet—compared to the instant web we enjoy today (Figure 6-6).

---

12 ConsenSys, "The Inside Story of the CryptoKitties Congestion Crisis."

Figure 6-6. User education in 140 characters or less

To further address the situation, they added a feature that updated users on the status of the Ethereum network. Then they added a transactional queue, so users could identify network "choke points" and refrain from bombarding the network with requests when it was already overloaded.

But the biggest difference was made with the addition of one simple button. When transactions were taking a long time to process, the button let users "Increase Gas Fee" and resubmit their transactions with higher gas prices. According to Dan, that little button—like offering a higher price to your Uber driver during peak hours—was the solution to the problem. It explained the issue, in a simple and elegant way, and put the user back in control.

These were the short-term fixes. The longer-term fixes, however, were more difficult.

First, Dan realized the number of transactions could be cut in half simply by removing parts that did not need to be recorded on the blockchain (or *on-chain*) and instead processing them locally (or *off-chain*). Alex Miller, cofounder of the blockchain energy project Grid+, introduced the idea of connecting multiple **side-chains** to the main Ethereum blockchain, allowing users to move between the chains.[13]

Definition

Sidechain: A parallel blockchain that runs alongside a main blockchain, allowing assets to be moved from one to the other (Figure 6-7). Imagine an overloaded conveyor belt on a factory floor, with side rooms that contain extra conveyor belts. Assets can be moved between conveyor belts, increasing overall capacity.

---

13 ConsenSys, "The Inside Story of the CryptoKitties Congestion Crisis."

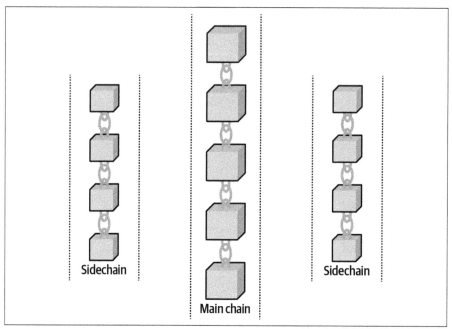

Figure 6-7. Side hustle

The CryptoKitties team realized that not everything needs to be on the block-chain: some transactions can be moved to sidechains, and some can be run locally. Since blockchain transactions are expensive (time, money, and processing power), the optimal blockchain solution involves using *just the right amount* of blockchain, only where it's needed.

Lessons Learned

People are locking up their CryptoKitties and taking out loans with their cats as collateral. People are using achievements in the virtual world to be able to get real benefits in the physical world, and we think that is magical.[14]

—*Roham Gharegozlou*

---

14 "CryptoKitties and the Future of Crypto," YouTube.

In its first month, more than 180,000 users signed up to play CryptoKitties, spending $20 million in Ethereum.[15] The average kitten sold for about $2, but prices for rare CryptoKitties could go up to $100,000. In May 2018, an art piece containing a Celestial Cyber Kitty (Figure 6-8) sold at auction for $140,000.[16]

Figure 6-8. This is what a $140,000 virtual cat looks like

In interviews, the members of the CryptoKitties team identified a few key lessons that can be applied across all blockchain projects:

Collaborative problem-solving
Just as a blockchain network increases in value as more users join it, these network effects apply to solving blockchain problems as well. Problems are more likely to be solved as more parties work together to solve problems. The Kitty Core team quickly grew into a "Kitty Crisis" team; this kind of decentralized development is common to successful blockchain projects.

---

15 Bowles, "CryptoKitties, Explained ... Mostly."

16 Michael del Castillo, "Exclusive: From CryptoKitties to Cardi B: Warner Music Joins $11 Million Investment in Ethereum Replacement," *Forbes*, September 12, 2019, *https://www.forbes.com/sites/michael-delcastillo/2019/09/12/exclusive-from-cryptokitties-to-cardi-b-warner-music-joins-11-million-investment-in-ethereum-replacement/#3b63f0d22b21.*

Educating and empowering users

Because blockchain is a different user experience—it takes transactions longer to settle, and transaction fees can be unpredictable—user education was important for setting expectations. A little education went a long way—and the Increase Gas Fees button let the users decide for themselves how much they really wanted that kitten.

Getting the right team

At a time when most blockchain teams were made up of developers and technologists, the CryptoKitties product team was unique. Since they considered the whole product—a funny concept, a user-friendly interface, an innovative token structure, and an addictive marketplace—CryptoKitties stood out like a pink cat in a herd of sheep.

According to Mack, you can implement all these lessons learned into your own blockchain enterprise, except for one: launching in November 2017, at the height of the Blockchain Boom.

Shortly after CryptoKitties solved its scaling problems, Axiom Zen spun off the team as a new venture, Dapper Labs, which quickly attracted $39 million in funding from investors including Google Ventures, Andreessen Horowitz, Samsung, and Union Square Ventures.

Further, Warner Music Group invested $11 million in Dapper Labs to work on *Flow*, a new public blockchain designed to address the challenges of scalability and accessibility. Flow is designed to handle higher transaction volumes than Ethereum and can validate the authenticity of unique digital objects, like artists or bands who want to issue their own digital assets to fans, who can buy and collect them.

CryptoKitties was just the beginning. Soon everyone would be able to issue their own blockchain-based crypto collectible. But just creating a collectible isn't enough: as with everything in blockchain, the first thing you have to collect is a community.

Next Steps

Although CryptoKitties is likely a short-lived fad, it suggests the diversity of uses of smart contracts. Digital assets that can be sold and transformed could have serious applications in finance and other business domains.[17]

—Kevin Werbach, professor of Legal Studies & Business Ethics, the Wharton School

The lasting legacy of CryptoKitties was the ERC-721 standard for non-fungible tokens, a framework that can be used for any one-of-a-kind asset. As Mack met with Roham, now the new Dapper Labs CEO, they discussed which of the following opportunities they should pursue next.

- Should the team create *unique, tradeable digital collectibles*? If so, where should they go next? Dogs? Giraffes?

- Should they consider *licensing deals with celebrities*? The team discussed collectible highlight videos of well-known athletes, or collectible limited edition songs from pop stars. Would superfans buy them?

- Should they consider *licensing deals with brands*? Longtime brands like Harley-Davidson and Coca-Cola already had a sizable collectible market, but were their aging fans ready for this new technology?

- Should they capitalize on their technology expertise around ERC-721 tokens? For example, they could do the following:
  - Create a collectible prototype that can be easily modified to launch new projects
  - Offer consulting services to assist other collectible creators
  - Create their own collectible wallet with improved features, such as security
  - Use blockchains to connect fans directly to artists (eliminating the traditional intermediaries), thus building new communities to be monetized

---

17 Werbach, *The Blockchain and the New Architecture of Trust*, 66.

— Build out the CryptoKitties ecosystem with more marketplaces and tools

- Finally, should they *seek approval from the SEC* so that investors could convert CryptoKitties into legitimate securities—like a stock—that could be traded on traditional public markets?

If you were running Dapper Labs, which strategy would you fancy?

7

Voatz: Blockchain-Based Voting

I will make sure you guys never succeed, because I don't believe elections should ever be electronic. They should all be on paper, because that is the safest thing in the world.[1]

Nimit Sawhney, cofounder of the blockchain voting platform Voatz, was surprised to hear this from an elderly woman the first time his app was publicly demonstrated, but it led to an important realization: simply having a great technology is not enough. You have to *earn the public's trust.*

The Story of Voatz

Nimit grew up in a Sikh family in India during the turbulent 1980s, when the assassination of Indian Prime Minister Indira Gandhi led to a religious backlash against Sikhs. Although not yet old enough to vote, Nimit tagged along with his grandfather to the polls on election day. There, he witnessed people, including his grandfather, forced to vote at gunpoint, with their thumbs being pressed against an inkpad to verify their votes—vivid memories that he still carries to this day. Although he couldn't comprehend the full scope of what he was seeing, he knew that this was something bad and that he should work to prevent it from happening again.

Fast-forward to 2014. While Nimit and his brother Simer were attending the annual South by Southwest (SXSW) conference in Austin, Texas, they

---

1 Emma Wright, "Founder's Spotlight: Nimit Sawhney of Voatz," CIC, January 14, 2018, *https://cic.com/podcasts/founders-spotlight/voatz.*

accidentally stumbled upon a hackathon entitled "Hack for the Future," with the goal of generating ideas for a better future. Drawing upon his childhood memory for inspiration and his decades-long background in mobile security and payments technology, Nimit and his brother developed a prototype with one purpose: to create a trustworthy platform that would enable citizens to vote from home.

Since no one was able to vote from a phone at the time, Nimit and Simer feared that they would be laughed off the stage. To their surprise, after pitching their prototype, they won. The prize package included $10,000, one bitcoin, and 30 minutes with an investor, who promptly advised them not to pursue the idea.

Nimit didn't heed that advice. In 2015, he quit his job to focus full-time on what became Voatz, a company working to make voting more accessible, transparent, and secure by combining smartphone hardware, biometrics, and blockchain technology. After a few years of development, the founders earned a spot in the elite 2017 Techstars accelerator program. Next, they won the $50,000 first prize in the 2017 MassChallenge competition, then followed that up by receiving the Microsoft Civic Innovation Scholarship.

These early successes set Nimit and Simer on a journey around the world, where they discovered there was a lot more than their company on the line: literally, the fate of the free world was at stake.

How It Works

The Voatz elections platform combines three technologies: smartphones (to make voting easy), biometric identity (to make it secure), and blockchain (to make it tamper-resistant):

Smartphones

In a digital age, it seemed quaint and old-fashioned to still use paper ballots, especially when increasing numbers of people—especially young people—lived on their mobile phones (Figure 7-1). Voatz set to work on creating an app that could identify individual voters and securely record their votes.

Biometrics

The Voatz app was designed to run on iPhone and Android models with embedded security features like fingerprint and facial recognition. Voters were authenticated using this biometric information, plus the smartphone's camera to scan their driver's license and their face.

Blockchain

Each voter was given one token for each possible choice on the ballot. As the voter made a selection, the token was altered, much like filling in an oval on a paper ballot. Once the ballot was verified, the tokens were subtracted (debited) from the voter's ledger, then added (credited) to the selected candidate's ledger.

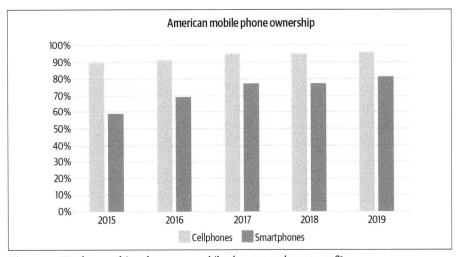

Figure 7-1. We do everything else on our mobile phones, so why not vote?[2]

These transactions (votes) were stored on multiple, geographically distributed servers. To clarify, this does not mean that some votes were stored on some servers and other votes were stored on other servers; rather, all votes were stored on all servers, giving each server its own copy of the complete voting record. Even if one server were to fail or be hacked, the complete voting record would still be intact.

Voatz chose to build its app on the Hyperledger Fabric blockchain platform, an open source version developed by IBM and currently managed by the Linux Foundation. Although Hyperledger is more often associated with business applications (Ethereum being the choice for consumer apps), the company was impressed with Hyperledger's close association with IBM, a company with decades of experience in government consulting.

2 "Demographics of Mobile Device Ownership and Adoption in the United States," Pew Research Center, June 5, 2020, *https://www.pewresearch.org/internet/fact-sheet/mobile.*

Hyperledger also offered the ability to create a permissioned blockchain that would allow control over who has the authority to validate and record transactions. In other words, users would need to live in the US and undergo a vetting process in order to run a node on the Voatz blockchain network. Thus, the added benefit of Hyperledger was that it most closely mirrors how elections are currently run.

Note

Although there are many options for choosing a blockchain platform, the three most common choices are Hyperledger, Ethereum, or building your own.

As we explored in Chapter 3, Voatz had to weigh the trade-offs between permissioned and permissionless systems. The tricky balance was to keep the system *decentralized* (anyone could run a node), while *centralizing* it enough to keep it free from foreign influence (nodes were carefully vetted and could be shut down if needed).

Then there was the problem of *scale*. Unlike public blockchains, on a permissioned blockchain, all nodes must be vetted (or approved). Scaling on a blockchain, however, has advantages because of network effects. By increasing the number of nodes from 4 to 16, for example, we don't just quadruple the system capacity; thanks to the **quadratic growth** of network effects, we increase it by a factor of 20.

Definition

Quadratic growth: Using the law of network effects (see Chapter 3) and the associated formula,

$$\frac{(n)(n-1)}{2}$$

in which n represents the number of nodes, we can see that adding a single node increases the number of connections quadratically (some people mistakenly call this *exponential* growth). Our favorite analogy is the Wii Bowling video game, in which the system adds a new row of bowling pins each round, providing a fun visual of quadratic growth of triangular numbers: increasing at an increasing rate.

To further ensure the integrity of the system, Voatz initiated a public **bug bounty program** in which hackers would be paid for identifying potential security breaches. These bounty programs are emerging as a best practice for companies that wish to develop bulletproof blockchains.

Definition

Bug bounty programs: Offering to pay for any bugs found by volunteer testers can help you create "bulletproof" blockchains and technology systems, especially in high-stakes applications like voting.

To further build trust in its system, Voatz recorded each vote in triplicate (Figure 7-2):

- Each voter received a digital receipt that showed that voter's ballot selections, and an anonymous copy of this receipt was also sent to election officials.

- An anonymous paper ballot was also printed at local election headquarters, where it could be tabulated using the same equipment as traditional paper ballots.

- Each choice on the ballot was recorded as a vote transaction on the blockchain.

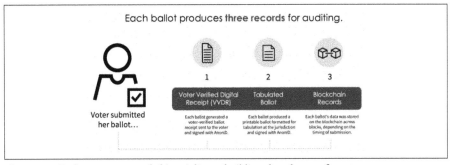

Figure 7-2. Each vote was recorded in triplicate, building three layers of trust

Recording each vote in triplicate created a three-way paper trail for post-election audits: local officials could validate their paper ballots against the electronic record of anonymous, voter-verified digital receipts, then audit these tallies against the blockchain data, thus ensuring 100% accountability.

Even with all this security infrastructure, one big hurdle remained: getting voters to trust the system.

The First Elections

Nimit and his team quickly learned that voting has both logical and emotional components. Building trust was not just about the *technology*; it was also about the *psychology*.

As a result, Nimit's team rolled out the Voatz platform in a series of small local elections starting in 2016, working to build this trust. Over the next few years, they recorded more than 80,000 votes in 40 US elections ranging from churches, unions, universities, towns, cities, and up to primaries for major political parties.[3] Initially, these elections were done for free; in 2017, the company started to receive paid contracts from state political parties that were eager to use the technology to reach more voters.

Voatz also built relationships with trusted industry experts such as Larry Moore, founder and CEO of Clear Ballot, one of the top companies running paper ballot elections. Clear Ballot collaborated with Voatz by providing test data that enabled Voatz to assess, refine, and validate the performance of its system.[4]

However, Nimit realized that this low-risk, low-reward strategy would get the company only so far. As he looked for a bigger opportunity, he was keenly aware that one blemish on the company's reputation could mean the end of Voatz. When the company's big break finally arrived, he knew the team had to get it right.

In 2017, that big break came.

The West Virginia Election

Nimit and the Voatz team had been attending *industry conferences* for the National Association of Secretaries of State (NASS) and the National Association of State Election Directors (NASED). Because Voatz was the new kid on the block, no one was keen to talk to the team, but these conferences turned out to be tremendous learning and networking opportunities.

Tip

Industry conferences are where you'll make the most valuable connections in the blockchain industry. Even though blockchain is a digital technology, the relationships are still forged face-to-face (80% of success is just showing up).

---

3 Voatz FAQ. Voatz. Accessed October 27, 2019. *https://voatz.com/faq.*

4 Larry Moore would eventually join the Voatz team as a senior vice president.

At one of these conferences, the Voatz team met Mac Warner, West Virginia secretary of state. Warner was a former officer in the US Army who had served in both Afghanistan and Iraq, so he knew firsthand the challenges of voting while serving overseas. With four children in the military, Warner was also passionate about improving voting access for the military, as well as other US citizens living abroad.[5] His rationale was clear: only 7% of citizens living abroad actively voted, compared to 72% for those living in the US.[6]

West Virginia was a good fit for the Voatz platform: the state had relatively low voter turnout (45th out of 50 states), with multiple points of failure in its absentee voting process. It was expensive and difficult for West Virginians living abroad to cast a vote, since it cost up to $50 to mail a ballot internationally.

Nimit and his Voatz team pitched Mac and his elections team on their solution. They kept the project small and manageable, focusing only on absentee voters for the state of West Virginia. The Voatz team spent much of its time educating the government team on the benefits of blockchain, with real-life examples of how the voting app had worked in elections to date (Figure 7-3).

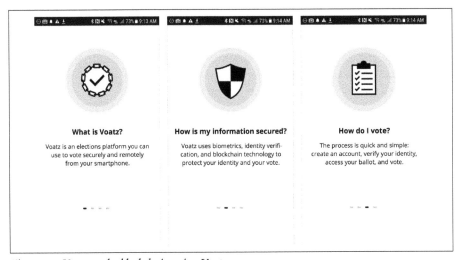

Figure 7-3. Votes on the blockchain using Voatz

5 "Built on Blockchain: Episode 2—One Block One Vote," Udacity, YouTube, September 14, 2018, *https://www.youtube.com/watch?v=6T94Uf4ML5A*.

6 "Overseas Citizen Population Analysis Report," Federal Voting Assistance Program, accessed October 31, 2019, *https://www.fvap.gov/info/reports-surveys/overseas-citizen-population-analysis*.

The elections team was impressed by the user-friendliness, security, and instant validation of the voting platform and agreed to implement the Voatz solution for its absentee balloting in the next state election. At last, the time had come.

The Run-up to the Election

Voatz placed absentee voters into three segments: military, disabled, and citizens working or studying abroad. The challenge was that Voatz didn't have easy access to these voters: some were just lists of names, without accurate contact information. How would Voatz market this service to people without knowing how to reach them?

To make the project a blockchain success story, Nimit knew they had to get three things right:

Awareness

Voatz worked with the secretary of state to actively publicize the program, launching campaigns on YouTube and social media (Figure 7-4). Since the military was a key demographic, Voatz also spread the word through military communication channels, as well as through the Federal Voting Assistance Program (FVAP). Any absentee voters with a valid email address received an email notifying them of the opportunity to vote using the Voatz mobile app.

Education

Voatz developed a step-by-step guide and videos demonstrating for users how to record their votes, start to finish. The team faced the challenge of making the guide both user-friendly and thorough: too much information would overwhelm voters, but too little could potentially lose a vote.

Technical support

Finally, Voatz needed to provide 24-hour technical support, not only to answer any questions but also to quickly correct any technical issues during the election.

Figure 7-4. Publicizing a blockchain platform: equal parts education and information

Despite these assurances, West Virginia still wanted to execute a test run prior to the November elections. Warner and elections director Donald Kersey had the idea to pilot the absentee voting in two counties, Monongalia and Harrison. Each had county clerks with decades of experience and a drive for innovation.[7]

Conveniently, Warner's son Scott, a West Point graduate and captain in the US Army serving in Italy, would be the first person to test this pilot. On March 18, 2018, Scott Warner earned the distinction of becoming the first US citizen ever to use mobile voting in a federal election.[8]

While serving overseas, his existing options to vote were by mail, email, or fax. Using the international mail system would have been both expensive and risky. Using fax or email would not be private, as the ballot would be received by a county clerk—and Warner wanted his vote to stay private.

According to Warner, the Voatz mobile voting process was simple and intuitive. Making his selections was easy, and the use of biometric facial recognition

---

7 "Built on Blockchain: Episode 2," YouTube.

8 Hilary Brasath, "Voting from the Sky: The First Mobile Blockchain Vote in History," *Blog @ Voatz*, Voatz, June 26, 2019, *https://blog.voatz.com/?p=976*.

technology was "cool." History will remember Warner's description of being the first human to vote using blockchain: "pretty sweet."[9]

Election Day Results

In November 2018, the state of West Virginia used the Voatz blockchain platform to successfully support absentee voting on a mobile app for 144 citizens living abroad in 31 countries.[10] Most encouraging: of the 200 voters who learned about the new program, roughly 75% voted, *increasing absentee voting by a factor of 10* (Figure 7-5).

Note

By moving a cumbersome and time-intensive voting process onto a blockchain-powered mobile app, Voatz increased voter participation by 10 times.[11]

Figure 7-5. Results of West Virginia blockchain vote[12]

9 Brasath, "Voting from the Sky."

10 "West Virginia Not Planning to Expand Use of Blockchain Voting," Govtech.com. e-Republic, November 9, 2018, *https://www.govtech.com/products/West-Virginia-Not-Planning-to-Expand-Use-of-Blockchain-voting.html.*

11 "Overseas Citizen Population Analysis Report," Federal Voting Assistance Program.

12 Hilary Brasath, "Remote Mobile Voting: Answering Questions, Addressing Misconceptions," *Blog @ Voatz*, Voatz, May 1, 2019, *https://blog.voatz.com/?p=721.*

Voter response was overwhelmingly positive, with only two voters reporting difficulty using the app.[13] Michael Graney, a West Virginian graduate student living in China, offered a typical voter response: he appreciated the ability to log in to his account multiple times, giving him the opportunity to research candidates before making his final selections and casting his vote. He also understood that his vote would be both secure and private on the blockchain, and he could confirm that his vote was counted, unlike a vote sent in by mail. Above all, Graney was proud that his home state was leading the country in mobile voting.[14]

From a technical perspective, the pilot ran smoothly. All absentee ballots were successfully recorded and verified by multiple independent security auditors, including former members of the FBI's Cyber Division, who also verified that no hacking had occurred. According to Kersey, "The West Virginia County Clerks were quite pleased with their ability to audit the ballots printed from the blockchain."[15] (One opportunity for improvement, however, was in making the audit process more accessible for those with limited technical backgrounds.)

After the election process was complete, the state of West Virginia issued an official announcement stating that its election officials were pleased with the results. State officials intend to continue using the Voatz mobile app in the future for absentee ballots.[16]

Lessons Learned

Looking back on this important milestone in his company, Nimit identified a few key lessons for blockchain technology leaders.

KNOW YOUR USERS

Most blockchain systems have different groups of users, and technology leaders should carefully analyze the needs of each user group. In the case of Voatz, think about how the solution must work for three very different user groups: voters, local election officials, and elected representatives (Figure 7-6).

---

13 "West Virginia Not Planning to Expand Use of Blockchain Voting," Govtech.com.

14 Hilary Braseth, "10,000 Miles from the Far East to Charleston WV," *Blog @ Voatz*, Voatz, July 13, 2019, *https://blog.voatz.com/?p=948*.

15 Braseth, "Remote Mobile Voting: Answering Questions, Addressing Misconceptions."

16 "West Virginia Not Planning to Expand Use of Blockchain Voting," Govtech.com.

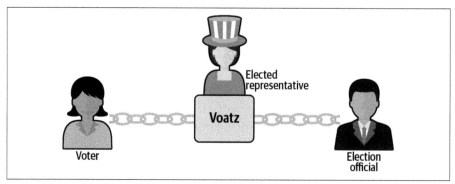

Figure 7-6. Blockchain is the Internet of Value, and the value exchanged here is votes

While a secretary of state was the "target customer" (i.e., the one who would write the check), the voters and local election officials were the real "end users" (the ones who would use the app). Even though Voatz was selling to government officials, it was the user-friendly product—for both voters and local election officials—that ultimately sold the platform.

APPLY A BEGINNER'S MINDSET

To become successful, a blockchain application needs to be simplified to a level that everyone—even the most nontechnical users—can understand. To address this challenge, the Voatz team hired marketing and communications professionals into senior leadership positions, who were able to apply a beginner's mindset in creating visuals and producing instructional videos (Figure 7-7).

Further, Voatz was able to position its messaging to meet the needs of both voters and election officials. Voters don't see the blockchain; they just want a user-friendly voting experience. Election officials just want a secure, auditable process that integrates with their existing voting systems.

As Voatz Director of Product and Communications Hilary Braseth said: "Voatz isn't just a company trying to bring a new product to market. We are trying to shift a methodology, a whole ideological framework of how we govern ourselves: that everyone should vote, regardless of their circumstances."[17]

---

17 Nimit Sawhney, interview with the author, October 8, 2019.

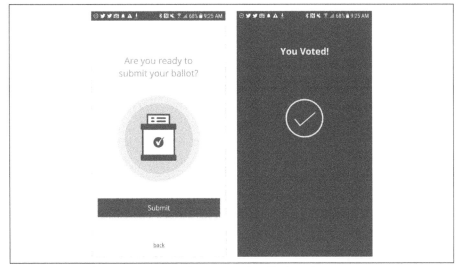

Figure 7-7. Blockchain doesn't get much more user-friendly than this

BUILD TRUST

Voatz learned that security is often a matter of perception, and perception does not always match reality. Voting has both a logical component and an emotional component. Many voters believe that paper is safer—even as the 2016 US elections proved that traditional voting systems can be hacked.[18]

Thus, the *public* must be educated that blockchain-based voting systems are more secure than old-fashioned paper ballots. The *government* must be educated that more citizens will vote when we make it as simple as a few taps on an app. And *local election officials* must be educated on how easy it is to audit mobile votes in real time, building faith in this system with each digitally verified vote.

Next Steps

For Nimit, the greatest reward from this experience was not just achieving a successful election but seeing the reactions of his fellow citizens to the Voatz platform. He was proud to learn that Warner, as an emerging thought leader in the

---

18 "2016 Presidential Campaign Hacking Fast Facts," CNN, October 18, 2019, *https://www.cnn.com/2016/12/26/us/2016-presidential-campaign-hacking-fast-facts/index.html.*

electoral space, had been invited to speak at the Bipartisan Policy Center to share his experience with the Voatz pilot program.[19]

As Nimit reflected on the success of the West Virginia absentee initiative, he realized that he needed to use this achievement as a catalyst for obtaining another round of financing. He was hoping to raise $5 million to $10 million dollars, and already had interest from Medici Ventures, Techstars, Oakhouse Partners, and the Urban Innovation Fund.

Assuming he'd raise the funds, he was then left with the big question: *what next?*

He knew that one of his biggest challenges was the small number of blockchain projects at the US state government level: only Wyoming, Rhode Island, and Ohio had made any significant efforts in support of blockchain. Without a critical mass of high-profile successes, trust would still be an issue, especially from risk-averse politicians.

He was also aware that international governments had been far more supportive of blockchain: for example, the Smart City Initiative in Dubai; the Crypto Valley of Zug, Switzerland; and blockchain-based real estate initiatives in Estonia.

Therefore, should he:

- *Find more states to use the Voatz mobile app for absentee voting?* This should be an easy sell in this 50-state market, given that the technology already existed, and the success of the West Virginia pilot.

- *Convince states to move beyond absentee voting?* Making blockchain-based mobile voting available to more voters—not just those living overseas— would be the next logical step, but it would also increase project complexity.

- *Participate in the US census?* Another opportunity might be to leverage the technology for a huge government initiative like the US census, which takes place every 10 years and is not as politically sensitive as voting.

---

19 "The Voting Experience: 2018 and the Future," Bipartisan Policy Center, February 14, 2019, *https:// bipartisanpolicy.org/event/the-voting-experience-2018-and-the-future*.

- *Target the solution to international governments?* This could be a huge win—especially in countries where citizens have low trust in existing voting systems—but it could be difficult to garner the support of all relevant parties to obtain buy-in.

If you were on the board of Voatz, where would you place your vote?

8

Binance Charity Foundation: Doing Good with Blockchain

I believe my purpose is to empower the bottom billion people in this world.[1]

—Helen Hai, head of Binance Charity Foundation

On her seventh birthday, Helen Hai's father took her on a trip to Beijing. It was the mid-1980s, the beginning of China's industrial revolution, and change was in the air. The streets were buzzing with bicycles; the sky was crisscrossed with cables and power lines; the ancient gates and walls seemed to sing with new life. For a young girl, the experience was dizzying and wonderful.

As a treat, Helen's father took her to one of the city's first five-star hotels. She slowly entered the lobby, mesmerized by its grandeur.

"How much for a room?" her father asked the hotel concierge.

"$100 a night," came the response.

"It's too expensive," her father said, whisking Helen away.[2]

That moment changed Helen Hai. She remembered thinking, *This will never belong to me.* She wondered how many other young girls shared the feeling that

---

1 Gina Clarke, "Binance Charity Set to Solve UN Sustainability Goals Believes New Chief Helen Hai," *Forbes*, September 21, 2018, *https://www.forbes.com/sites/ginaclarke/2018/09/21/binance-charity-set-to-solve-un-sustainability-goals-believes-new-chief-helen-hai/#31a2939118a9.*

2 Wang Chao and Andrew Moody, "The Enlightenment of Helen Hai," *China Daily*, February 21, 2018, *http://www.chinadaily.com.cn/kindle/2014-02/21/content_17298230.htm.*

this hotel represented a world they would never enter, a world they would be denied because of lack of opportunity.

Over the course of her life, Helen seized those opportunities, or created opportunities where they didn't exist. After receiving her education from Cass Business School in London and the graduate business school INSEAD, Helen became the youngest female partner in the history of insurance brokerage Jardine Lloyd Thompson, before joining Zurich Financial Services to become the chief actuary for China.

Her career took Helen to many exotic locations. On a 2011 trip to Ethiopia, she found herself in a five-star hotel, enjoying evening walks through its formal gardens. Looking around, she noticed that the hotel guests were Asian, European, and American—but none were African. She flashed back to her childhood experience in Beijing. How many young Africans passed by this hotel, only catching a glimpse of what was inside, believing it would always be beyond their reach?

Drawing on these two memories, Helen felt that she had to find a way to empower the people of Africa in the same way that her life had been empowered by China's industrial revolution. She would find this opportunity a few years later, when offered the position of heading up the new Binance Charity Foundation, a blockchain project for good.

The Origin Story

Changpeng Zhao—or CZ—was rich.

His Binance exchange, where people could trade bitcoin and altcoins, had made him a blockchain billionaire. CZ had followed up this achievement by creating Binance Coin (BNB), which quickly became one of the most valuable altcoins on the market. (For more on CZ's remarkable story, see Chapter 3.)

But like a grand master playing chess, the young entrepreneur was already thinking many moves ahead. One of the ideas incubating in his mind was a blockchain-enabled charity, a way to use these new digital assets for social good. There was little doubt he had the digital wealth to do it.

While a new financial technology like blockchain might widen the gap between the haves and the have-nots, CZ wanted to ensure that those with limited access to technology and financial services would be able to participate in the blockchain revolution—which was founded on principles like freedom, equality, and democratization.

On a 2018 trip to Davos, Switzerland, while attending the World Economic Forum's annual conference, CZ was introduced to Helen Hai, who was serving as a goodwill ambassador for the United Nations. CZ and Helen immediately bonded over their shared upbringings, as well as their shared vision for using technology for social good.

Helen had become a believer in the power of creating jobs to spur economic growth. She had spent the previous five years leading the Made in Africa Initiative, serving as an economic consultant to African governments to help stimulate local economies. She had made friends in high places, with access to the leaders of many African nations.

She arranged a meeting for CZ to meet the presidents of Togo and Uganda, and the four discussed ideas for charitable ventures on the continent. After a half-hour meeting, these leaders, without technical backgrounds, were receptive to the potential benefits of blockchain technology and how it might spur more charitable giving.

Further, Yoweri Museveni, president of Uganda, saw blockchain as a way for his country to leapfrog the rest of the world. As other governments struggled to understand blockchain, Uganda would move quickly to put it into practice. He invited Binance to set up its foundation and a localized exchange—Binance Uganda—in his country.

Soon after, CZ offered Helen the position of leading the charity arm for Binance. Helen realized that this could be the vehicle for helping her realize her vision of serving the "bottom billion" of society. If blockchain is the Internet of Value, that value should be shared more freely and more fairly. Just as the internet allows everyone to share information, blockchain could allow us to share the wealth.

She took the job.

Helen set about making a splash. She first built a coalition of international support around a new initiative called Blockchains for Sustainable Development. This consortium introduced the initiative at the United Nations World Investment Forum 2018, where Binance also launched its donation platform and started a charitable fund with a commitment of $10 million to seed initial pilot projects.[3]

Binance Charity Foundation was live. The money started to pour in—but so did the problems.

---

3 Clarke, "Binance Charity Set to Solve UN Sustainability Goals."

How It Works

In most charities, the donation process is not transparent. On binance.charity, we send donations directly to the end beneficiaries, not a third party. The funds go directly to the individuals.[4]

—Jill Ni, deputy head, Binance Charity Foundation

The idea was simple: a charity built on blockchain.

Well, like everything involving blockchain, it wasn't quite *that* simple. Binance Charity Foundation (BCF) was a blockchain-powered charity to which people could donate digital assets—bitcoin or altcoins—that were then sent to various charities. Recipients *received those donations in the same digital currency.*

This was the crucial point: instead of converting dollars to digital, or digital to dollars, BCF dealt exclusively in digital currency. The entire flow of funds took place on the blockchain. The recipients also received these digital assets directly—as opposed to a traditional charity, with its layers of administration and reliance on third parties (Figure 8-1).

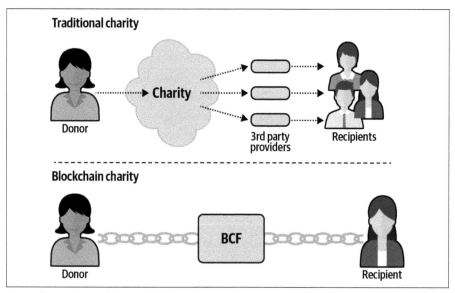

Figure 8-1. Traditional charity versus Binance Charity Foundation

---

4 Jill Ni, interview with the author, November 26, 2019.

BCF was also a *platform*, like Kickstarter. This meant donors could propose new philanthropic projects, from solar panels to school lunches. Like a crowd-funding campaign, new donors could choose any available project on the binance.charity website, which showed a real-time total of funds raised (Figure 8-2). Donors could also contribute to the Binance Charity Wallet, which was simply a global fund—a shared pool of digital money—that was allocated at Binance's discretion.

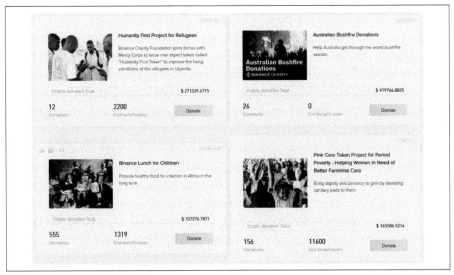

Figure 8-2. The "marketplace" of BCF projects

By storing all transactions on the blockchain, BCF created a fully transparent charity: users could see each transaction on the ledger, along with where the money went. Thus the tagline: Making Giving Transparent.

Binance covered the operational and administrative costs of BCF pro bono. The company also donated all of Binance's **token listing fees** to BCF, ensuring a steady flow of new donations, recorded on chain, with full transparency to the public.

Definition

Token listing fees: To get a new token listed on a reputable digital exchange like Binance, the issuing company pays a token listing fee. Think of this like getting your stock listed on NASDAQ or a similar stock exchange—it's a necessary step for attracting enough buyers and sellers to give your token liquidity. In the case of Binance, these listing fees were donated to BCF.

BCF represented a new model for the philanthropic industry in three important ways.

First, it was a *more efficient use of donations*—not only was there no overhead, but BCF also worked with local communities to develop solutions to their most pressing problems. Traditional charities—as well as government foreign aid programs—can fall into the trap of blindly sending money overseas, without working with locals to find out where resources would be most beneficial.[5] By engaging directly with the communities they were supporting, BCF could quickly test, refine, and scale its solutions to maximize their social impact.

Second, it *required end beneficiaries to use digital currencies*, enabling them to participate in the new Internet of Value. Just as traditional foreign aid was designed to build goodwill for the donating country, BCF had a secondary goal of building goodwill around digital currencies. As in other areas of blockchain, simply providing technology isn't enough; rather, the challenge is to get people using it in a positive way.

Third, it *provided a new channel for donors to give*—and many of these donors were newly wealthy after the blockchain boom of 2017. This had two interesting effects. Just as traditional charities will often take donations in stocks or bonds, BCF became the de facto standard for accepting digital assets. It also encouraged major industry players like Ripple and Zcash to send over large donations denominated in their own token. By accepting any digital asset (as opposed to, say, only its own token), BCF was able to quickly attract large donors, allowing the foundation to start from a position of financial strength.

In its first year, BCF helped 40,000 end beneficiaries with the use of contributions from more than 1,000 donors to initiatives like disaster relief, refugee support, and end-of-life care.[6] As of this writing, BCF has received over 1,200 donations on the blockchain, totaling $6,300,000, which they have transferred to over 100,000 beneficiaries in Uganda.[7]

5 William J. Lederer and Eugene Burdick, *The Ugly American* (New York: W. W. Norton & Company, 1958).

6 Scott Thompson and Christina Comben, "Binance Charity Foundation: Harnessing Blockchain Tech for Social Good," Coin Rivet, July 28, 2019, *https://coinrivet.com/binance-charity-foundation-harnessing-blockchain-tech-for-social-good*.

7 Binance Charity, "Binance Charity Showcases Cryptocurrency's Role of Improving Lives in Africa," ACCESSWIRE, September 6, 2019, *https://www.accesswire.com/558699/Binance-Charity-Showcases-Cryptocurrencys-Role-of-Improving-Lives-in-Africa*.

Why Uganda?

We didn't choose Uganda; Uganda chose us.[8]

—Jill Ni

BCF's partnership with Uganda serves as an excellent success story illustrating the benefits of blockchain to forward-thinking governments.

Although BCF was holding all donations in digital currency, it still needed "off-ramps" to redeem digital currencies for local currencies (you can't buy a school lunch with bitcoin). Unfortunately, its model wouldn't work anywhere digital currencies were outlawed or discouraged. We might call this the **last mile problem**: getting the donations into a currency the end recipients could spend locally.

Definition

Last mile problem: Blockchain makes it easy to send money anywhere around the globe—but converting it back into your local currency can prove difficult. Like the last mile problem of getting broadband access into individual homes, blockchain's last mile problem is getting digital currency into individual wallets.

Because of the complex regulatory issues surrounding digital currencies, government cooperation was key to setting up Binance Uganda. A regulated gateway was required for converting **crypto to fiat**, which provided an easy way for recipients to cash out their digital donations into Ugandan shillings.

Definition

Crypto to fiat: Converting digital currencies to traditional currencies (think of currency exchange kiosks at the airport). A crypto-to-fiat gateway is a website or exchange that allows you to convert a digital currency like bitcoin (BTC) to a traditional one like Ugandan shillings (UGX).

Uganda, a country of 44 million people, was already an African leader in blockchain technology, supporting conferences, associations, and communities. Binance—a company that began in China, on the heels of the industrial revolution—saw investing in Africa today like investing in Asia 50 years ago.

---

8 Ni, interview.

Whereas a developed economy may view blockchain technology as a threat, an emerging economy can view it as an opportunity. In other words, blockchain can disrupt inefficient financial systems in existing economies, but it can *become* the system for emerging economies.

Ugandan government leaders hoped that access to blockchain-based financial services would have systemic effects. Blockchain-based microloans could make it easier for Ugandan entrepreneurs to borrow capital for new businesses. Inflation-resistant stablecoins could make it easier for them to save for retirement. And because no banks were needed—just a mobile phone—blockchain could introduce millions of rural Africans into the global economy for the first time, opening the floodgates of modern finance.[9]

What's more, Binance Uganda was not limited to Ugandans. Any resident of a country that allowed digital currency ownership could create an account at Binance Uganda, using Ugandan shillings to buy bitcoin and altcoins. This would further stimulate the Ugandan economy, introducing more flow into its national currency—even if that flow was driven by digital currencies.

Thus, a valuable partnership between Binance and the Ugandan government was forged. It is these public-private partnerships—between private companies and public governments—that we wish to highlight as a model for successful blockchain projects, particularly nonprofits.

You can't airdrop bitcoin into a country and hope that it will do some good: as BCF proved, you need an infrastructure with easy donations, trustworthy custodians, fiat off-ramps, and local partnerships to ensure that the donations go to where they can do the most good (Figure 8-3).

9 Benjamin Rameau, "10 Reasons Why Binance Labs Is Fully Committed to Africa," Medium, August 31, 2018, *https://medium.com/@benjaminrameau/10-reasons-why-binance-labs-is-fully-committed-to-africa-3aeaaa32fe9e.*

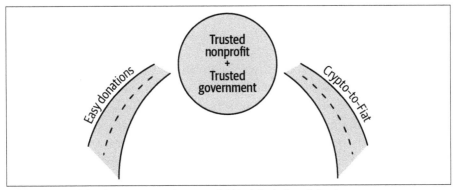

Figure 8-3. High-level components of a successful blockchain-based charity

Let's now look at how these elements came together in the first successful BCF project, where digital currencies quite literally came to the rescue.

The Pilot Project

In the past...the beneficiaries passively received the goods that donors perceive fit their demand. Binance Charity is using the new model to engage end beneficiaries, which is the most critical element in charitable giving, by clicking a payment button themselves.[10]

—Helen Hai

The torrential rains that came down in October 2018 were unlike anything the residents of Bududa, Uganda, had ever seen.

The unrelenting downpour caused the Suume River to burst its banks, triggering a massive landslide that wiped out two villages, including a schoolhouse with 200 children inside.[11] The ensuing floods swallowed up crops, drowned livestock, and washed away low-lying villages. All told, the disaster claimed the lives of 51 people, with 400 missing, 1,000 displaced, and more than 12,000 affected.[12]

---

10 "Empower Bududa," Blockchain Charity Foundation, accessed December 18, 2019, *https://www.binance.charity/empower-bududa.*

11 Samuel Okiror, "At Least 36 Dead in Uganda Landslides as School Disappears beneath Mud," *The Guardian*, October 12, 2018, *https://www.theguardian.com/global-development/2018/oct/12/uganda-landslides-36-dead-school-disappears-beneath-mud-bududa.*

12 "Empower Bududa," Blockchain Charity Foundation.

Rather than just sending money, BCF worked with local aid providers to ask, *what do the survivors need?* They quickly learned that one of the most immediate needs was containers to hold clean water.

Next, BCF worked with the CryptoSavannah Foundation (CSF) to find reliable, quality suppliers who could produce these goods at affordable prices. Simultaneously, CSF sent in volunteers to educate victims on how to open digital wallets and transfer payments to suppliers, in order to create relief baskets containing rice, soaps, bedsheets, cooking oil, saucepans, jerricans, and basins.

On January 21, 2019, roughly three months after the disaster, the first relief trucks arrived with 625 donation baskets for the first group of recipients. It was a victory for both BCF and CSF, showing that blockchain donations could be deployed into real-world emergencies, at the local level, even in developing nations.

Even better, the process involved the participation of the end beneficiaries (i.e., the disaster victims who received the help): BCF wasn't just helping, it was empowering the people to help themselves. According to Helen Hai, these local communities "know that they own the control, and that their voices will be heard."[13]

Thus, something destructive gave way to something constructive. The Ugandan pilot project ultimately delivered relief baskets to 1,328 recipients, while enabling BCF to refine its processes and build out its website to facilitate transparent donation tracking.

Small successes often lead to big ones—especially in the highly networked world of blockchain. "Once you have shown a successful model," Jill Ni explained, "people will start to notice." As BCF's successful pilot project started to generate buzz, major blockchain industry players began to pledge big donations.

But BCF's approach still had problems. The volatility of digital currencies was a big one: how could it accurately predict the number of relief baskets that could be produced from one bitcoin, if the price of bitcoin varied so widely? The business model evolved quickly, and within a year had incorporated the concept of *tokenization*.

---

13 "Empower Bududa," Blockchain Charity Foundation.

The Pink Care Token

Women are the base of any society. Women are the most powerful. But they don't know how much power they have and what they can do.

—*from the documentary* Period. End of Sentence.

Jill was sitting in a Ugandan classroom, surrounded by African schoolgirls who were receiving a lesson on feminine hygiene.

A volunteer from AFRIpads, BCF's partner organization, was holding up a pink sanitary pad and giving a lesson to young girls on that most delicate of subjects: menstruation.

"Your period is a natural, life-giving function that gives birth to the next generation," she explained, "without which your communities could not grow. Rather than being ashamed of your period, you should be proud of it." Some schoolgirls giggled; others shyly looked away.

The AFRIpads volunteer handed out pamphlets and then read stories from girls about their first experiences with their periods. The volunteer explained that many women use rags or cassava leaves during their monthly cycle, even strips of old clothing—whatever is available. She explained that reusable menstrual pads are a safe and sanitary solution, using how-to videos to show how to properly use and maintain them.

In a country where menstruation is still a source of social stigma, the mission of AFRIpads is to provide young women with feminine hygiene education and products—to end the so-called "week of shame." During their monthly period, many African schoolgirls stop going to school altogether for fear of embarrassment. In some villages, women are still expected to leave the community during their monthly cycle, reinforcing the sense of shame that begins as schoolchildren.

It all seemed a world away from the Yale campus where Jill had received her MBA while running the Responsible Investing Club. "I wasn't really into blockchain, or even technology," she explained later. "But I met Helen Hai, and we both had an interest in impact investing, especially in Africa. So I learned."

In one of BCF's early projects, to fund school lunches in Uganda, a female employee had noticed that girls were often missing from school for several days at a time. She soon learned that the need for feminine products—not to mention education around them—was among the most pressing for Ugandan schoolgirls.

Outside of the humanitarian concerns, the economic benefits were clear: when girls excel in school, they are empowered for employment outside the home, which grows the economy. Educated women are also less likely to become trapped in childhood marriage and early pregnancy, a generational cycle from which it is difficult to escape.

Education is a clear means to economic development. Education to destigmatize menstruation is particularly effective for young Ugandan girls: helping them understand that it is natural, not shameful, and that your monthly period does not mean you must refrain from engaging in society.

To address the issue, Binance created a new Pink Care Token Program with the focus on improving feminine health in developing countries. This alliance of 47 companies and organizations, including Ripple, Quantstamp, and Blockseed Ventures, launched the Pink Care Token (PCAT), a new type of stablecoin that was redeemable for one thing: an individual one-year supply of sanitary pads.

Throughout the success stories in this book, we've seen how tokenization can be applied to a wide variety of assets: votes, wireless connections, and collectibles. But how do you tokenize menstrual pads?

How the Cycle Works

We've seen how Binance Uganda—a local exchange—was necessary to convert digital currency to local currency. But how to convert that local currency into sanitary pads?

In the disaster relief project, a central coordinator distributed physical goods. Here, BCF wanted to allow individuals—young women or their parents—to obtain the pads directly. They couldn't send digital currency to each recipient and expect them to buy the pads; nor could they centrally handle distribution of the pads across all of Uganda. They would need to work with local suppliers, like pharmacies and village stores.

But this introduced a new problem: how could they send digital currency to a local pharmacy, ensuring that it would be used only to provide sanitary pads? The answer was tokenization (Figure 8-4).[14]

---

14 "Pink Care Token Project for Period Poverty—Helping Women in Need of Better Feminine Care," Blockchain Charity Foundation, accessed December 18, 2019, *https://www.binance.charity/period-poverty*.

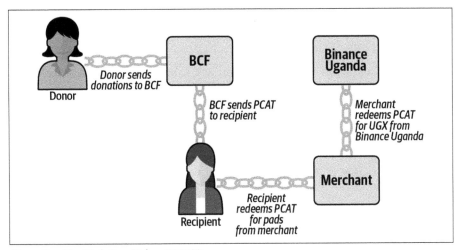

Figure 8-4. The Pink Care Token (PCAT)

Think of it like food stamps: the PCAT holds a unit of value that can be redeemed from the pharmacy in the form of sanitary pads. You could also think of it like a digital coupon: the pharmacy or shop owner can then redeem the PCAT back into Ugandan dollars on the Binance Uganda exchange (just as a US grocery store can redeem coupons back into dollars).

For this system to work, the recipient must install a digital wallet on her mobile phone, which stores the PCAT until she redeems it at the local pharmacy. In this respect, it's like transferring bitcoin, or any other digital currency, between wallets. However, unlike bitcoin, this is a *redemption-only token*, issued on the Binance blockchain, that can't be otherwise bought, sold, or traded.

This new type of token—let's call it a **crypto coupon**—was an immediate success. At the end of 2019, more than 10,000 Ugandan girls had redeemed Pink Care Tokens to receive their sanitary pads.[15]

Definition

Crypto coupon: A redeemable-only digital token that functions like traditional coupons or food stamps. The recipient exchanges the token for a physical good, and then the merchant is reimbursed for the price of that good in digital currency or dollars. Crypto coupons cannot be bought, sold, or traded.

---

15 Binance Charity, "Binance Charity Showcases Cryptocurrency's Role of Improving Lives in Africa."

The AFRIpads partnership also had another economic benefit: with headquarters in Uganda and sales offices in Kenya and Malawi, the company manufactured the pads locally, with a 90% female staff. In addition to empowering girls to stay in school, it created more than 200 jobs for women, providing financial independence and job skills while contributing to the Ugandan economy.[16]

Binance Charity Foundation now had multiple successful pilot projects, an innovative tokenomics model, and valuable public-private partnerships. What could go wrong? As it turns out, plenty.

Lessons Learned

It is normal for people to have questions or even misconceptions when a new concept is introduced. We think skepticism indicates that the public cares about our work.[17]

—Athena Yu, executive director, Binance Charity Foundation

As you've seen throughout this book, successful blockchain pioneers must balance both the *technical* and *political* challenges of their work, handling "the code" and "the crowds" in equal measure. As with our other success stories, BCF's first challenges required the skill of a programmer and the style of a politician.

TRANSPARENCY

Transparency sounds great, but most traditional charities don't really want to expand transparency beyond legal requirements. Transparency means that donors see how much money goes to operational costs and executive salaries—not to mention the endless cycle of your donations being spent to raise even more donations.

This issue of transparency presented a problem for many charitable organizations that reached out to BCF for partnerships. Once they understood that blockchain represented a new level of transparency—as you can see literally every donation, on the shared ledger—these conversations often became difficult.

Another challenge of transparency was that everyone could see your every move, including your mistakes. Imagine your accountant having a team of

---

16 AFRIpads.com, accessed December 18, 2019, *https://www.afripads.com*.

17 Thompson and Comben, "Binance Charity Foundation: Harnessing Blockchain Tech for Social Good."

people—in fact, the entire world—watching every transaction, and you get a sense of the new reality.

In December 2018, for example, BCF made a mistake: a donation intended for the L-Istrina Campaign was sent to the wrong internal wallet. When the blockchain community called out the mistake, the funds were immediately sent back to BCF under the transaction "Adjustment to BCF" in the amount of 15,313.94 BNB.[18] This example illustrates that just because a blockchain transaction is permanent doesn't mean that it can't be "undone." As with any accounting error, we can simply make an opposite or counterbalancing transaction. Fully transparent nonprofits, BCF learned, would need to quickly acknowledge and correct accounting errors.

Other members of the blockchain community called out BCF on why some donations were not immediately showing up on the blockchain. The foundation explained that donated funds weren't shown on the blockchain until they were allocated to a charity. For example, the TRON blockchain project made a donation of $3 million, to be gradually allocated on a project-by-project basis.[19] These funds showed up only after they were committed to specific projects.

Is transparency a feature or a bug? That is the question that blockchain innovators may ask themselves. Does a public ledger lead to more rigorous accounting and therefore to more trust? Or does it lead to more questions from a skeptical public and consequently to less trust? The early BCF challenges show that blockchain accountants will need to practice scrupulous honesty and radical openness—especially about their mistakes.

VOLATILITY

How do you maintain a reserve fund of digital currencies when the value of that fund is a yo-yo?

At the time of this writing, for example, BCF has received donations of 466 BTC. This has a value of about $3.3 million, but that could range from $2.5 million to $4 million in one week. Clearly, this volatility can make the allocation of funds a complicated endeavor.

BCF has chosen to hold donations in whatever form they were donated, be it BTC, ETH, BNB, or even USD. This undoubtedly keeps things easy from a

18 Binance Charity Foundation, accessed December 18, 2019, *https://www.binance.charity/about*.

19 Ibid.

conversion perspective: BCF is simply the trusted custodian of those donations, paying them out to the appropriate projects. It's a pass-through.

This means, however, that they assume the volatility risk, which could have either positive or negative effects. The Pink Care Token was a way of reducing some of the risk, by creating a stable store of value—but the money paid back to the merchant for redeeming that token is still being held in volatile digital assets.

These problems could be solved by converting all donations into stablecoins, or even traditional currencies—but this presents new complexities, especially for those who want to "see where the money is going." Simplicity means volatility; conversion means complexity.

INFRASTRUCTURE

In developed nations, we take our infrastructure for granted. Our financial systems, educational systems, postal systems, technology systems, and even our highway systems are all vital "pipelines" that carry our money, our communications, and our groceries. They make our modern lives go.

In emerging nations, infrastructure is often the greatest challenge. In the case of AFRIpads, volunteers have to get the pads to remote rural communities, but the roads and bridges may be unpassable. In the case of Binance Uganda, merchants need a computer or smartphone, but wireless connections may be spotty. And people can use blockchain only if they understand how it works—but blockchain education systems are hard to find.

For blockchain to thrive, a country needs the following infrastructures (Figure 8-5):

Physical infrastructure
> The ability to transport goods where they are needed (whatever blockchain is buying)

Financial infrastructure
> "On-ramps" and "off-ramps" to convert local currency to digital currency, and vice versa

Technology infrastructure
> Reliable internet connections, with access to the rest of the world (not firewalled)

Regulatory infrastructure
> Government support—or at least a government "sandbox"—that allows digital assets to fearlessly be converted into local currency

Educational infrastructure
  A public system to explain blockchain, with both its benefits and its risks

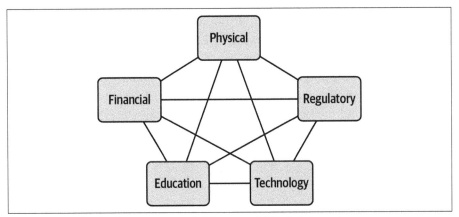

Figure 8-5. The local infrastructures needed for successful blockchain projects

  As BCF looked at new countries to enter, it thought carefully about these issues. Which nations had these infrastructures in place—or the political will and capital to build them?

Next Steps

Helen had come a long way since her childhood experience in Beijing. As she and Jill prepared to present their accomplishments to BCF's board meeting at the United Nations General Assembly in New York, they kept returning to their goal of serving the "bottom billion" of society. How could they unify BCF projects toward this larger global goal?
  Described as a "shared blueprint for peace and prosperity," the United Nations Sustainable Development Goals focus on 17 issues ranging from ending poverty, to improving health and education, to tackling climate change by the year 2030.[20] By strategically focusing on projects that tie into the United Nations 2030 Agenda, Helen and Jill hoped they could multiply the impact of new BCF projects—and attract new partner governments as well.
  They also wanted to *measure results*. Their idea was to create an impact model to monitor the social impact of each of their projects, and then publish an impact

---

20 "Sustainable Development Goals," United Nations, accessed January 6, 2020, *https://sustainabledevelopment.un.org/?menu=1300.*

report for each project. In the spirit of transparency, these reports would be freely available to the public.

BCF's early projects showed promise. But by far the project with the most donations was the Binance Charity Wallet, the "open fund" that could be disbursed as BCF chose. But *which projects should receive these donations?*

While Helen had many valuable political connections, *government relations* would clearly be a big part of BCF's success. How much time and energy should they focus on these efforts, and in which countries?

These were big questions, and they were a small team. While blockchain technology could multiply their efforts many times over, they were still making up a new model of philanthropy as they went along. If you were in Helen and Jill's shoes, how would you reach the "bottom billion"?

9

Cardano Foundation: Blockchain Governance

Cardano will be valuable based upon hard work, real-world use and the utility of the platform. I'm not here to make day traders rich. I'm here to change the world.[1]

—Charles Hoskinson, founder of Cardano

Like so many successful people in blockchain, Nathan Kaiser had an unusual skill set.

He grew up in Switzerland during the personal computer revolution, teaching himself BASIC programming and beginning his lifelong love of technology. As a young man, he entered law school, eventually earning bar membership in Zurich, Berlin, Hong Kong, and Taipei. Over the next 20 years, he combined his love of law with his passion for PCs, practicing international law with a focus on technology.

In 2011, a now-famous *Wired* article on bitcoin captured Nathan's interest.[2] He quickly became a blockchain believer, delivering passionate presentations on bitcoin and decentralization. A few years later, he facilitated one of the first bulk purchases of bitcoin: the client, a bitcoin miner in China, needed a contract drafted. Many lawyers didn't even know about bitcoin; few understood it. Nathan did.

1 Charles Hoskinson, Twitter, February 1, 2018, *https://twitter.com/iohk_charles/status/959076402912927744*.

2 Benjamin Wallace, "The Rise and Fall of Bitcoin," *Wired*, November 23, 2011, *https://www.wired.com/2011/11/mf-bitcoin*.

To his skill stack of technology lawyer, bitcoin expert, and blockchain speaker, Nathan now added *entrepreneur*. He bought one of the first bitcoin ATMs, installing it in an ice-cream parlor in Taiwan. With the help of the other partners in his law firm, Nathan learned how to manage and operate the ATM with full legal compliance. Although the business venture didn't make money, it was a tremendous learning experience and a stepping stone for what was to come.

As the bitcoin ATM experience was wrapping up, Nathan received a phone call from a new tech company called Input Output Hong Kong (IOHK). A blockchain luminary named Charles Hoskinson had heard that Nathan was a lawyer working with bitcoin in Hong Kong, and he asked if Nathan could help the company with legal matters, as it was creating a new blockchain project called Cardano. The relationship started with small, simple tasks, but quickly grew to more complex projects. It then became Nathan's main client, when he accepted the position as general counsel of IOHK.

One of the interesting aspects of the global, distributed nature of blockchain organizations is that it wasn't until two years later that Nathan and Charles finally met face to face. Nathan is a genial, good-natured tech lawyer with an easy smile; Charles is a bearded, passionate tech visionary with strong opinions. The Swiss lawyer and the blockchain programmer were an unlikely pair, but the pairing seemed to work well.

So well, in fact, that soon Charles would present Nathan with an even greater opportunity: to run the Cardano Foundation.

What Is Cardano?

Launched in 2017 by Ethereum cofounder Charles Hoskinson, Cardano is one of the world's leading blockchain platforms. It is a self-described *third-generation* platform, seeking to improve on the first-generation (bitcoin) and second-generation (Ethereum) models.

If Ethereum can be described as a platform for building new decentralized applications (dapps), the vision for Cardano might be described as a *better Ethereum*. Specifically, Cardano seeks to be a blockchain development platform that's more scalable and more interoperable, two areas where Ethereum has struggled (see our CryptoKitties case study in Chapter 6). Developers, in other words, can use Cardano as a foundation for creating new blockchain applications—like Ethereum, but better.

Charles built Cardano around a research-driven approach, more in the vein of a rigorous academic model than a go-go internet startup. Developers and engineers from top schools like the Massachusetts Institute of Technology (MIT), University of Edinburgh, and Tokyo Institute of Technology give peer review on proposed changes and updates to Cardano, through a *blockchain development process* that serves as a best practice for technology leaders.

Blockchain Development Process

All major features at Cardano are developed using this process (Figure 9-1):

1. *Call for papers*: Cardano sends messages to its community, outlining problems and requesting solutions.

2. *Whitepaper*: Developers or academics submit documents explaining their proposed solution.

3. *Peer review*: Others stress-test, improve, and refine the solution; rinse and repeat.

4. *Specs*: Eventually, developers create detailed technical specifications (like a blueprint) for the solution.

5. *Proof of concept*: Developers build a small-scale version of the solution to see if it works.

6. *Testnet*: Developers release the solution on a small scale to beta testers.

7. *Mainnet*: The completed solution is released to the world.

This "open source" process—used by leading blockchain projects like Ethereum and Hyperledger Fabric—generally achieves more creative, more rigorously tested, and lower-cost solutions than those developed by closed teams.

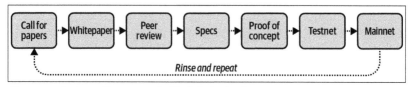

Figure 9-1. Best practice process for blockchain development

One of the first projects built on top of Cardano was its own digital asset called ADA (a.k.a. Ada). Just as Ether (the currency) is the unit of account for Ethereum (the platform), ADA is the unit of account for Cardano, serving as the "money" that other applications can use as payment.

ADA runs on "payment rails" called the Cardano Settlement Layer (CSL). On top of this payment network sits the Cardano Computation Layer (CCL), which runs blockchain-based **smart contracts**.

Definition

Smart contracts: If you're just joining us, these are contracts that are executed (or signed) automatically between two or more parties, written into code and executed on blockchain. Think if/then, as in, "*If* I receive 10,000 ADA in payment, *then* you will automatically be emailed the key to my apartment rental." (For a refresher on smart contracts, see Chapter 3.)

Finally, Cardano pioneered a new **consensus protocol** called Ouroboros, based on Proof of Stake but with a random process to choose validator nodes.[3] This reduces the potential for the "rich to get richer" through their consolidation of staking power (in the same way jury duty randomly selects citizens to judge the fates of their fellow citizens).

---

3 "Ouroboros," Cardano, accessed June 14, 2020, *https://www.cardano.org/en/ouroboros.*

Definition

Consensus protocol: To review, this is the process by which blockchains arrive at consensus, or agreement, across a widely distributed network. In the Proof of Stake flavor of consensus, those who hold more of a token generally have more voting power (they have more *at stake*).

The downside to this method of decentralized decision-making, as we covered in Chapter 2, is that this means power can become centralized in the hands of a few (which we call the *Consensus Paradox*). Ouroboros tries to solve this problem through random selection (like jury duty).

Cardano had sophisticated technology overseen by thoughtful academics, but plenty of blockchain projects have had great tech, only to crash and burn when the human element came into play. As you've seen throughout this book, this human element—the leadership and decision-making process, also known as **governance**—is just as important as the code.

Definition

Governance: In blockchain, the rules of the system that allow people to make decisions and move projects forward. Because blockchain is decentralized (owned by the users, as a government is owned by the citizens), good governance is a blockchain best practice.

It is in governance that Cardano made some of its biggest innovations, with a three-tier governance system, much like the three branches of the US government. This tricameral system provides checks and balances to help ensure a balance of power. Here's how they work.

The Three Columns of Cardano

By way of analogy, the US government has three branches, each with its own structure and responsibilities:

- Executive (President)
- Legislative (Congress)
- Judicial (Supreme Court)

Similarly, Cardano comprises three organizations:

- Cardano Foundation, which drives adoption and grows the community
- IOHK, which manages Cardano development
- EMURGO, an incubator for Cardano startups

Each entity—together, the *Cardano columns*—has its own governance, ownership, and leadership (Figure 9-2). We'll explain each of these in turn.

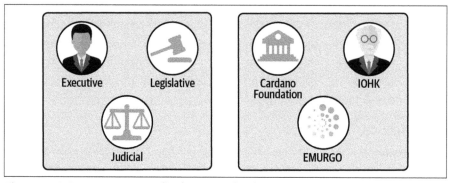

Figure 9-2. US governance (centralized) compared with Cardano governance (decentralized)

CARDANO FOUNDATION MAKES CARDANO GROW

Based in Zug, Switzerland, the Cardano Foundation is a nonprofit organization that drives new Cardano partnerships, builds the community, and works with companies and governments to pave the way for future growth of the Cardano platform.

Because blockchain is global, the foundation works to develop communities and partnerships in countries around the world, from Nigeria to the United Kingdom to the Republic of Mauritius.[4]

The Foundation team consists of the following:

---

4 Bakyt Azimkanov, "Cardano Foundation to Work with African Nations to Develop Blockchain Governance," Cardano Foundation, November 21, 2019, *https://forum.cardano.org/t/cardano-foundation-to-work-with-african-nations-to-develop-blockchain-governance/28487*; Charles Hoskinson, "Davos Special —Global Fintech Ecosystem and Industry Trends," Cardano Foundation, YouTube, January 22, 2020, *https://www.youtube.com/watch?v=HonNZUW1Zf8*.

Foundation Council

This five-member team provides centralized direction for the decentralized Cardano project.

PR Team

Led by Bakyt Azimkanov, the communications team strategically positions Cardano in leading media outlets and publications, building its brand.

Community Management Team

The six-member team focuses on the management and growth of the Cardano user community, including an Ambassador Program that we'll discuss shortly.

Operations Team

The seven-member team advises the Foundation Council on "getting stuff done," with an emphasis on efficiency, growth, and accountability.

Tech Team

Consists of two people who understand the technology aspects of the business and who interface with IOHK (coming up next).

IOHK IS CARDANO'S CORE DEVELOPER

IOHK is a separate technology company founded by Charles Hoskinson and Jeremy Wood, contracted to work on Cardano at least through 2020.[5] IOHK writes the code and develops the protocols for new Cardano features and releases.

IOHK has also built regional centers for education and development around the world, where they teach locals how to code on Cardano.

EMURGO IS CARDANO'S STARTUP INCUBATOR

EMURGO serves as the for-profit, investment arm of Cardano. It supports the Cardano ecosystem by nurturing companies that are building enterprise applications on Cardano. The philosophy is not to reinvent entire industries (i.e., the financial system); rather, EMURGO looks for opportunities to build blockchain solutions on top of existing systems.

---

5 Guy, "Cardano Review: What's Up with ADA?" Coin Bureau, YouTube, October 7, 2019, *https:// www.youtube.com/watch?v=DKuV-_sicNo.*

EMURGO startups are located all over the world, tackling problems as diverse as land registries (tracking who owns what), supply chain (tracking what goes where), and identity management (tracking who's who).[6]

Government Versus Governance

From a higher perspective, we might contrast the three-branch system of government with Cardano's three-branch system of blockchain; see Table 9-1.

Table 9-1. *Comparing US government and Cardano governance*

Government	Blockchain
Executive: sets objectives	Foundation: drives strategy
Legislative: makes laws	Development: writes code
Judicial: develops legal ecosystem	Incubation: develops business ecosystem

Just as a national government serves its citizens, the Cardano governance serves its users. Most of these users are ADA investors (people who have bought ADA and are invested in its long-term success). Others are developers or companies that have built projects or businesses on the Cardano platform.

Like the citizens of a government, these Cardano users are theoretically "all in it together," but they have a wide variety of needs, priorities, and opinions. In blockchain, as in government, how these needs are heard, prioritized, and communicated matters a lot. Without a strong governance system, the mobs can get angry and storm the gates of government with torches and pitchforks (today this is mostly done on Twitter).

A three-branch governance system can provide a check on a single, all-powerful founder, who in the best case will be a "benevolent dictator" and in the worst case will become a despot. The trade-off is that this system of checks and balances will be slower. It means that thoughtful debate will be needed to find the best solutions together, always listening to the needs of the users.

The takeaway is that the governance system matters. It's not something that can be easily grafted onto a blockchain project later; it should be planned thoughtfully from the start.

---

6 Bakyt Azimkanov, "Cardano Foundation Strengthens Its Support to Blockchain-Related Research Initiatives," Cardano Foundation, August 12, 2019, *https://cardanofoundation.org/en/news/cardano-foundation-strengthens-its-support-to-blockchain-related-research*.

The Blockchain Balancing Act

At its core, blockchain is about people.

At the core of blockchain, you have *nodes that make up the network*. Nodes are managed and maintained by people. You have developers, who are also people (mostly). You have holders of the digital asset (in this case, ADA): people with a financial stake in the system.

Quickly, the governance of blockchain becomes a people problem.

This is why, like designing a traditional government, designing blockchain governance is tricky business. There are no perfect solutions for managing people, but there are *principles*. Managing this balancing act of centralized and decentralized systems, as you've seen throughout this book, is the key principle (Figure 9-3).

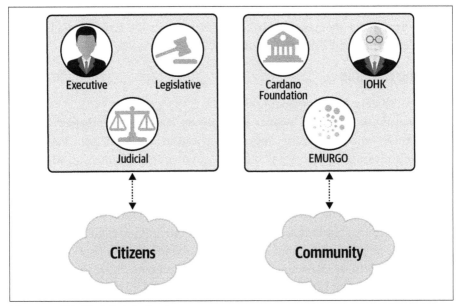

Figure 9-3. The blockchain balancing act

In a government like the US, the three branches work together as a centralized organization reporting to the people, who are decentralized. The people (the citizens) can influence policy, but governments do the work.

With Cardano, the balance is similar: the three centralized Cardano organizations are all accountable to the decentralized Cardano community (ADA investors, developers, and users who manage the nodes). This community can suggest and assist, but the central columns hold it all together.

To summarize, within Cardano's system, the Foundation (a nonprofit growth engine) works hand in hand with IOHK (a for-profit developer), building new companies through EMURGO (a nonprofit incubator). This "government" ultimately reports to the Cardano community (the "citizens"). One important caveat is that they are not elected officials—remember that Charles appointed Nathan—which could lead to possible conflicts of interest.

Why do citizens care? Because this government even has its own "currency" in the form of ADA, and most of the citizens hold that currency. It is in everyone's best interest to see this economy grow, by building the ecosystem and making the Cardano platform a global standard.

When Charles asked Nathan to lead the Cardano Foundation, then, it was a momentous decision: from the chief lawyer at IOHK to the head of the Foundation. It was also a momentous challenge, as heading the Cardano Foundation meant reporting to the Cardano community. And a storm was brewing.

Righting the Ship

Cardano's citizens were demanding change.

If you think traditional politics is tough, try running a blockchain project. People loudly voice their complaints across social media, blockchain news sites, and public message boards. Small disputes can turn into a flame war, which can harden into an ideological impasse.

This was the case by the end of 2018, when many in the Cardano community felt that the Foundation wasn't moving quickly enough on its development road map. Community members took to Twitter and Telegram to call for the Foundation chair to step down. Nathan, with his legal background, was put in charge of negotiating this tricky transition, bringing it to a successful and diplomatic agreement. It was then that Charles asked Nathan if he would fill the chair position on an interim basis.

Nathan accepted the offer.

Now the real work began. Nathan saw that Cardano had a powerful blockchain platform, a successful cryptocurrency, and a strong governance structure. He also knew that he had to balance the centralized and decentralized aspects of the project, which were formalized as the *Cardano Council* and the *Ambassador Program* (Figure 9-4).

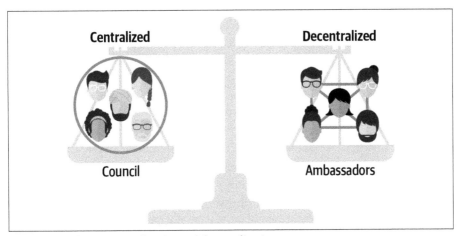

Figure 9-4. Balancing centralization and decentralization

Nathan saw that Cardano needed better coordination among the three Cardano columns. Communication was cumbersome, and *someone* had to keep the ball moving forward. He had in mind a council, which is like a board of directors except that it does not represent shareholders (since there are no shareholders). The council is more like a steering committee that represents the interest of the Cardano project as a whole. It serves Cardano.

The first question was, who would be on this new council to drive the direction of Cardano? The easy answer was IOHK founders Charles and Jeremy, as well as Nathan, but this would have been controversial, giving IOHK undue influence over the Cardano Foundation.[7]

Nathan wanted a better option: appointing a small team of smart people to represent the three organizations:

- Nathan was the first member; upon accepting the position, he made it clear to Charles that even though his background was with IOHK, he would not automatically vote according to Charles's wishes. His fiduciary duty as a member of the council would be to the Foundation.

- The second member, vice-chair Manmeet Singh, was the CIO of EMURGO, which was separate from IOHK. Bringing a strong background

---

7 Remember, IOHK was still just a separate contractor, but Charles founded both Cardano Foundation and IOHK because he didn't want the centralized IOHK running the nonprofit Cardano Foundation.

in entrepreneurship, his eyes were on the prize of incubating new projects to help the Cardano platform reach its potential.

- The third member, treasurer Domino Burki, brought over 15 years of experience in banking, international investing, and compliance, with a focus in digital asset management. He served as the independent voice, with allegiance to neither IOHK nor EMURGO.

Eventually, the Council would add two new members, IOHK chief of staff Tamara Haasen and EMURGO chief technology officer Nicolás Javier Arqueros Rojas, to maintain the balance. Bringing a woman and a South American to the Council also increased diversity.[8] With five members spread across time zones, the Council meets monthly via video to discuss the Cardano project, solve problems, and make high-impact decisions.

The Council provided a much-needed decision-making framework for Cardano's centralized core. Simultaneously, the Cardano Foundation team built out a growth framework, the Cardano Ambassador Program, for its decentralized community. Here's where things got interesting.

The Ambassador Program

Ambassador Status is something that must be earned. We believe in decentralization, and that a strong community led by those who contribute the most is extremely important.[9]

—Cardano Foundation

The idea was simple: bring in people who want to grow the Cardano community and then empower them to do it.

Ambassadors were people with specialized skills (like blogging or translating) who would help spread the Cardano message. Cardano would give these Ambassadors a suite of messaging tools and direction on how to use them; Ambassadors in turn would function as the Foundation's "eyes and ears," relaying community chatter back to the Foundation.

---

8 Bakyt Azimkanov, "The Cardano Foundation Strengthens Its Council with Two New Members," Cardano Forum, December 3, 2019, *https://forum.cardano.org/t/the-cardano-foundation-strengthens-its-council-with-two-new-members/28728*.

9 "Ambassadors," Cardano, accessed March 4, 2020, *https://cardano.org/ambassadors*.

Why would people sign up for an Ambassador role, at no pay? *Because they own the token.*

Here again we see the power of blockchain-based units of value (in this case, Cardano's ADA tokens) in driving the growth of a blockchain project. Just as a shareholder of Apple is more likely to evangelize Apple products, so an ADA token holder is going to evangelize Cardano. More users leads to increased network effects, which often (but not always) leads to increased token prices (see Chapter 3).

Cardano Ambassadors could choose from a few roles, as described to the Cardano community:[10]

Meetup organizer

Form local communities by holding regular Cardano events in your area. The standard is to host at least one meetup every three months, with a minimum of 10 attendees, and then share recaps of the meetups on the Cardano Forum.

Moderator

Manage online communities like the Cardano Forum by answering questions, sharing content, and relaying important internal information. You must already be active on the channel, and your performance will be validated by platform metrics (e.g., upvotes).

Content creator

Develop content like blog posts and videos to provide deeper insight into the Cardano project. You must audition with three pieces, showing positive community feedback (views, likes, shares), and then continue sharing at least one post each month.

Translator

Help grow international awareness by translating content into local languages. You must translate at least 3,000 words in total and continue to translate 1,000 words a month. Translated content may be shared or posted on any platform.

---

10 Cardano, "Cardano Ambassador Program Roles Details," Cardano Forum, August 28, 2019, *https://forum.cardano.org/t/cardano-ambassador-program-roles-details/26114.*

Besides increasing the Cardano "economy," there are other benefits to Cardano Ambassadors. "I've learned a lot, and I've built lots of relationships," said Ambassador Josh Munday in a promo video (Figure 9-5). "I'm always helping people, and it's quite rewarding."[11]

Figure 9-5. "Compared to other blockchains, I feel that we have the strongest community...we strive to help each other all the time."

Since communication is a two-way street, the Ambassadors have two roles: not just getting the Cardano message out to the public, but also bringing the public message back to Cardano. Ambassadors have their own Slack channel: the Foundation's "ear to the ground" on what the community is saying.

The Council members, in turn, have a responsibility to communicate frequently with Ambassadors. It is their job to spread the message on what the centralized part of the organization (the *hub*) is doing, receive feedback from the decentralized community (the *spokes*), and then rinse and repeat (Figure 9-6).

11 Cardano Foundation, "Cardano Foundation Meets Cardano Ambassadors," YouTube, May 5, 2020, *https://youtu.be/HqWLe7sT_rl.*

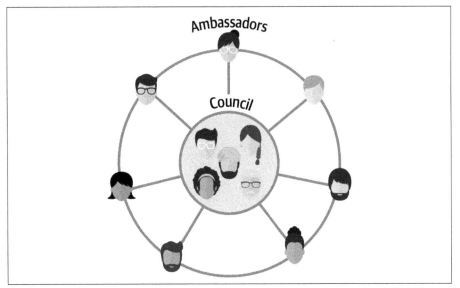

Figure 9-6. The hub-and-spokes model of blockchain communication

The valuable feedback the Council members receive from Ambassadors, and vice versa, creates a relentless and constant feedback loop that can't just be delegated to a public relations firm. The Ambassadors allow the leaders to get their messaging into every medium—online, offline, small groups, and large events—and receive feedback in return.

This is a fundamentally different way of communicating with the public. Most organizations issue bland, boring press releases, favoring corporate-speak over clear communication. Working with a blockchain community requires transparency and rapid response (Figure 9-7).

Managing online communities is like managing citizens, but on steroids. Small disagreements can turn into flame wars; rumors can spread like forest fires. Amplified by Reddit and Twitter, a few unhappy users can quickly burn down months of hard work, just by being the loudest voices in the room.

Rather than reacting like firefighters, blockchain projects will do well to proactively communicate with their users, with a goal of clarity and transparency. That's the goal of Cardano Ambassadors: to keep communication flowing and to watch for smoke.

jonmoss   2 ✐ Sep '18

Statement from Cardano Foundation

Cardano Foundation (CF) is aware of the concerns of some in the community via comments on social channels. In light of this we would like provide some further context on the issues raised around the audit and also about the work of the Foundation.

With regards to our audit work, back in November 2017, IOHK invited the CF to audit the build of Cardano SL. Ensuring stakeholder accountability is one of the key objectives of CF so this was an exciting prospect and a natural fit. The audit of Cardano SL was proposed with the intention to thoroughly review the code, technical documentation and operating procedures of Cardano's Development team. CF engaged FP Complete, an independent Haskell specialist firm, to carry out these audits.

The first audit report was shared with IOHK in December 2017 and reports have been sent every month since, the last one being August. The idea, agreed and supported by IOHK, was that the reports would become public for full transparency.

The first public audit report was released ₁₉ in February 2018, it was agreed with IOHK that CF would share these reports with the community monthly. Since the first public report was released, CF have not received feedback from IOHK on the audit points raised, CF felt it counterproductive to highlight audit points to the community without showing a balanced response from the auditee. In order to release fair and objective audit reports, CF believe the best approach is to allow IOHK time to adapt to the process and CF remains hopeful of releasing the next audit very soon.

CF believes that this collaborative approach is in the interest of project harmony and will benefit Cardano in the long run. CF is excited to be able to share the extensive and valuable work carried out by FP Complete over the past 9 months.

Figure 9-7. Communicating with a blockchain community

The Cardano Foundation had a goal of bringing on 100 Ambassadors by the end of 2019, but ended the year with about half that many. Nathan considered the concept a partial success, but he realized people would work for free for only so long; the Foundation would ultimately need to pay its Ambassadors.

Moreover, managing decentralized communities was messy. Blockchain governance, like traditional government, involves drama, disagreement, and debate. People have financial fortunes tied up in the project; one community member even had a Cardano tattoo!

How do you manage these passions while also managing the project?

Lessons Learned

You live with the fact that you will always have opponents, but someone different is unhappy every time. There is no magic solution. It is neither beautiful nor elegant; it is rough, but in the end, everyone will be happier than they are today. The only wrong decision is not making any decision.[12]

—Nathan Kaiser, chair, Cardano Foundation

Now that Cardano had state-of-the-art blockchain technology, a governance structure with the Foundation Council at the center (the hub), and a decentralized Ambassador program (the spokes), how would Nathan "herd the cats" to govern effectively and move the Cardano project forward? He reflected on some lessons learned.

RELY ON EXPERTS, BUT ALLOW EVERYONE TO WEIGH IN

Just as in traditional government, your in-house experts understand how the system works, while the larger community sees mostly the results of that system. Let's say you're a politician hearing from your citizens that homelessness is a problem. You can have an open period during which you hear ideas from citizens, but then you need policymakers to hash out details and find a workable solution.

Similarly, strategic decision-making at the Cardano Foundation is impacted by the feedback the Foundation Council receives from the community. To work through issues, the Council relies on experts: IOHK, EMURGO, Cardano Foundation staff, and their academic partners. But the extended Cardano community can weigh in on proposed solutions, just as citizens can vote on a proposed law.

You simply can't put an entire project in the hands of a community, since most don't have the technical skill or deep understanding. Nor can you completely centralize the decision-making, because then you have a dictatorship. (Even benevolent dictators eventually fall.) You must strike a balance.

In blockchain, as in any community, some people have a disproportionately loud voice but do not necessarily represent the community opinion. Since blockchain is largely discussed via online forums and Twitter, these voices can generate a good deal of online drama, without ever having to show their faces.

---

12 Nathan Kaiser, interview with the author, February 4, 2020.

In blockchain, as in government, not everyone will be happy with every decision. But the minority consents to be governed by the majority. Nathan, much like a politician, must balance the needs of all his stakeholders, doing what's best for the Cardano ecosystem.

AVOID RIGID DECISION-MAKING STRUCTURES; EMBRACE FLEXIBILITY

Nathan has consistently opposed overly formalized decision structures (such as spreadsheets with lists of open issues or bug fixes), because real decisions are not made that way. In practice, either no one fills out the spreadsheets or they're only partially filled out, and no one reads them.

Real decisions, he believes, are made by a combination of people talking to each other and gut feeling. The Foundation does hold monthly formal Council meetings with an agenda, discussion, voting, and meeting minutes. The Council members receive feedback from the Cardano community and from the Ambassadors—but ultimately they meet, discuss, vote, and then measure the results.

Most of the Foundation's decisions are not sexy: they simply see something wrong and then fix it. There are always some unhappy stakeholders, who feel that project X should be addressed before bug fix Y, but the important thing is to keep moving forward. This practice is consistent with many other blockchain success stories you've seen throughout this book. It is better to act, fail quickly, and learn rather than to wait for perfect information, timing, and agreement, which never seems to happen.

DOING IT RIGHT IS STILL MORE IMPORTANT THAN DOING IT QUICKLY

Speed is not Cardano's only goal. For example, team members don't focus too heavily on quarterly goals; they'd rather make sure that something is done properly than push it through before it is ready. They also don't rush to keep up with potential competitors like Ethereum and Algorand: they believe that in an emerging technology, the market is continually expanding (and you can often beat competitors on quality, not speed to market).

KEEP MOVING FORWARD

The important thing is that much like a shark, we *always need to be moving forward*. As Nathan said, "In crypto space, to not move is sure death."[13]

---

13 Kaiser, interview.

The Road Ahead

This year has been transformational for the Cardano Foundation on multiple accounts, and [next year] promises to be even more monumental. We have built our team and grown our collective skill set. To continue our expansion, the new Council members will empower the Foundation to have even more holistic decision-making, provide additional expertise, and bring new perspectives."[14]

—Nathan Kaiser

Day after day, the Foundation kept moving forward. Nathan and the Council continued to build out their framework of centralized and decentralized governance, attracting top talent to their centralized team, while improving the quality and quantity of their decentralized community members. By the end of 2019, they had a lot to show for it.

In just one year, they had accomplished the following:

- Appointed two new Council members
- Significantly expanded their Community Management Team and Ambassador Program (Figure 9-8)
- Increased their presence in the Americas, Asia-Pacific, Africa, and Europe, now operating out of 16 locations in 12 countries
- Included 17 nationalities among organization members, with almost a third women
- Substantially grown the worldwide Cardano community

These achievements led to better governance, not only for the Cardano Foundation, but for the entire Cardano ecosystem.

---

14 Azimkanov, "The Cardano Foundation Strengthens Its Council."

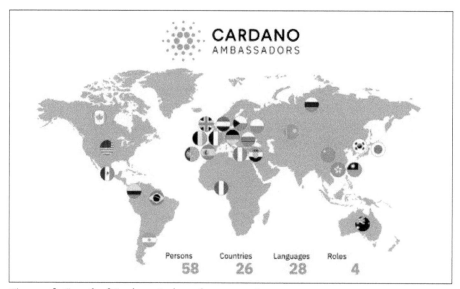

Figure 9-8. Growth of Cardano Ambassador program[15]

Further, Cardano had worked collaboratively with other organizations that were building industry applications around supply chain, logistics, identity management, real estate, and IoT. Despite these efforts, however, the ADA cryptocurrency remained the primary use case of Cardano—and the price at the end of 2019 was lower than the beginning of the year (Figure 9-9).

15 Bakyt Azimkanov, "Cardano Foundation Launches Phase 2 (Rewards) of Its Ambassador Program," Cardano Foundation, April 30, 2020, *https://cardanofoundation.org/en/news/cardano-foundation-launches-phase-2-rewards-of-its-ambassador-program.*

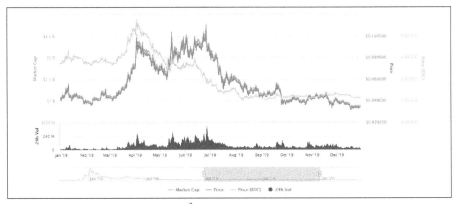

Figure 9-9. ADA price history for 2019[16]

Finally, by raising brand awareness of Cardano with legislators and regulators, Cardano promoted both adoption and interoperability. In other words, when governments finally figured out the laws for digital assets, Cardano would be ready with those relationships they'd already built.

After a few years, however, the Cardano logo, brand, and website were starting to become less clear. Nathan felt they needed a brand refresh, realigning everyone on the ultimate goal, which was to make Cardano the world's leading blockchain platform.

Thus, as 2019 came to a close, the Cardano Foundation announced it would be teaming up with McCann Dublin, a creative agency with a roster of clients including Microsoft, LinkedIn, and Anheuser-Busch InBev. Their new marketing campaign would realign the Cardano brand with the Foundation's mission.

Next Steps

Nathan's skill stack had served him well. His passion for tech, law, and blockchain proved to be a perfect foundation for running the Foundation. Now, more than a year after taking the chair position and rebuilding the Council, Nathan reflected on the results. While various community members were still unhappy about one thing or another, Nathan felt the governance structure was a success: it had allowed Cardano to steadily move forward, while staying true to the five pillars of the Foundation's mission.

---

16 "Cardano (ADA) Price, Charts, Market Cap, and Other Metrics," CoinMarketCap, accessed May 6, 2020, *https://coinmarketcap.com/currencies/cardano.*

The question: on which of these pillars should Cardano focus next?

Expanding and diversifying the community
> For example, continuing to build out the decentralized community and enhancing the Ambassador program

Driving the adoption and standardization of Cardano
> For example, launching Cardano-based financial protocols or pursuing more real-world applications in various industries

Shaping legislative and commercial standards
> Educating and building relationships with policy makers, regulators, and industry partners

Ensuring stakeholder accountability
> Working to disentangle, or at least clarify, possible conflicts of interest between the Cardano Foundation, IOHK, and EMURGO

Facilitating partnerships
> Finding strategic partners (such as large tech companies) to embed Cardano technology in products and solutions

There were many options on the table. If you were betting on Cardano, on which card would you play?

10

Chamber of Digital Commerce: Blockchain and Government

It is necessary to strengthen basic research, enhance innovation...and strive to let China take the leading position in the emerging field of blockchain.[1]

— Xi Jinping, president, People's Republic of China

When Xi Jinping made this statement in the fall of 2019, it drew a line in the sand: China was getting serious about blockchain.

Those in the blockchain community already knew that China had been quietly expanding its expertise in the emerging technology, while the US still had no formal government policy on blockchain. While the US was a confused mishmash of regulations, China was publicly taking the lead.

It was a Sputnik moment. But unlike the 1960s space race, this one would play out in cyberspace.

Perianne Boring had seen it coming. Years earlier, she had founded the Chamber of Digital Commerce in preparation for this moment. In spite of encouraging a *proactive* approach, she saw that the US would now have to be *reactive* if it was going to catch up to China and the rest of the world.

---

1 Perianne Boring, "The Race Is On: China Plans to Gain 'New Industrial Advantages' via Blockchain Technology," Chamber of Digital Commerce, April 22, 2020, *https://digitalchamber.org/blockchain-china-beating-us.*

She and the Chamber had built their organization to galvanize US response and get the wheels of blockchain innovation turning. The big question: who would listen?

The Origin Story

Having the opportunity to cover bitcoin in 2013 was the greatest gift a journalist could ask for.[2]

—Perianne Boring, founder and president, Chamber of Digital Commerce

Perianne was working on Capitol Hill when she first learned about bitcoin in 2011. As a legislative analyst covering financial services and monetary policy, she was intrigued by the idea of a digital currency that was not issued or controlled by government. Like so many of the leaders we've covered in this book, she fell down the rabbit hole to learn everything she could about bitcoin.

In 2013, Perianne was invited to join RT America, an international television network, to launch and host a finance program that aired live daily to millions of viewers across the world.

Perianne was a new type of journalist who sat at the intersection of economics and technology—what we have previously called *techonomics*—but with the added perspective of working in government (Figure 10-1). Her newfound knowledge of digital assets was itself an asset, as she became one of the first broadcast journalists to cover bitcoin on an international network.

---

2 Perianne Boring, interview with the author, May 7, 2020.

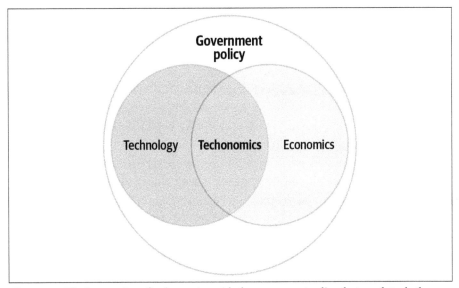

Figure 10-1. The intersection of techonomics, with the government policy that regulates both

Bitcoin made international headlines in 2013, when the government of Cyprus approached the European Union for a bailout. Its two largest banks, which held a large amount of Greek government debt, were on the verge of financial collapse. Panicked investors began pulling their cash from the banks, to which the government responded by limiting money movement out of the country.

This type of **bank run** is common in unstable economies and is frequently accompanied by a *flight to safety*, or buying assets that investors believe will hold their value. In this case, that asset was bitcoin.[3]

Definition

Bank run: A rush to withdraw money from banks (converting deposits to paper currency) that frequently occurs when investors lose confidence in the stability of an economic system. They may also buy up other safe-haven assets like gold that they believe will hold their value. The classic bank run can be seen in the American holiday movie *It's a Wonderful Life.*

3 Mark Thompson, "Cyprus Banks to Reopen with Strict Cash Limits," CNN Business, March 28, 2013, *https://money.cnn.com/2013/03/27/news/economy/cyprus-capital-controls/index.html.*

Driven by this newfound demand, the price of bitcoin began to skyrocket, from about $13 in December 2012 to $250 by April 2013.[4] This domino effect—from Greece to Cyprus to the price of bitcoin—began to ripple through other parts of the blockchain ecosystem.

Mt. Gox, the largest bitcoin exchange at the time, filed for bankruptcy after more than $450 million worth of its customers' bitcoin went missing.[5] Dark web markets like Silk Road began to thrive, accepting bitcoin as a primary means of payment. Governments began to take notice.

In the US, the Financial Crimes Enforcement Network issued guidance on how virtual currencies should be regulated under the Bank Secrecy Act to prevent money laundering, and the SEC issued a warning on the dangers of bitcoin.

Perianne saw that bitcoin was gaining momentum as a new kind of international digital money, which made her even more excited about working in this space. Further, it solidified in her mind what was needed: a dedicated organization to work with policy makers on the emerging world of digital assets.

Her vision was a professional organization, made up of industry experts, that could lead and advise governments as they struggled to make sense of this strange new world of bitcoin. They could also advise government policy makers on crafting smart laws around these new digital currencies.

This vision, which eventually became known as the *Chamber of Digital Commerce*, started slowly. Perianne studied nonprofit law for six months, eventually deciding it should be a 501(c)(6) nonprofit organization to help educate and advocate for smart regulation around this new world of digital commerce.

Still, the devil was in the details. As she mapped out her vision, Perianne found herself facing questions with no precedent. Chief among these:

- How do you advocate for a technology with no CEO and no clear governmental regulatory agency?

- How could this organization serve as an independent, unbiased advocate—and avoid conflict-of-interest issues?

---

4 "History of Bitcoin," Wikipedia, May 21, 2020, *https://en.wikipedia.org/wiki/ History_of_bitcoin#Prices_and_value_history.*

5 Nathaniel Popper and Rachel Abrams, "Apparent Theft at Mt. Gox Shakes Bitcoin World," *New York Times,* February 25, 2014, *https://www.nytimes.com/2014/02/25/business/apparent-theft-at-mt-gox-shakes-bitcoin-world.html.*

Perianne's experience in starting the organization was much like that of any entrepreneur. It was hard work, spending countless hours in stuffy conference rooms, evangelizing her idea to people who had no idea what she was talking about. No one in Washington was working on bitcoin full-time, so it wasn't even clear if she was talking to the right people. It was a grueling, thankless task—and even worse, *she wasn't getting paid.*

But bitcoin investors *were* getting paid. As the price of bitcoin climbed above $1,000 by the end of 2013, the US government began to respond in a series of confused, lurching steps. As Senator Joe Manchin of West Virginia asked regulators to ban bitcoin, the Federal Election Commission announced that it would accept bitcoin as donations to political committees. Meanwhile, the Internal Revenue Service announced it would treat bitcoin as *property* for tax purposes, making it difficult to use as a *currency.*[6]

Against the backdrop of these developments, Perianne readied the formal launch of the Chamber of Digital Commerce. Things were about to escalate quickly.

The Launch

We believe that...putting in place appropriate regulatory standards for virtual currencies will be beneficial to the long-term strength of the virtual currency industry.[7]

—Ben Lawsky, head of the New York State Department of Financial Services

For Perianne and the Chamber, their public policy work began on day one: actually, on day minus one. On July 17, Benjamin Lawsky, the head of New York's Department of Financial Services (NYSDFS), drafted the first regulatory framework for cryptocurrency, called the BitLicense (see Chapter 5). As soon as the Chamber launched, Perianne was immediately asked, "What is your position on the BitLicense?"

---

6 "Manchin Demands Federal Regulators Ban Bitcoin," US Senator Joe Manchin of West Virginia, February 26, 2014, *https://www.manchin.senate.gov/newsroom/press-releases/manchin-demands-federal-regulators-ban-bitcoin.*

7 Ben Mezrich, *Bitcoin Billionaires: A True Story of Genius, Betrayal, and Redemption* (NY: Flatiron Books, 2020), 239.

At the time, Perianne was attending the North American Bitcoin Conference in Chicago. While on a plane to the next industry event in San Francisco, she sat next to her attorney, going through the new BitLicense proposal line by line to craft a position. Here was a new regulatory regime for cryptocurrency, and there were still so many unknowns. They were building the plane as they were flying in it.

There was a 30-day comment window, but Perianne and her attorney felt that 30 days would be insufficient for reviewing and commenting on such a massive, comprehensive proposal. As a result, they petitioned the NYSDFS to extend the comment period. NYSDFS consented, so just days into the launch of the Chamber, it had already achieved its first win.

At the time of launch, the inaugural members of the Chamber were all start-ups. Established institutions, Fortune 500 companies, and banks were exploring the technology, but public companies wouldn't admit for another year that they were looking at bitcoin, which still had a stigma.

But as it persisted in its advocacy work—including holding its first Congressional Bitcoin Education Day—the Chamber then began to grow quickly, adding its first publicly traded companies: Microsoft, IBM, USAA, NASDAQ, and Overstock. The onboarding of these companies showed that industry leaders were taking bitcoin and blockchain technology seriously, and that they were combining their resources to focus on public policy issues.

Like any advocacy group, the Chamber presented a simple choice to these large organizations: you can either have a seat at the table to help shape regulation, or you can sit it out and let others decide the fate of these new technologies for you. The more tech leaders who joined, Perianne found, the more who wanted to join.

Building on this momentum, the Chamber launched the *Blockchain Alliance*, a public-private forum in which industry and law enforcement agencies worked together to address public concerns about blockchain technology and to fight illegal activity.

2016 proved to be a watershed year for the Chamber. After the Chamber hosted the first DC Blockchain Summit, its testimony before Congress led to the passage of House Resolution 835, which recognized the potential for blockchain technology in a variety of relevant sectors. The Chamber was finally getting real leverage with real legislation.

That's when the call came.

Every year, the Federal Reserve System, the International Monetary Fund, and the World Bank hosted a three-day event in Washington, D.C. This year, the Fed asked the Chamber to lead a series of discussions on blockchain technology for the heads of the central banks from around the world. After years of tireless effort, Perianne and her group—consisting of representatives from Chain, NAS-DAQ, Goldman Sachs, and Bloq—would speak to the leaders of the world economy.

Blockchain was going big time.

The Meeting at the Fed

Perianne took a deep breath.

The Board Room—the official meeting place of the Board of Governors of the Federal Reserve System—was dominated by an enormous conference table, like the one attended by the US president and staff. In its polished mahogany and ebony surface sparkled the reflection of the two-story chandelier hanging overhead. Enormous, high-draped windows on either side of the table opened to a cavernous ceiling, giving the room magnificence. At the far end of the room, a seal of the US hung over the fireplace, flanked by a pair of flags.

The walls were infused with history. This was once considered the most secure meeting place in D.C. and was used as an essential meeting room during World War II. Seated around the table were the shapers of the global economy: dozens of central bankers from around the world, the Federal Reserve (the central bank of the US), the World Bank (the international bank that aims to reduce global poverty), and the International Monetary Fund (like the United Nations of money).

Federal Reserve Chair Janet Yellen spoke first. "You should be learning everything that you can about blockchain technology," she urged these world leaders. In a passionate 30-minute talk, she discussed how financial technologies continually change the course of humanity.

She used the example of how derivatives in the agriculture industry had enabled farmers to completely transform their standard of living. Rather than relying on the whims of fate—a good crop this year, a bad one the next—farmers were able to sell **futures** at a slight discount.

Definition

Futures: Financial contracts that let you buy a future asset at an agreed-upon price today. Instead of buying rice at $500 a ton for this year's crop, you could buy next year's crop—in advance—at $450 a ton. By getting the money up front, the farmer is able to invest in next year's harvest and protect against financial difficulty. The buyer of the future may get a discount by buying in advance.

New financial technologies, in other words, weren't just a threat: they were also an opportunity. This wasn't just about bitcoin as a competitor to the dollar, but about the power of the underlying technology to change the economic system —and to improve living conditions for humanity as a whole.

Yellen's talk gave the Chamber and its members the first insights into the Fed's thinking on blockchain. Afterward, Chamber member Adam Ludwin, CEO of Chain, gave a live demo to show the power of peer-to-peer transactions by making a donation in bitcoin to the Wikimedia Foundation using his smartphone. The audience may not have understood the significance: Ludwin sent the first bitcoin from inside the Federal Reserve that day.

In just two years since the Chamber's launch, Perianne realized, the government's discussion had progressed from "we have no jurisdiction over bitcoin," to "this technology is potentially powerful," to "when will we start building a digital dollar?"

Perianne felt that the Chamber had also moved the needle within the bitcoin community. Many of bitcoin's early users had anti-establishment, anti-government beliefs and were adamant that bitcoin should be left unregulated. When Perianne announced that the Chamber would be the first organization to work with the government on blockchain issues, she had no idea what type of response she would receive. Much to her surprise, she received standing ovations.

Perianne heard her name, interrupting her reverie. Now it was her turn to speak. She took a deep breath.

The Structure

We went from warnings, and anxiety, and fear...to so many doors being opened throughout the policy circles. Regulators are very interested in this, but it does require a degree of education, and it also requires a willingness to engage.[8]

— Perianne Boring

Today, the Chamber of Digital Commerce comprises more than 200 members and has become the world's leading trade association for the digital asset and blockchain industry. The Chamber focuses on three top priorities: education and advocacy, anti-money laundering and terrorist finance prevention, and regulatory clarity for digital tokens. We'll explore each of these in turn.

EDUCATION AND ADVOCACY

To promote understanding of blockchain technology among government leaders, members of the Chamber actively participate in a variety of legislative and regulatory organizations. To coordinate these efforts, the Chamber issues regular whitepapers, called Chamber Reports (Figure 10-2).

These Chamber Reports cover a range of topics including Legality of Smart Contracts, Chinese Patent Strategies, Understanding Digital Tokens, Blockchain Cybersecurity, Securitization, Regulatory Sandboxes, Healthcare Policy, and Financial Inclusion.

Education has always been a challenge with government leaders, who are short on time and long on priorities. If you are fortunate enough to get on their calendars, you typically have a 15-minute window to explain the technology and your position. (Meanwhile, you've spent 10,000 hours preparing.)

---

8 "Perianne Boring of Chamber of Digital Commerce on Hyperledger," Hyperledger, YouTube, February 3, 2018, *https://www.youtube.com/watch?v=oh8Rlx9ONjA*.

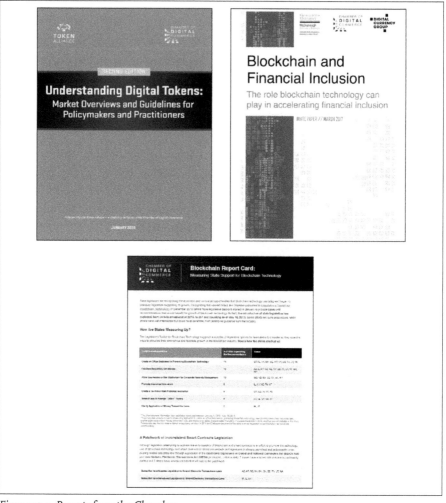

Figure 10-2. Reports from the Chamber

Education is also a relationship business: government leaders are just people, and people tend to trust people they know. Building relationships and resources can't be a hobby: it is a full-time job. It's hard to build an advocacy group entirely out of volunteers because even the most passionate part-timers soon find that life gets in the way, and the advocacy work goes on the back burner.

Education is further complicated by any type of negative press. Anytime the press runs something negative about bitcoin, you will hear about it, and you need full-timers who can educate government leaders on the full picture.

While Perianne and her team took no salary in the early days of the Chamber, the dues paid by larger corporate members now make it possible for them to work full-time, without conflicts of interest. This full-time approach is what makes the Chamber unique in influencing public policy.

ANTI-MONEY LAUNDERING AND TERRORIST FINANCE PREVENTION

The Chamber understands that digital currencies have an image problem: many still think bitcoin is anonymous. The truth is that *cash* is anonymous; bitcoin is **pseudonymous**. When bad actors use bitcoin, it is easier to trace.

Definition

Pseudonymous: Like writing under a pseudonym, bitcoin is linked to a specific account—or wallet address—that is written permanently on the blockchain. While users can keep their identities private, their transactions are public. (Compare this with cash, which is truly anonymous, so it can be used for terrorist activities or political bribes.)

Over the years, the US has introduced an alphabet soup of acronyms to track the criminal movement of money: the Bank Secrecy Act (BSA), the Office of Foreign Assets Control (OFAC), know your customer and anti-money laundering (KYC/AML) laws, and customer due diligence (CDD). Digital currencies can simplify these efforts, but working within these existing legal frameworks is the challenge: a "translation layer" is needed to explain why digital currencies are fundamentally different from cash.

Thus, the Chamber cofounded the Blockchain Alliance, which brings the public and private sectors together to share information, educating lawmakers and law enforcement on how digital currencies can help achieve the ultimate objective: to create an orderly functioning of the marketplace.

REGULATORY CLARITY FOR DIGITAL TOKENS

Of all the working groups in the Chamber, the largest and most active is the *Token Alliance*, composed of more than 400 industry leaders. Their work centers around one key question: *how should we legally classify digital tokens?*

As we've discussed in previous chapters, this question holds enormous importance for the US economy. A digital token—a unit of value, recorded on the blockchain—can variously be described as a security, a currency, a commodity, property, or some weird mashup of all these assets.

Simply stated, different laws govern these different types of assets—and no one is sure how blockchain tokens should be treated. Should tokenized ownership of a company be considered a security, like shares of stock? What if the company has no revenue? What if there's no company?

These issues quickly get murky, so the Chamber's Token Alliance educates and advocates with stakeholders like the SEC, Commodity Futures Trading Commission (CFTC), and Congress with the goal of achieving a predictable legal environment for tokenized assets. This type of environment will allow a new wave of blockchain-based innovation and entrepreneurship.

Tip

Here are two regulatory rules of thumb:

If it's not predictable, it's convictable.
> Regulatory uncertainty leads to fear of breaking the law, which stifles innovation.

With clarity comes prosperity.
> If we understand the rules, we can innovate and a thousand flowers can bloom.

In addition to these high-level priorities, the Chamber pursues other priorities through a variety of working groups, especially in the areas of accounting, smart contracts, and tax reform. "No matter how much you do," Perianne says, "there's always more to do."

Perhaps the biggest priority, then, is keeping membership money flowing. This involves constantly communicating with Chamber members about the value of investing in public policy outside their own company; simply hiring a lobbyist is not an effective long-term strategy.

When the Chamber pitches new members on joining, companies often ask why they should give money to an organization that is already doing business with their competitors. The answer is simple: by bringing everyone together to establish the rules of the road, they can all get it right from the start.

Coordination is better than confusion. When everyone works together to grow the industry pie, everyone's slice of pie will be bigger. That is the purpose and value of a trade association. When an industry speaks with one voice, a government is more likely to listen.

ORGANIZATIONAL STRUCTURE

Our position is always going to be whatever is best for the ecosystem as a whole.[9]

—Perianne Boring

How do you create a group of member companies without the member companies taking over the group?

This is the classic problem with trade associations: one or two large companies can sway the entire organization. To avoid these conflicts, the Chamber has a two-tiered governance structure composed of the Chamber's executive committee and advisory board.

The executive committee and advisory board meet quarterly to set the general policy directives of the Chamber. By doing so, they set policy *topics* without setting policy *positions*.

Member companies can choose from these levels of participation:

- Executive committee (members include Accenture, Binance.US, Citi, Deloitte, Docusign, DTCC, Fidelity, IBM, JP Morgan, MakerDAO Foundation, Medici Ventures, and Ripple)

- President's circle (members include Bitmain, Bitwise, ErisX, Hedera Hashgraph, and Stellar)

- Industry members (reserved for startups only)

These levels, which serve as the funding mechanism for the Chamber, are determined by the amount that members pay to the organization. The higher levels give companies more access to the "platform" (i.e., more member benefits); however, membership levels do not affect the shaping of official Chamber positions.

To the contrary, the Chamber has the goal of maximizing benefits to the entire blockchain ecosystem. As a result, every member, regardless of their financial contribution, has the same voice in crafting policy positions. Quite often,

---

9 Boring, interview.

decisions are reached only after tough conversations: some positions are not beneficial to individual members but benefit the growth of the ecosystem as a whole.

With higher levels of membership comes more access to the Chamber's platform. For example, the Chamber receives many speaking requests for experts. Higher-level members are the first to be referred to these opportunities. More financial leadership leads to more thought leadership.

The Chamber also offers private briefings on new developments, giving members-only access to the most knowledgeable experts on public policy for blockchain and digital assets. If a company needs to understand the potential impact of new regulations, these private sessions help them quickly get up to speed.

In summary, the Chamber's tiered membership structure allows those who pay more to enjoy more exclusive benefits, while allowing all members to have an equal voice in determining policy positions.

Lessons Learned

We are calling on the US government to do two things: the first is to demonstrate national leadership through strong, public support at the highest levels of government. The second is to adopt a national action plan to coordinate all of the stakeholders.[10]

—Perianne Boring

For several years, the Chamber, through all its initiatives and events, had been setting the stage. As 2019 began, it was time to unify the US. The Chamber called the nation to action, through a **national action plan.**

Definition

National action plan: A comprehensive and coordinated strategy for supporting an emerging technology, in order to grow jobs and grow the economy.

Blockchain wasn't the only technology in which the US had been lagging behind. It wasn't until early 2019, for instance, that the US created an official policy for artificial intelligence. A comprehensive national strategy is important for encouraging new technologies to grow: a unified vision will inspire

---

10 "National Action Plan for Blockchain," Chamber of Digital Commerce, YouTube, April 29, 2019, *https:// www.youtube.com/watch?time_continue=45&v=12peiLmH9qg&feature=emb_logo.*

entrepreneurs, incentivize small businesses, and inject new investment into blockchain innovation.

In February 2019, the Chamber summarized all the lessons it had learned into a national action plan for blockchain, with these guiding principles for US legislators:[11]

Establish a predictable legal environment
Blockchain innovators (and their lawyers) can then understand the rules of the road.

Roll out the red carpet
Welcome blockchain innovation through incentives and support (instead of simply staying out of the way).

Create government pilot programs
These programs can be used as a Proof of Concept for using blockchain technologies in real life.

Recognize blockchain as the New Normal
Much like the early days of the internet, understand that new innovations like bitcoin are not a novelty, but the future.

Think globally
Digital currencies, for example, have the potential to reshape the global economy, knocking the US dollar off its perch.

Match China's investment
The three e-commerce giants in China—Alibaba, Baidu, and Tencent—were building the infrastructure for a state-owned digital currency. The US, which had no such financial infrastructure, was only beginning to talk about a digital dollar.[12]

---

11 "Key Thought Leaders from Government and Industry Come Together to Promote a Coordinated Strategy for Blockchain Technology—A Readout on the Day's Discussion," Chamber of Digital Commerce, January 9, 2020, *https://digitalchamber.org/americancompetitivenessroundtable.*

12 Alun John, "China's Digital Currency Will Kick off 'Horse Race': Central Bank Official," Reuters, November 6, 2019, *https://www.reuters.com/article/us-china-markets-digital-currency/chinas-digital-currency-will-kick-off-horse-race-central-bank-official-idUSKBN1XG0BI.*

Develop a sense of urgency

Without the government's quick action, the smart money would simply leave the US—and in the borderless world of blockchain, that was already happening.

The call for a national action plan was supported by US Congressman Tom Emmer, co-chair of the Congressional Blockchain Caucus, who called it "a necessary step forward" for the industry. "Before we stifle," he stated, "we must encourage the private sector to develop these technologies. The National Action Plan...provides a needed call for clear regulation."[13]

Perhaps the spirit of the call was best summed up by Brett McDowell of the decentralized Hedera Hashgraph network: "This is the American Way—embracing the promise of new technologies, and the opportunities they create."[14]

Working with States

While the Chamber was located in Washington, focused on issues at the national level, local blockchain bills were being introduced by states. Although the bills were well-intentioned, Perianne felt that many of them were getting the details wrong, erring on key definitions, and neglecting relevant policy principles.

To help legislators get the language right, the Chamber began partnering with other organizations that were focused on state issues. They fueled these efforts by creating the *Legislator's Toolkit for Blockchain Technology* to guide these lawmakers in their policy-making efforts.

As seen in Figure 10-3, by using an open source, non-copyrighted approach to these reports, the Chamber can influence policy simply by giving lawmakers freedom to copy and paste sections of their Chamber Reports into proposed legislation.

Perianne stated that, by putting the right tools in the hands of the right people, more than 50 bills were introduced by legislators who utilized language from the Toolkit within one year of its introduction.[15] The Chamber had discovered a powerful way to create new laws: copy, paste, and pass.

---

13 "National Action Plan for Blockchain," Chamber of Digital Commerce, February 3, 2020, *https://digital-chamber.org/blockchain-national-action-plan*.

14 "Key Thought Leaders from Government and Industry Come Together to Promote a Coordinated Strategy for Blockchain Technology," Chamber of Digital Commerce.

15 Boring, interview.

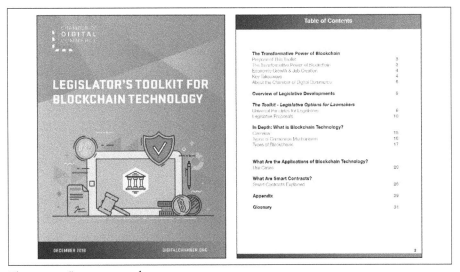

Figure 10-3. Copy, paste, and propose

Next Steps

It is critically important for American and western policymakers to understand how serious China and other nations are taking digital currencies and blockchain technology. It is crucial to become conscious as to what we can expect to see from those who seek dominance in the space, implications for the international monetary and financial system, and, more pointedly, for the US dollar.[16]

—Perianne Boring

In this weird new world of economics, technology, and politics, two pervasive thoughts drew Perianne's attention.

The first was the emerging "new world order." The industry was moving from decentralized currencies like bitcoin to privately issued stablecoins by the likes of JP Morgan and Wells Fargo, and it became apparent that central banks (like the US Federal Reserve) would soon be introducing their own digital currencies. This would likely be followed by global digital currencies from international banking entities such as the World Bank and IMF. Private coins, national coins, and global coins, all powered by blockchain.

---

16 Boring, "The Race Is On: China Plans to Gain 'New Industrial Advantages' via Blockchain Technology."

Would these players merge? Would they collide? What would this future of money look like?

Perianne's second thought centered on who would lead this new monetary system. Would it be a one-world global money overseen by the IMF and tied into each nation's digital currency? Or would the US quickly introduce a digital dollar, maintaining its hold on the world's dominant currency?

Despite the efforts of the Chamber, China was clearly in the lead on developing a national digital currency, and the US was not really even in the game. It seemed clear that if it remained on the current trajectory, the US was in danger of losing its status as the world's reserve currency.

From the time she heard Xi's speech on blockchain in late 2019, Perianne had worked relentlessly to pull US lawmakers together. Blockchain would likely determine the future of the global economy—and with it, the future of the world. The Chamber's challenge was getting lawmakers to take it seriously.

She reflected on where the Chamber should focus its efforts next:

Central bank digital currencies
Upgrading the US financial system to prepare for blockchain-based digital currencies that are issued and supported by central banks

Stablecoins
Creating better understanding and support for *stablecoins*, independently issued blockchain tokens that are redeemable for US dollars

Digital securities
Providing guidance on how to update securities laws in the age of blockchain (as we covered in Chapter 3, regulatory clarity leads to prosperity)

Building support
Increasing political support for pro-blockchain candidates

"We are now six years into the Chamber's journey," Perianne reflected, "yet it feels like we are still just getting started."[17]

If you were Perianne, where would you start next?

---

17 Boring, interview.

The Power of the People

In a sense, you *are* Perianne: someone who has the power to influence blockchain laws in your own state or country. Where does blockchain legislation stand in your local government? Can you write your local representatives, petition your national leaders, maybe even start—or join—a group like Perianne's?

Where should *you* start next?

Everledger: Blockchain and the Supply Chain

We have so much wealth, yet we stay so poor. I can understand why you Americans say you don't want to buy our diamonds. Instead of blessings, our diamonds bring us nothing but misfortune.[1]

—Zacharie Mamba, head of mining, Tshikapa, Democratic Republic of the Congo

Tshikapa is rich in diamonds. Sadly, many of the people who mine those diamonds are desperately poor.

Since these precious gems were discovered there in 1907, the small city in the Democratic Republic of the Congo, located in south-central Africa, has become a mining hotspot. The growth of these mining operations was accompanied by appalling human rights violations: from child labor to violence and rape.

In a poverty-stricken country, wracked by years of civil war and rebel uprisings, discovering a single diamond can mean putting food on the table and getting much-needed medical help for a miner's family. So the workers spend hours in back-breaking labor, sweating under the sweltering sun, hoping to find a single rough gem. When the surface mines tunnel underground, workers shovel gravel inside dark pits, always with the threat that the mine may collapse around them, burying them alive.

---

1 Aryn Baker, "Blood Diamonds," *Time*, accessed June 17, 2020, *https://time.com/blood-diamonds*.

Time magazine reports from one of these mining sites:

> Knee-deep in water pumped from the nearby river, three men sluice pans of gravel through small sieves.
>
> [The miner] gives an excited yelp, fishes out a sliver of diamond the size of a peppercorn and hands it to an overseer sitting in the shade of a striped umbrella. The overseer folds it into a piece of paper torn from a cigarette pack and puts it in his pocket. It's worth maybe $10, he says. That find will be split between the owner of the mine site, who gets 70% of the value, and the 10 members of the sluicing team, who have been working since 9 a.m. and will continue until the sun sets around 6 p.m. If they are lucky, they will find two or three such slivers in a day.[2]

From there, the diamond changes hands through a chain of agents, before it is finally bought by a shop in Tshikapa, where the streets are unpaved and residents bicycle past hand-lettered signs advertising diamonds for sale.

Some of the diamonds, running through networks of diamond buyers, will make it out of Tshikapa and will eventually make it into high-end showrooms around the world—and from there, onto the fingers of happy newlyweds.

Perhaps nowhere is the gap between rich and poor more pronounced than in this supply chain. On one side are young people risking their lives in labor for luxuries. On the other hand—literally—are young people giving these diamonds to each other as a symbol of love and wealth.

While many of these diamonds are now "sustainably sourced," thanks to an international certification standard introduced in 2000,[3] this certification is still easy to counterfeit or work around.[4] Although the colloquial name for these gems is *blood diamonds*, the diamond industry has softened this term to *conflict diamonds*. Still, this conflict, in the form of local warfare over these territories, results in blood. Their blood is literally on our hands.

---

2 Baker, "Blood Diamonds."

3 "The Kimberley Process (KP)," Kimberley Process, accessed June 17, 2020, *https://www.kimberleyprocess.com*.

4 Theo Leggett, "Global Witness Leaves Kimberley Process Diamond Scheme," BBC News, December 5, 2011, *https://www.bbc.com/news/business-16027011*.

The Origin of Everledger

*This is fast becoming a business and political ultimatum: prove your cre-
dentials or step aside.*[5]

—Leanne Kemp, founder and CEO of Everledger

Leanne Kemp is a fast-moving, quick-thinking Aussie who never seems to sit
still. As the chief entrepreneur for the state of Queensland, Leanne is busy communicating, from giving talks to government policymakers to interviews with
CNBC, painting a picture of a world that is "greener, smarter, and fairer."[6]

Her precise skillset is harder to pin down—as is Leanne herself. As we prepared this case study, we conducted our interviews with the serial entrepreneur
over videoconference: once from a moving car, and once in an elevator. (We lost
contact briefly when the elevator started moving.)

Like her whirlwind schedule, Leanne is a force of nature who started as a
self-taught engineer with a background in accounting and commerce. She began
her entrepreneurial ventures in the mid-1990s, first with radio frequency technology (RFT), then with track-and-trace technologies (what we would today call
supply chain) for Australian goods like Wagyu beef steak.

In 2007, Leanne invested in a jewelry business and began to understand
firsthand the challenges of sourcing ethically produced diamonds: there was no
"single source of truth" for a diamond's origin, fraud was rampant, and diamonds were frequently smuggled across borders to launder their origin.

Several years later, she discovered bitcoin, and it was a revelation. "We went
through the Satoshi whitepaper and started thinking about what challenges we
could solve," she remembered.[7] As in other stories in this book, the aha moment
came from combining the open-ledger principles of bitcoin with a hard-to-track
asset (like Leanne herself). If blockchain is the Internet of Value, the thing of
value for Leanne would be *diamonds.*

---

5 Leanne Kemp, "How Can E-Provenance Transform Supply Chains into Value Chains?" *Forbes*, March 16,
 2020, *https://www.forbes.com/sites/leannekemp/2020/03/16/how-can-e-provenance-transform-
 supply-chains-into-value-chains/#26d22a4f128f.*

6 Credit for this phrase goes to Kristalina Georgieva, "The Great Reset," International Monetary Fund, June
 3, 2020, *https://www.imf.org/en/News/Articles/2020/06/03/sp060320-remarks-to-world-economic-
 forum-the-great-reset.*

7 Leanne Kemp, interview with the author, May 13, 2020.

Specifically, Leanne found herself interested in blockchain's unique combination of transparency and privacy. Like a Google Sheet, the shared ledger is open to everyone: it's transparent. But user information can be encrypted, as with an anonymous wallet address: it can also be private.

More important, blockchain could reduce or eliminate many of the middlemen (mostly men) in the supply chain, from that local network of agents in Tshikapa to the global network of buyers and sellers that end at the display case in the jewelry store.

Leanne applied to the prestigious Techstars accelerator program, where she was accepted into the 2015 startup cohort. There, she and her team created the first version of their blockchain-based diamond-tracking system that would eventually become Everledger. The problem they were trying to solve could be described in one word: provenance.

The Eye of Provenance

Being a conscious consumer means leaving the world in a better place. Individual stewardship matters.

—Leanne Kemp

Back to our diamond example, we'll pose the following questions: how can the young couple know if the diamond they have just used to seal their wedding vow is sustainably sourced? How can they know they do not have blood on their hands?

How do we know, for that matter, that our lattes and sneakers and iPhones are not produced for us at the cost of human suffering? A common argument for vegetarianism is to end the needless suffering of animals. By being aware of the everyday products we consume, can we also end the needless suffering of humans?

The historical information associated with products as they move through our supply chains is often lost because it's considered to be of limited value. A new generation of consumers, however, is looking for insight into where their products are sourced. You see this everywhere, from Fair Trade food and beverage products, to Sustainably Sourced clothing and furniture.

We call this history of a product, as it moves through the supply chain from producer to buyer, **provenance**.

Definition

Provenance: The complete history of a product, from origin to end consumer.

The lines are blurry around the criteria for calling a product Ethically Sourced, but there's no question that from a marketing perspective, the right piece of provenance can significantly increase the value of an item. (Consumers will pay more for the adjectives.)

Unfortunately, the selective use of provenance can often mislead customers. Leanne saw an opportunity to track and trace products from the source—showing the complete chain of owners, like an auto title or property deed.

The early-stage prototype of Everledger was called *Blocktrace*, a mashup of the bitcoin network with a collection of MySQL and POSTGRES databases. Every diamond in the world could be registered on this shared public ledger, distributed to each of the nodes, in the same way bitcoin's ledger of transactions is stored on local computers (Figure 11-1).[8]

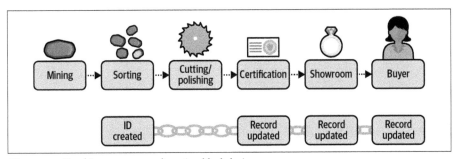

Figure 11-1. Tracking provenance by using blockchain

To Leanne, diamonds were only the beginning. She saw that provenance was important for other precious gems, rare earth minerals, and luxury goods like wine and art.[9] The question of provenance was also trickling down to consumers, who were beginning to ask about their everyday grocery purchases like bananas and coffee:

---

8 Rob Price, "The 25 Most Exciting Bitcoin Startups," Business Insider, March 23, 2015, *https://www.businessinsider.com/25-most-exciting-bitcoin-startups-in-the-world-ethereum-21-coinbase-coindesk-2015-3?op=1#25-edgelogic-stamping-out-diamond-thieves-1*.

9 Darryn Pollock, "Fidelity, Tencent, Rakuten Back $20 Million Round for UK Blockchain Provenance Firm," *Forbes*, September 25, 2019, *https://www.forbes.com/sites/darrynpollock/2019/09/25/fidelity-tencent-rakuten-back-20-million-round-for-uk-blockchain-provenance-firm*.

- Are these products sustainably sourced?
- How fair are their business practices toward local producers?
- What is the impact on the environment of their supply chain?
- Who exactly has worked on my product throughout its life cycle?
- Where has it been, and where is it going next?

Just as you look at a diamond differently when you realize it has been mined using slave labor, you look at your groceries and electronics differently when you know they have been created in conditions of extreme poverty. The diamond is a symbol of this gulf between the world's rich and poor.

By tracking that diamond from its source, buyers could better identify gems that were ethically sourced—for example, refusing to buy from countries with a history of war crimes or human rights violations. What's more, this could be verified at the consumer level, with a smartphone app that pulls up the complete history of the gem, verified on a public blockchain: a certification that can't be forged.

Rather than just focusing on the four C's of carat, cut, color, and clarity, consumers can now add a fifth C: conflict-free.

The Launch of Everledger

We are excited to be able to offer Rock Solid Diamonds to our customers, as part of our ongoing commitment to responsibly sourced, transparent jewelry supply chains. Being able to provide a fully transparent and intimate connection between our customers and their diamonds brings real meaning and value to their precious investment.[10]

—Kristen Darrow, group vice president of Fred Meyer Jewelers

Like many successful entrepreneurs, Leanne had combined her specialized skill set—a knowledge of gems and a passion for blockchain technology—to launch Everledger into the market. A London Techstars event in June 2015 propelled her early-stage proof of concept into the eyes of investors, potential customers, and mainstream media.

---

10 "Tech for Good Blockchain Solutions," Everledger, April 21, 2020, *https://www.everledger.io*.

Now it was time to think bigger. Over 12 fast and furious months, Leanne built out the Everledger team across two locations—London (UK) and Brisbane (Australia)—which then built Everledger's customer base across the globe. The team began pursuing partnerships in earnest.

In the $80 billion global diamond market, they found willing partners who wanted to better track the origin, production, and value of a specific gem.[11] They developed partnerships with over 100 stores in the Fred Meyer Jewelers chain in the US; the Indian diamond manufacturer Sheetal Group; and the Gemological Institute of America (GIA), perhaps the most trusted gemological institute in the world.

Everledger also partnered with Spanish jewelry company Facet to launch DiamondByway, thus forming Europe's first completely traceable collection of jewelry.[12] It is currently tracking more than 900,000 carats contained in over two million diamonds, powered by an innovative marketing campaign.[13]

The diamond industry, of course, is no stranger to marketing, which is important when you're trying to essentially sell rocks. The industry tells prospective buyers that they "should" spend at least two months' salary on an engagement ring—as if this were a great law of the universe—and that "diamonds are forever."

The problem is that when diamonds—or any product—are ethically sourced, the price generally goes up. (Fair wages = higher prices.) How do you convince buyers that conflict-free diamonds are worth the extra cost, especially when *conflict* is not really what newlyweds want to hear?

DiamondByway talks about the *story* of the diamond, with the freshly mined gem receiving an identification number that stays with it through the cutting, polishing, and faceting process. The diamond is then graded and certified, and crafted into beautiful jewelry.

11 Rachel Wolfson, "New Blockchain Tool Provides Free Price Estimates for Diamonds, Showing Quality and Provenance," *Forbes*, August 9, 2018, *https://www.forbes.com/sites/rachelwolfson/2018/08/09/new-blockchain-tool-provides-free-price-estimates-for-diamonds-showing-quality-and-provenance/#4f3c66e43226*.

12 "Everledger Upgrades Blockchain Platform, Expands Beyond Diamonds," Ledger Insights, September 19, 2019, *https://www.ledgerinsights.com/everledger-upgrades-blockchain-platform-expands-beyond-diamonds*.

13 Michael del Castillo, "The Future Of Blockchain: Fintech 50 2020," *Forbes*, February 19, 2020, *https://www.forbes.com/sites/michaeldelcastillo/2020/02/12/the-future-of-blockchain-fintech-50-2020*.

As you've seen in the stories throughout this book, blockchain solutions are most successful when we hide the complexity from users. Behind the scenes, the diamond identification number is an entry on the Everledger blockchain. To the consumer, it is the *story of the diamond*. (See our example ad in Figure 11-2.)

Figure 11-2. Hide the complexity

Instead of simply moving the gem through the supply chain from miner to consumer, blockchain can turn this supply chain into a **value chain** that increases the value of products in the supply chain by adding provenance data to the product—in essence, telling its story.

Definition

Value chain: The set of processes that add value to a finished product as it moves through a supply chain. For example, the cutting and polishing of a diamond may not cost much in labor, but it adds tremendous value to the final cost of the diamond.[14]

---

14 Michael E. Porter, *Competitive Advantage: Creating and Sustaining Superior Performance* (New York: Free Press, 2008).

Whenever we tell the story of a product or a company, we generally add to its value. This is what we've done with telling the company stories throughout this book—which is called *Blockchain Success Stories!*—and why we advise all blockchain entrepreneurs to be able to tell the story of their companies and projects.

Blockchain-based provenance tells the story. That adds value.

Transparency: It Cuts Both Ways

Everledger was able to provide additional value in a partnership with online diamond retailer Rare Carat. Combining the Everledger blockchain (now rebuilt on the enterprise-grade **Hyperledger Fabric** platform) with AI-based statistical modeling, the "Rare Carat Report" was able to predict the value of any given diamond by using a free evaluation tool.

Definition

Hyperledger: An open source consortium for developing blockchain technology hosted by the Linux Foundation, with contributions from IBM, Intel, and SAP Ariba.
Hyperledger Fabric: The enterprise-grade permissioned blockchain platform upon which new projects can be built. (See Chapter 3.)

Simply entering the identification number of a diamond generates a report using AI and industry price data to make a fair estimate of the diamond's price, considering its finer qualities as well as its flaws. Rare Carat likens it to the Zestimate provided by Zillow, which factors in comparable real estate prices in a neighborhood to estimate a fair price for your home.

This level of transparency can be tremendously empowering for consumers, who are otherwise bewildered by the process of buying diamonds. Like the first-time homebuyer, the first-time diamond buyer has traditionally made a large purchase based largely on faith in a person they've only just met.

By making prices transparent, buyers and sellers can reduce the *information asymmetry*, or lopsided bargaining, that can occur around large purchases. While sellers (say, retail jewelry stores) may fear this leads to lower prices and reduced profit margins, they can once again add to the value chain by leveraging this price data as an unbiased third-party resource. "Let's look at the Rare Carat report," they can offer, thus forming a trusted one-to-one relationship with the buyer that online sellers can't provide.

"Consumers are often frustrated by a lack of transparency when buying a diamond engagement ring," said Apeksha Kothari, Rare Carat COO and fifth-generation diamond industry member. "The Rare Carat Report fills a key role as the industry addresses this problem with its newest generation of buyers, helping build trust between buyers and sellers."[15]

Leanne predicts that more price comparison sites will come to market, but price information alone will provide neither the trust nor the story that consumers crave. As diamonds are passed from hand to hand throughout the diamond supply chain, she sees Everledger as the "connective tissue" across the industry.[16]

That vision is coming true: with a network of partnerships across the industry, Everledger's reach now encompasses 40% of all diamonds in circulation.[17] For an industry that prides itself on clarity, it was finally getting some.

15 Wolfson, "New Blockchain Tool Provides Free Price Estimates For Diamonds."

16 Wolfson, "New Blockchain Tool Provides Free Price Estimates For Diamonds."

17 Ian Allison, "Everledger Looks Beyond Blood Diamonds with ESG Supply Chain Collaboration," CoinDesk, March 25, 2020, https://www.coindesk.com/everledger-looks-beyond-blood-diamonds-with-esg-supply-chain-collaboration.

Note

For Everledger, moving to the Hyperledger Fabric blockchain platform had three advantages over their early prototypes that were built on top of the bitcoin blockchain:

Different asset types

Whereas the bitcoin blockchain can track the movement of only bitcoin, Hyperledger Fabric allows the tracking of any digital asset. It also allows developers to create their own assets and set the value of those assets.

Support for states

Hyperledger Fabric allows for *states*, or snapshots, of current asset value across the blockchain. This is vastly more efficient than older blockchains like bitcoin, which can require reading through the entire log of transactions.

More standardized

Just as Ethereum began to develop a critical mass of developers and users (see Chapter 2), Hyperledger Fabric has built a consortium of enterprise sponsors, developers, and users. These network effects make it a standard that will likely stand the test of time.

Thus, Hyperledger Fabric was a blockchain platform that could support provenance for unlimited asset types, with scalable and efficient processing, and the confidence that the platform would be supported by the industry's leading companies.

Beyond the Diamond

If an asset doesn't have identity, it does not have ownership, value, or existence. In the high-end products market, authenticity—provenance as well as value—cannot be separated.[18]

—Leanne Kemp

Everledger began to set its sights even higher.

---

18 Nicky Morris, "Everledger Adds Blockchain DNA Tagging for Leather," Ledger Insights, October 19, 2018, *https://www.ledgerinsights.com/everledger-blockchain-provenance-dna-tagging*.

Just as Amazon used its early success as an online bookseller to become *The Everything Store*,[19] Leanne used her foothold in the diamond industry to expand into other high-end, luxury items where provenance (i.e., transparency and the story of a product) were valuable.

DESIGNER GOODS

One of Everledger's first applications outside of gemstones was with a company called Applied DNA Sciences, which uses molecular tagging to verify that luxury items are authentic, so consumers can avoid buying a knockoff designer handbag or watch. When the product is manufactured, it's embedded with a custom molecule that can be verified with a handheld scanner at any point in the supply chain. Whereas a QR code or designer label can easily be counterfeited, molecular identification cannot.[20]

Thus, Everledger creates a kind of **digital twin**, a blockchain-based record of a real-world physical object. This twin must match the physical product; a product without its matching twin is a warning flag for consumers, like buying Christian Louboutin boots off the back of a truck.[21]

Definition

Digital twin: A virtual record of a physical item, stored on blockchain. The physical object will ideally have a physical identifier that is difficult to counterfeit (think tamper-proof seals, or the CVV checksum on your credit card) that ties it back to its digital twin.

FINE WINE

The company also began to make inroads into the high-end wine market. Everledger was the first to record a bottle of wine on the blockchain: a bottle of 2001 Château Margaux, which today retails for over $1,000. As wine expert Johannes Selbach told *Wine & Spirits* magazine: "Counterfeit first-growth Bordeaux...has

19 Brad Stone, *The Everything Store: Jeff Bezos and the Age of Amazon* (New York: Little, Brown & Company, 2014).

20 "Everledger Upgrades Blockchain Platform, Expands beyond Diamonds."

21 Morris, "Everledger Adds Blockchain DNA Tagging for Leather."

certainly become a big problem, and for those wines, new tracking systems will certainly meet a demand."[22]

The value of tracking wine goes beyond weeding out counterfeit grapes: wine benefits greatly from proper handling and storage at every step of the chain. As with diamonds, Everledger provides transparency in the wine's journey from vineyard to table, which adds value by telling the story of the wine. As Alex Michas, COO of wine importer Vintus put it, "It seems self-evident that transparency into provenance will result in consumers ultimately having a better bottle on the table."[23]

ELECTRIC VEHICLE BATTERIES

Next, Everledger partnered with Ford Motor Company, the American auto manufacturer. With funding from the US Department of Energy, the two companies began work on a pilot project to track electric vehicle (EV) batteries throughout their life cycle.

Industry observers see electric vehicles as the future of transportation, with EVs making up half of new car sales by 2040, according to Bloomberg.[24] But their batteries cannot be thrown away, as they contain toxic chemicals that must be carefully recycled. These batteries, however, can have a second life powering smaller devices like refrigeration units and car-charging stations, even when they no longer hold a charge like when they were younger.

The Ford/Everledger pilot project creates a blockchain-based digital identity for each battery, so the battery can be monitored through its life cycle. In addition to tracking the number of miles on the battery, the digital identity can also track details like performance (for the battery's second career) and composition (for its eventual retirement).

22 Ed Zimmerman, "Bordeaux in the Blockchain," *Wine & Spirits*, February 23, 2017, *https://www.wineandspiritsmagazine.com/news/entry/bordeaux-in-the-blockchain.*

23 Zimmerman, "Bordeaux in the Blockchain."

24 David Stringer and Jie Ma, "Where 3 Million Electric Vehicle Batteries Will Go When They Retire," *Bloomberg*, June 27, 2018, *https://www.bloomberg.com/news/features/2018-06-27/where-3-million-electric-vehicle-batteries-will-go-when-they-retire.*

Definition

Circular economy: A system that reduces waste by reusing old materials to create new ones, creating a kind of virtuous circle. Circular business models are being used in industries as diverse as textiles (reusing old scraps and fibers), automobiles (manufacturing new cars using recycled parts), and farming (reducing artificial fertilizers in favor of natural manure).

In Leanne's opinion, batteries are just the beginning: "Capturing production, transport, and environmental data in real time allows us to keep track of products and materials, which in turn, increases opportunities to recover and recycle them."[25] This idea of a **circular economy** stands in stark contrast to our dominant economic model of "make, take, and trash" (Figure 11-3).

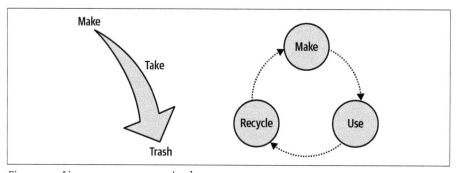

Figure 11-3. Linear economy versus circular economy

Securing Funding

Everledger's early days were funded by several seed rounds of investment, allowing the company to grow its platform and partnerships. In September 2019, Everledger completed its $20 million Series A funding round, led by Tencent, the Chinese internet giant.

While it holds investments in hundreds of companies, Tencent is perhaps best known as the creator of WeChat, one of the most powerful social media apps in China. Known as the *Everything App*, WeChat is like the full suite of apps on your phone, from instant messaging to ride sharing to digital payments, rolled into one.

---

25 Jennifer Kite-Powell, "Why We Need to Track the Lifecycle of Electric Vehicle Batteries," *Forbes*, January 29, 2020, *https://www.forbes.com/sites/jenniferhicks/2020/01/29/why-we-need-to-track-the-lifecycle-of-electric-vehicle-batteries/#50d3f1874cfc*.

By December, Everledger had piloted a WeChat Mini Program (like an app within the app) to allow retailers to offer diamonds with transparency and trust, potentially reaching a billion new users.[26] Partnering with Alrosa, the world's largest diamond producer, the new WeChat Mini Program allows full traceability of diamonds from mines to consumer: it even plugs into WeChat Pay, the company's digital payment solution.

Evgeny Gokhberg, head of the Europe division at Everledger, trumpeted the app release: "This is a groundbreaking initiative with the titans of the diamond and internet industries." It certainly was. But this partnership brought a new challenge: in the deep mines of WeChat, would anyone find their diamond in the rough?

Lessons Learned and the Road Ahead

In two to three years, no one will be talking about blockchain, just like today we don't talk about browsers, or HTTP, or SMTP, or email.[27]

—Leanne Kemp

Everledger's original vision was "to create a secure and permanent digital record of an asset's origin, characteristics, and ownership."[28] This transparency would add more value to the final product by allowing companies and consumers to see the story of their stuff. This, in turn, would speed the development of a circular economy, where products could be reused, recycled, and remanufactured, reducing waste and making the global economy more efficient.

Not bad for a self-taught engineer.

Every big vision starts with small steps, so the company began with products for which transparency matters most: diamonds, luxury items, and wine.[29] The first lesson, then, is to *start with what you know*. Leanne knew diamonds, so she started there, then looked for other opportunities that put a premium on

---

26 Yoana Cholteeva, "Alrosa and Everledger Introduce WeChat Programme for Blockchain-Enabled Diamonds," Mining Technology, December 23, 2019, *https://www.mining-technology.com/news/alrosa-and-everledger-introduce-wechat-programme-for-blockchain-enabled-diamonds*.

27 Leanne Kemp, "Leanne Kemp (CEO Everledger)—Working Blockchain Platform for Diamonds | BIC18," Blockchain Innovation Conference, YouTube, June 15, 2018, *https://www.youtube.com/watch?v=feWCOZpaac4*.

28 "Tech for Good Blockchain Solutions," Everledger.

29 Pollock, "Fidelity, Tencent, Rakuten Back $20 Million Round for UK Blockchain Provenance Firm."

provenance, transparency, and privacy. She saw that just as Amazon became the Everything Store, Everledger could become the Everything Ledger.

As Everledger expanded beyond diamonds to EV batteries, Leanne predicted that rare earth minerals—like the metals used in batteries—would be the next supply chain with conflict issues. Tantalum, a metal used in electronics components and as an alloy in jet engine parts, was being mined in Rwanda.[30] Lithium extraction in the Atacama Desert of South America was leading to "devastating environmental impact."[31]

Although Everledger is a for-profit company, a heavy dose of social good was wrapped up in its mission. The second lesson, then, was to *live your values*. Everledger was not just helping the environment through sustainable sourcing: it was also ensuring better wages, better working conditions, and better wealth distribution from New York jewelry showrooms to the diamond mines of Tshikapa.

The third lesson, then, was to *think of your supply chain as a value chain*, adding more real value to the product at each step in the process. Here so many opportunities existed: from tracking high-quality organic fabrics, to whole and healthful foods, to post-consumer recycled plastic. It was a challenge on a global scale: how could Everledger save the planet without "boiling the ocean"?

Putting yourself in Leanne's role, on what would you focus next?

- Would you focus on more high-value assets and luxury goods? Which ones?

- Would you turn your attention to more "killer apps" for consumers, like the Rare Carat Report and WeChat mini programs?

- Would you deep dive into bigger global industries, like automobiles or construction? Which industries?

- Would you focus more on social issues, working with human rights organizations and global consortiums?

- Would you go after higher-quantity, lower-value assets like textiles and plastics? How would you scale?

If you could put everything on the Everledger, whatever would you do next?

---

30 Allison, "Everledger Looks Beyond Blood Diamonds With ESG Supply Chain Collaboration."

31 Amit Katwala, "The Devastating Environmental Impact of Technological Progress," *Wired*, October 25, 2019, *https://www.wired.co.uk/article/lithium-copper-mining-atacama-desert*.

12

Learning Machine: Blockchain-Based Credentials

One of our primary motivations has been to empower students to be the curators of their own credentials. This system makes it possible for them to have ownership of their records and to be able to share them in a secure way, with whomever they choose.[1]

—Mary Callahan, registrar, Massachusetts Institute of Technology

The Massachusetts Institute of Technology (MIT) had a problem: its dean of admissions had fabricated her credentials.

Marilee Jones had sent in the bogus resume decades ago, while applying for an entry-level position at the prestigious school. Over the years, she had worked her way up the ladder, even becoming something of an academic celebrity: recently she had authored a self-help guide for stressed-out students trying to get into elite schools.[2]

As she rose in the ranks, she never corrected her credentials. Her resume listed degrees from three New York institutions, until it came to light that she had not earned a single undergraduate degree. Two of the three schools on her resume she had never even attended.

---

1 Elizabeth Durant and Alison Trachy, "Digital Diploma Debuts at MIT," MIT News, October 17, 2017, http://news.mit.edu/2017/mit-debuts-secure-digital-diploma-using-bitcoin-blockchain-technology-1017.

2 Marilee Jones and Kenneth R. Ginsburg, *Less Stress, More Success: A New Approach to Guiding Your Teen Through College Admissions and Beyond* (Elk Grove Village, IL: American Academy of Pediatrics, 2006).

"This is a very sad situation for her and for the institution," MIT chancellor Phillip Clay told the press. "We have obviously placed a lot of trust in her."[3]

Trust is at the very root of credentials. Think of all the experts you trust every day: your doctor, lawyer, clergy, teacher, or therapist. Few of us would want to hire an untrained professional to do mental work, much less dental work. When people claim to be licensed and certified, we trust them.

But the licensing, certification, and education, which we'll broadly call **credentialing**, are difficult to verify. Most graduate students know the hassle of requesting a college transcript from their undergraduate institution, but that's just the beginning. Schools go out of business. Professional organizations shut down. If a PhD falls in the forest, and there's no one to verify it, does it make any noise?

Definition

Credentialing: Broadly speaking, a stamp of approval issued by an outside authority, confirming that someone has the necessary skills and training to do the job well. Common credentials include medical licenses, industry certifications, and college degrees.

Nearly a decade after that credentialing crisis, MIT was still looking for a solution. In 2015, it partnered with a company called Learning Machine to create *blockchain-based credentials* that would be issued by the institution, held by the user, and verifiable by anyone.

As Learning Machine envisioned it, this solution would go way beyond college degrees. From displaced refugees providing proof of their profession, to citizens accessing benefits they need and deserve, this would become the worldwide standard for securing "high-stakes digital records," by anchoring them to a blockchain.

Like the companies in so many great technology stories, Learning Machine started years earlier, targeted to a completely different audience: art students.

---

3 Tamar Lewin, "Dean at MIT Resigns, Ending a 28-Year Lie," *New York Times*, April 27, 2007, *https://www.nytimes.com/2007/04/27/us/27mit.html*.

The Origin Story

The promise of [blockchain] technology is that it can give students their own official records—think diplomas, transcripts, professional certifications—that they can hold and share with others in a manner that's tamper-proof and trusted.[4]

  —Chris Jagers, CEO, Learning Machine

Chris Jagers saw a problem: it was hard to upload an online portfolio when applying to art school.

Originally trained as a painter, Chris received his bachelor of fine arts at Southern Methodist University, then enrolled in the master of fine arts program at the University of Washington. In his application to art schools, he saw firsthand that the process of sending in a physical portfolio (a showcase of your artwork for a college application) was cumbersome.

Think of all the different types of artwork, from sculpture to video to mixed media: how could colleges accept and review them all? Moreover, how could the college verify the work was original? Search engines were still in their infancy, and there was no easy way to spot forgery or fakes. Chris was physically mailing 35mm slides to schools.

The bearded, soft-spoken artrepreneur spotted an opportunity.

After graduating in 2007, Chris started a company called SlideRoom, a portfolio review system for art programs, that made it easy for prospective students to upload art portfolios, and easy for schools to catalog and review them. Over the next 10 years, he grew the business to become the official portfolio review partner to the Common Application. Today, any student who uses the Common App to apply to colleges with a portfolio requirement has used SlideRoom software.

Along the way, Chris and his business partner, Dan Hughes, saw another opportunity: most college transcripts and letters of recommendation were still being sent via paper. A new generation of students who grew up on text and Snapchat couldn't understand why the process of paperwork was so time-consuming and cumbersome.

---

4 "What the &$*% Is Block Chain?" Sandbox ColLABorative, YouTube, 2017. *https://www.youtube.com/watch?v=9qJchEhV-Eo.*

During this time, SlideRoom had established a relationship with MIT.[5] Around 2014, as bitcoin started to explode, Chris and Dan found themselves hanging around the MIT Media Lab, the world-famous incubator for emerging digital technologies. "How cool would it be," they asked themselves, "to verify digital credentials using blockchain?"

At that time, an MIT research team happened to be developing an open source project to verify digital credentials. They struck a deal: SlideRoom would hire engineering talent to contribute to the project in collaboration with MIT. This project became known as *Blockcerts*.

As we covered in Chapter 1, blockchain technology can be described as an Internet of Value, an easy way to share items of value, everything from digital money to tokenized assets. In this case, the "thing of value" would be *credentials*.

The Blockcerts project team imagined using the blockchain to **anchor** and verify digital records of achievement. Blockcerts would piggyback on the infrastructure Satoshi outlined in the original whitepaper for bitcoin, but instead of sharing money, people could share diplomas, certificates, examinations, photo IDs, even access badges (Figure 12-1).

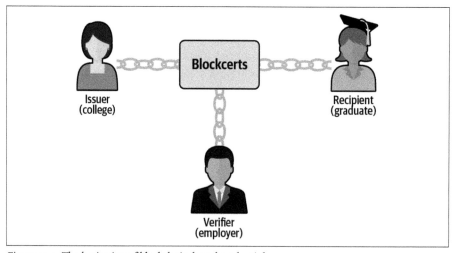

Figure 12-1. The beginning of blockchain-based credentials

5 Danny Crichton, "With MIT Launched, Learning Machine Raises Seed to Replace Paper with Blockchain Credentials," TechCrunch, May 7, 2018, *https://techcrunch.com/2018/05/07/learning-machine-credentials*.

Definition

Anchoring: Instead of *storing* data on a blockchain, we can *anchor* data to a blockchain. The data is stored somewhere else, but the anchor serves as a record that the data is authentic. Think of this as a *digital fingerprint* (like your fingerprint that unlocks your phone) confirming that a credential is real.

Blockcerts was launched in 2016 as an open source project that anyone could use to develop their own blockchain-based records. Published under an MIT Free and Open Source Software (FOSS) license, Blockcerts was offered to developers free of charge, with the goal of becoming the global standard for digital credentials.

In 2017, SlideRoom was acquired by the education services provider Liaison —with a condition. Chris and Dan negotiated a deal to spin out the Blockcerts blockchain team into its own company. That company became Learning Machine.

The team's challenge: how would they build a company around a free infrastructure? Learning Machine was about to learn.

How Blockcerts Works

This is the magic of open source: you get some of the best programming talent and crypto talent in the world all pulling their resources to solve a common problem, which then anyone can use as the infrastructure for the technologies that come next.[6]

—Natalie Smolenski, SVP Business Development, Learning Machine

Blockcerts is short for *blockchain certificates*, which neatly describes what it does (Figure 12-2).

---

6 Natalie Smolenski, interview with the author, February 3, 2020.

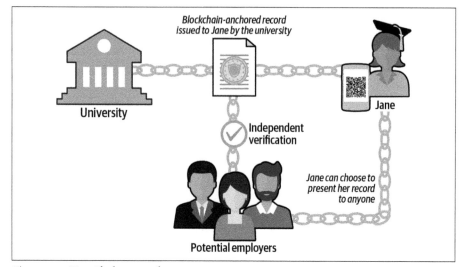

Figure 12-2. How Blockcerts works

From a user perspective, users download the Blockcerts Wallet, a free app available for both iOS and Android, that manages their public and private keys (like a username and password), enabling access to their records of achievement: degrees, licenses, certifications, and so on—which they now own. This is a fundamental shift in perspective: instead of contacting your school for a transcript, you now *own the transcript*. Instead of requesting a verification of your professional certification, you now *own the certification*.

From the institution's perspective, the Blockcerts app creates and manages the credentials for, say, every member of a graduating class, empowering them to own their degrees.[7] This, too, is a change in perspective: rather than charging students to essentially shuffle paperwork, schools can now send transcripts quickly and digitally.[8]

In summary, Blockcerts decentralizes our credentials, so we own them. If our school goes bankrupt, if a natural disaster hits, or if we move to a country with political instability or war, we don't have to worry about bureaucratic or

---

7 "Government of Malta Launches Learning Machine's Blockchain Records Platform," Learning Machine, accessed February 27, 2020, *https://learningmachine.newswire.com/news/government-of-malta-launches-learning-machines-blockchain-records-19978449.*

8 "Project Digital Academic Credentials," MIT Media Lab, accessed February 27, 2020, *https://www.media.mit.edu/projects/media-lab-digital-certificates/people.*

economic roadblocks holding up our credentialing. The Blockcerts standard eliminates a single point of failure when it comes to our hard-earned expertise.[9]

But here we must reiterate a key point: *the digital credential is not stored on the blockchain*. Rather, a *record* of the digital credential is stored on the blockchain. This record is known as a **hash**.

Definition

Hash: Broadly, an encrypted sequence of letters and numbers, like a code. In blockchain, a hash can be used to store a trusted, timestamped record of an event (such as the time that someone registered a copyright or earned an academic degree).

Store Just Enough on Blockchain, but No More

A common misconception about blockchain is that the data itself must be stored on the blockchain—the equivalent of putting your graduate degree online. Instead, picture the blockchain record as a digital fingerprint of your graduate degree, which you hold in a **JSON** file on your hard drive. (Your school also holds a copy of the JSON file, just in case; see Figure 12-3.)

Definition

JSON: Short for *JavaScript Object Notation*, it is a simple text file format that's easy to read, for both computers and humans.

Put another way, you hold a file that holds your degree. That file has a unique digital fingerprint that is stored permanently on a blockchain. If you change the file, the fingerprint of the changed file will no longer match the fingerprint on the blockchain. The institution also has a copy of the file, with the same digital fingerprint.

---

9 "Government of Malta Launches Learning Machine's Blockchain Records Platform," Learning Machine.

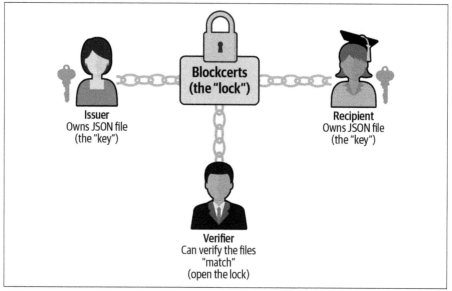

Figure 12-3. Store just enough on the blockchain, but no more

Now let's say a potential employer wants to verify your degree. You send a copy of your JSON file to that company, which checks the file against the blockchain record by using the open source Blockcerts Verifier. If the two digital fingerprints match, you can be sure no one has tampered with the record. The Blockcerts Verifier also checks the integrity of the document's digital signature (i.e., makes sure no one is impersonating another issuer) and the status of the credential (whether it has been revoked or expired).

By design, then, Blockcerts does not upload any document data to the blockchain itself, which is what also makes it easy to anchor records to multiple blockchains. Because hashes of records can be recorded on most blockchains—bitcoin, Ethereum, you name it—Blockcerts can work with any of them.

Tip

Blockchain best practice: Don't store sensitive information on a public blockchain, which anyone can see. Instead, store an anchor, or a *hash of the record* on the blockchain, which serves as the digital fingerprint to validate a file that users manage themselves (more on this in Chapter 13).

Blockcerts creates a new power dynamic that we illustrate throughout the case studies in this book: by giving people ownership of their own information, they not only become personally empowered but also receive personal responsibility. ("With great power comes great responsibility.")

In summary, *there is no Blockcerts blockchain*. Blockcerts is not an app. You can't buy or install Blockcerts software, any more than you can buy WiFi or TCP/IP. Instead, Blockcerts is the infrastructure technology, or **protocol**, that allows the following:

- The institution to record the issuing of a credential (say, a student earning an undergrad degree) on a blockchain
- The issuer and recipient to receive a JSON file for safekeeping
- The student to self-verify by sending the JSON file to the verifying institution (for example, when the student applies to graduate school)
- The institution to compare the JSON file with the blockchain hash to verify the credential

Definition

Protocol: A communication standard for allowing computers to talk to each other. In the same way that open protocols like HTTP and SMTP are the "rails" that let us transport information on the internet, digital standards for verifiable credentials may be considered protocols—the rails—that let us transport credentials on the Internet of Value.

Natalie Smolenski, senior vice president of business development, worked with Chris and Dan at SlideRoom and became one of the first employees in the spin-off of Learning Machine. She points out that the internet is great for sending and receiving information, but not so great at *verifying* information, especially high-stakes information like credentials. The Blockcerts standard provides that verification.

The Learning Machine team worked with the World Wide Web Consortium (or W3C), the standards-setting body for the internet, to adapt the Blockcerts project into a new global standard, Verifiable Credentials.[10] Chris explained, "The W3C credential standards are analogous to TCP/IP or GPS: open protocols that

---

10 "Verifiable Credentials Data Model 1.0: Expressing Verifiable Information on the Web," W3C, *https://www.w3.org/TR/vc-data-model*.

enabled the internet and geolocation revolutions."[11] Whenever you use a web browser or Google Maps, you're making use of those base-level protocols, approved by the W3C, that have allowed these technologies to flourish.

Tip

Blockchain best practice: Start your project with a commitment to working collaboratively. Developing open source frameworks with open standards can *future proof* your solution for potential customers. For example, institutions can adopt the Blockcerts standard without fear about Learning Machine's future because Blockcerts is an open *standard* as well as open *source*. This makes adoption easier because anyone can build on it and use it for verification, and the use of shared standards creates cross-platform interoperability.

Paradoxically, giving it away can make it more likely that the market will buy it.

Like so many of the case studies in this book, Learning Machine started by developing an open source standard, then giving it away. Which begs the question: if you're giving it away, *how do you make money?*

The answer: SaaS on top of open source.

The Learning Machine Revenue Model

Software as a service (SaaS) is the blockchain revenue model that Learning Machine pursued—that is, a monthly or annual subscription fee for an enterprise-ready implementation of the open source Blockcerts platform. Learning Machine followed in the footsteps of companies like Red Hat, which grew quickly by charging subscriptions to its enterprise-grade services and support built on top of the open source Linux (Figure 12-4).

---

11 "Future Proof," Hyland, January 13, 2020, *https://www.learningmachine.com/future-proof.*

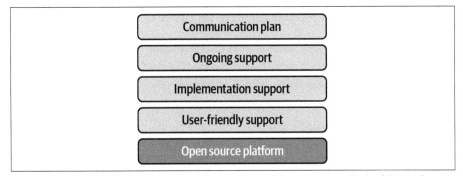

Figure 12-4. The blockchain business model: SaaS on top of open source. Think of this as the value stack.

The Learning Machine platform allowed customers (like universities) to easily design custom credentials (like a branded school degree), import their data, and manage credentials at scale—all in an easy, web-based interface. Learning Machine took the geeky command-line interface of open source code, in other words, and made it *user-friendly*.

As we've reiterated throughout the book, *blockchains are useful only if people use them*. Learning Machine's solution was a bundle of product, services, and support that helped customers successfully use Blockcerts with the following:

- *A ready-made web application*, which eliminated the need for customers to hire developers to build and support Blockcerts issuance and management

- *Quality assurance and technical support* when users ran into problems, as well as *implementation support*

- An *implementation road map*, complete with key performance indicators (KPIs) and a paper-to-digital transition plan

- A *communications plan* to build awareness, convey value, and promote participation across the institution

The more Learning Machine team members talked to potential customers, the bigger they saw the potential opportunity. This went far beyond diplomas and degrees: blockchain technology could be used for any high-stakes credentialing: examination results, ID cards, even security clearances.

The team rapidly made business development a priority, winning partnerships in three key industries: education, government, and healthcare.

Education Use Case: Massachusetts Institute of Technology

It was the perfect confluence: technology developed at MIT and a vendor who was aware of MIT's culture as a community that values learning, at a time when a comprehensive record of lifelong learning was an evolving need.[12]

—Mary Callahan, MIT registrar

After the dean of admissions debacle, MIT had to ensure that its faculty really held the credentials they claimed. But the reverse was also true: the school had to ensure that people who claimed to have MIT degrees really did.

Learning Machine's early history with MIT was a win for both organizations. MIT found a solution to its credentialing challenges, and Learning Machine was able to list the school as a high-profile use case, when 619 students from the MIT graduating class of 2018 were given the option of receiving a digital version of their diploma (Figure 12-5).[13]

From an institutional perspective, the digital diploma needed to have the aesthetics of a traditional MIT diploma. Using Learning Machine's platform, the layout designer created a template that could be populated with student data, and then transformed into a JSON file and hashed to the blockchain.

To verify the credential, MIT hosted a website where users could paste a link or upload a file, verifying that the hash of the uploaded diploma matched the hash stored on the blockchain. Because verification is open source, all Blockcerts can also be verified at the Universal Verifier available at Blockcerts.org. This site acts as a Google for digital document verification, so that anyone can look up any credential's authenticity as long as they have the file or a link. "There are a lot of people who pretend to graduate from MIT with fake diplomas," said Chris. "This provides a format that people can't fake."[14]

---

12 "Massachusetts Institute of Technology: Digital Diplomas," Hyland, accessed February 27, 2020, *https://www.learningmachine.com/customer-story-mit.*

13 Frankie Schembri, "Digital Diplomas: Blockchain Technology Gives Grads Control over Their Digital Credentials," MIT Technology Review, April 25, 2018, *https://www.technologyreview.com/2018/04/25/143311/digital-diplomas.*

14 Lindsay McKenzie, "MIT Introduces Digital Diplomas," Inside Higher Ed, October 19, 2017, *https://www.insidehighered.com/news/2017/10/19/mit-introduces-digital-diplomas.*

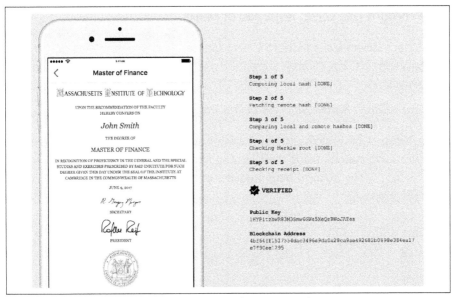

Figure 12-5. The MIT Digital Diploma (no cap and gown required)[15]

The test pilot was encouraging: by the end of April, 214 students had already downloaded the Blockcerts Wallet. Based on these results, MIT registrar Mary Callahan announced that starting in June 2018, all MIT graduates would have the option of receiving a digital diploma.

After the success of the MIT pilot, more universities and community colleges have selected Learning Machine as the issuer of their digital credentials. As Colin Van Ostern, vice president of Workforce Initiatives at Southern New Hampshire University (SNHU) put it, "This is what a modern transcript would be: digital, portable, owned by the student. Employers don't need to call up SNHU to verify that information; it's already self-verified."[16]

---

15 "Massachusetts Institute of Technology: Digital Diplomas," Hyland.

16 "Our Approach," Hyland, accessed February 27, 2020, *https://www.learningmachine.com/our-approach.*

Government Use Case: Republic of Malta

It's self-sovereign, trustworthy, transparent, and impossible to destroy because it's not simply stored on databases in some government building.[17]

> —Evarist Bartolo, minister of Education and Employment, Malta

Malta became the first country to implement blockchain-based credentialing in its educational system, using the Learning Machine platform, which launched in October 2017. The goal: to help students transition more easily into the workforce (Figure 12-6).

Figure 12-6. Using paper signatures to usher in the age of digital signatures in the Republic of Malta[18]

Upon completion of a program—from graduating college to finishing vocational training—graduates received Blockcerts digital certificates verifying their

---

17 "Our Approach," Hyland.

18 "Government of Malta Launches Learning Machine's Blockchain Records Platform," Learning Machine.

achievements. These blockchain-based credentials could then be used to apply for jobs: students could share them with prospective employers, who could easily verify them.

For *Maltese workers*, this new technology simplified the job application process and reduced wait times to begin working. For *employers*, it eliminated paperwork, streamlined the hiring process, and created a new layer of trust with new hires.

To ensure consistency and aggregate data across the nation, a new Maltese Credentialing Framework was built into each school's issuing platform in order to standardize the digital certification process. This also enabled the government to have a *single source of truth*, a bird's-eye view on where educational initiatives were working and where they needed help.

According to Minister of Education and Employment Evarist Bartolo, "Maltese business will find hiring workers with the right qualifications has gotten much easier. This is a win/win for Malta, whose skilled workforce is among the primary drivers of its economic success."[19]

Healthcare Use Case: Federation of State Medical Boards

Verification of medical education and related credentials is a critically important endeavor.[20]

—*Michael Dugan, chief information officer at FSMB*

Perhaps there is no field in which the cost of credentials is as great as medicine: *human lives* are on the line.

The Federation of State Medical Boards (FSMB) is a US nonprofit that provides licensing and credential services for medical practitioners, working with over 70 medical boards. In October 2017, the FSMB became the first professional membership organization to issue official documents—degrees, transcripts and verifications—by using the Learning Machine platform.

---

19 "The Republic of Malta: A Better Pathway," Hyland, accessed February 27, 2020, *https://www.learning-machine.com/customer-story-malta*.

20 "Federation of State Medical Boards: Professional Certification," Hyland, accessed February 27, 2020, *https://www.learningmachine.com/customer-story-fsmb*.

In plain language, doctors now had their own digital certificates that verified their ability to practice medicine, which they could take anywhere—say, into a war-torn country, an epidemic hot zone, or just another state (Figure 12-7).

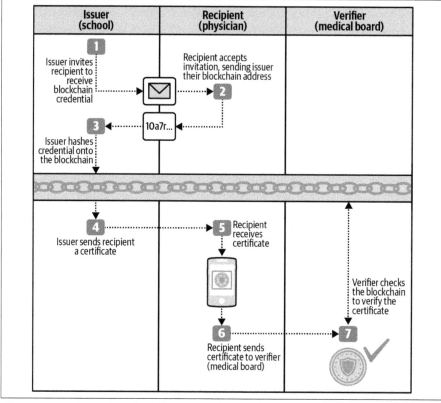

Figure 12-7. The FSMB's credentialing process: from med school to physician to medical board[21]

According to Natalie, this is a fundamentally different model than many blockchain applications that still place vendors at the center. "Learning Machine is building a social infrastructure that will outlast any company or issuing institution. We are building for the long-term future."[22]

---

21 Federation of State Medical Boards, *http://www.fsmb.org/blockchain*.

22 "Federation of State Medical Boards: Professional Certification," Hyland.

The Road Ahead

*By the end of three years, we want to see blockchain-based records...
start to enter the public consciousness.[23]*

—Chris Jagers, 2017

As the Learning Machine team members looked to the future, they took time to reflect on the road they had traveled. Throughout this journey, they had maintained a consistent vision of digital credentials based on an open source, open standard platform.

From the beginning, Learning Machine and MIT were on the same page: an open standard was the best way to ensure worldwide adoption. But when Learning Machine began to seek outside funding in 2018, many investors didn't get it. They were looking for a competitive advantage—a "moat"—and saw open source and open standards as counterintuitive.

Rather than accept any offer, no matter how big, Learning Machine stuck to its open standard principles. Eventually, it raised $3 million of seed funding from three lead investors who supported this approach:[24]

- PTB Ventures, a venture capital firm focusing on early-stage companies in the digital identity ecosystem

- Omidyar Network, a philanthropic investment firm that looks for "impact investments" in areas like education and financial inclusion

- Learn Capital, one of the largest VC firms focusing on the global education technology sector

With this funding in place, Learning Machine was able to build a world-class team to build out its platform and partnerships. It wasn't long before the company was faced with its next decision: how to build even bigger.

---

23 Crichton, "With M.I.T. Launched, Learning Machine Raises Seed to Replace Paper with Blockchain Credentials."

24 Learning Machine, "Learning Machine Raises $3M Seed Financing to Drive Growth of Blockchain Records and Identity Platform," PR Newswire, June 27, 2018, *https://www.prnewswire.com/news-releases/learning-machine-raises-3m-seed-financing-to-drive-growth-of-blockchain-records-and-identity-platform-300643382.html.*

Lessons Learned and Next Steps

If blockchain is going to work in the enterprise, deep expertise, traditional business models, and open standards appear to be the potentially winning formula.[25]

—*Chris Jagers*

The Learning Machine team had learned a great deal.

SlideRoom had improved college applications; Learning Machine had improved college graduations. Along the way, the leadership team had introduced a world-changing technology that let anyone own their credentials. In the future, instead of hanging diplomas on the wall, we might all print and frame our Blockcerts.

Throughout this journey, Learning Machine had learned several blockchain best practices:

Using open-source standards
> This ensured widespread adoption of the Blockcerts protocol, instead of trying to build a "walled garden."

Using a SaaS-based platform on top of this protocol
> This ensured an enterprise-ready level of service and support for customers, as well as a predictable revenue model for Learning Machine.

Identifying the digital asset
> In this case, keeping a laser-focus on the *digital credential*: this is the "thing of value" on the Internet of Value.

Storing the bare minimum on-chain
> The credential itself was held by the user and the issuing institution. Only the hash, or "proof," of that credential was stored on the blockchain.

Moving from paper to paperless
> We call this the **Law of Digital Migration**: anything that can move from paper to digital, will. Entrepreneurs need only look for legacy paper processes—in this case, school transcripts—for business opportunities.

---

25 Crichton, "With M.I.T. Launched, Learning Machine Raises Seed to Replace Paper with Blockchain Credentials."

Definition

Law of Digital Migration: Anything that can move from paper to digital, will.

As 2019 ended, the question became where to go next. The team discussed three options:

- Continue to grow organically
- Seek another round of funding
- Acquire, merge, or be acquired by another company

It wasn't long before an opportunity presented itself. It was the decision so many entrepreneurs dream about: the opportunity to be acquired.

The offer came from Hyland, an Ohio-based company that specialized in content services solutions that connect information, processes, and software across the enterprise. Hyland had been actively involved in blockchain at the local and international level, and many of its customers were in healthcare, financial institutions, government, and higher education.

The rationale for the deal, according to Hyland president and CEO Bill Priemer, was that by adding Learning Machine's digital credentialing to Hyland's content services platform, customers could generate, manage, share, and verify digital documents. From Chris's perspective, Learning Machine's customers would benefit from the value created by Hyland's software platform.

As an example, more than 800 higher education institutions already leveraged Hyland's content services platform. Using Learning Machine's platform to tie into Blockcerts would give Hyland customers a unique digital advantage—not to mention huge cost savings.

Still, Learning Machine would face challenges based on seamlessly integrating its product into Hyland's existing platform offerings. The team would also have to figure out a fair price. Further, as with any acquisition involving organizations with different physical locations, they'd have to figure out communication and coordination.

If you were advising the Learning Machine team, what would you recommend?

13

Conclusion:
Blockchain in Action

The Massachusetts economy is facing clear headwinds, given the current global challenge around COVID-19, but our world-class Innovation Economy will help us address the challenges posed by this crisis and can bolster the Commonwealth's resiliency.[1]

—Mike Kennealy, Massachusetts secretary of Housing and Economic Development

As we were finishing up this book, the COVID-19 pandemic hit.

For those readers in the distant future, it's hard to describe how quickly the pandemic took most of us by surprise. We had read about the initial outbreak in Wuhan, China, but it seemed distant and improbable that it would affect those of us in other countries.

We had no life experience—no mental map—of a fast-moving, global pandemic. Even when it began to spread to other countries, we had no idea how quickly things would change.

Overnight, it was like a zombie outbreak straight out of *World War Z* or *The Walking Dead*. One day, society was functioning normally; the next day, everyone was ordered to quarantine. Movie theaters shut down; restaurants closed. Streets were empty; cities were quiet. It was eerie and bewildering.

Digital transformation, long a buzzword, now became a necessity. Businesses had to quickly pivot to videoconference and online collaboration tools. Schools

---

1 "The Annual Index of the Massachusetts Innovation Economy, 2019 Edition." Innovation Institute at the MassTech Collaborative, February 2020, *https://masstech.org/sites/mtc/files/documents/2019-Index/MAInnovationEconomyIndex-2019Edition.pdf*.

had to quickly learn how to manage distance learning. Churches and synagogues had to quickly invent new digital rituals.

It required a massive upgrade to humanity's tech infrastructure. What might have taken 10 years was crammed into 10 weeks. Companies that had invested early in digital transformation were rewarded with a smoother entry into the New Normal, where others had to learn it in a time of crisis.

And it *has* been a time of crisis. As more than 36 million people have contracted COVID-19, and more than 1 million have lost their lives, healthcare systems and hospital workers have struggled to cope with the demands.[2] Governments have struggled to make the difficult decisions between saving the economy and saving lives. Parents have struggled to work while taking care of kids. Kids have struggled to live in the same house as their parents.

The pandemic has been difficult for everyone, but everyone's difficulties are different. Whether you are a child living in an abusive household, or a refugee trying to leave a country where the borders have been sealed shut, it has been difficult. Even if you live in a stable home, with a good technology job and reliable internet access, the constant grind of online meetings and lack of real human contact has made day-to-day life an endurance marathon—except a marathon has a clear finish line. Here there has been no end in sight.

There have been unexpected pleasures, though. A return to simplicity, with home-cooked food and long walks in nature, provide comfort and a sense of normalcy. At the grocery, the demand for simple essentials like flour and eggs have shown that people have been rediscovering the joy of making bread and omelets. In Italy, quarantined residents have been singing together from their balconies in nightly serenades.[3]

A strange cognitive dissonance has arisen between seeing the ghost-town parking lots of shopping malls and the almost supernatural vibrancy of nature during this time. With reduced pollution and a renewed appreciation for being outdoors, it has felt as if nature were in 8K, like a Pixar film in real life.

This combination of exquisite beauty and excruciating difficulty has been both surreal and disorienting. It's been a dystopian novel come to life, a wartime

---

2 "Coronavirus Map: Tracking the Global Outbreak," *New York Times*, January 28, 2020, *https://www.nytimes.com/interactive/2020/world/coronavirus-maps.html.*

3 Christopher Mele and Neil Vigdor, "Singalongs from Windowsills Lift Spirits During Coronavirus Crisis," *New York Times*, March 23, 2020, *https://www.nytimes.com/2020/03/23/us/coronavirus-window-singalong.html.*

without a war. People have described it as "weird" and "strange," but those words don't really capture *how* weird and strange it's felt: it has been a kind of silent chaos, a funhouse without the fun.

In the midst of this madness, in the spring of 2020 we saw opportunity. If ever there was a technology that could deal with a decentralized, distributed, peer-to-peer virus, it was blockchain. As we were wrapping up this book, confronting COVID-19 felt like a **capstone project.**

Definition

Capstone project: The final project that ties together all the lessons learned in a degree or course of study. This case study serves as the capstone project for both you and your authors. (We're in this together.)

Who would implement these blockchain solutions? As fate would have it, we had just started working with one of the most forward-thinking governments in the world: the Commonwealth of Massachusetts.

Massachusetts: The Hub of Technology

Founded in 1788, the state of Massachusetts was one of the earliest tech hubs in the US. The first reason is that early colonies invested heavily in education, building excellent institutions modeled after the universities of Britain, like Harvard University and (later) MIT.

Second, there were fewer workers in the US than in England, which meant a greater need to automate tasks. (Necessity breeds innovation.)

Third was location: many Massachusetts cities were located near waterways or seaports, giving rise to textile mills, industrial machinery, and global trade—not to mention a steady flow of innovative ideas from across the pond.[4]

Fast-forward to the War of 1812, which cut off the supply of industrial goods from Britain into Massachusetts seaports. The need to produce these goods at home fueled a renewed investment in technology, transforming America from an agricultural economy to an industrial superpower.

This development was further accelerated by the military-industrial-academic partnership during World War I and World War II, with the great Massachusetts physicist Robert Goddard launching the first experimental rockets from the

---

4 "Technological and Industrial History of the United States." Wikipedia, June 1, 2020, *https://en.wikipedia.org/wiki/Technological_and_industrial_history_of_the_United_States*.

campus of Clark University, which led to the Space Race, and, four decades after Goddard's launch, the first moon landing.[5]

The Massachusetts *128 belt*—so named for Route 128, which circles the belly of Boston—became a hive of activity for technology companies from the 1960s through the 1980s. An early *Business Week* article referred to it as "the Magic Semicircle," as it attracted tech unicorns like Digital Equipment Corporation, Wang Technology, Honeywell Information Systems, Polaroid, EMC, and Autodesk.[6]

During the dot-com boom of the 1990s, Boston's influence on the American technology scene began to wane, as Silicon Valley and New York became the new hot spots for young tech companies. But in the internet era, the city of Cambridge reinvented itself as the hub for life sciences, with the support of a 10-year, $1 billion investment from Governor Deval Patrick.[7] Today, the area around Harvard and MIT boasts over 120 biotech and biopharma companies: the highest concentration of life sciences development in the world.[8]

Against this backdrop—a highly-educated workforce, a history of scientific innovation, and a government that's willing and able to invest in long-term technology plays—we began our journey into blockchain.

Our story with the state started several years before the pandemic. It started, in fact, over lunch.

Collaborating with the MassTech Collaborative

Jasmijn van der Horst-Rompa was new to Massachusetts and to the United States. She had recently moved from the Netherlands, where she spent seven years with Brainport Development, an economic development agency that created jobs and grew the local innovation economy by supporting collaboration among stakeholders across industry, education, and government.

With an easy smile and a slight Dutch accent, Jasmijn explained to John that she had been recently hired as the director for Industry & Program Assessment

5 "Robert H. Goddard," Wikipedia, June 12, 2020, *https://en.wikipedia.org/wiki/Robert_H._Goddard.*

6 "Massachusetts Route 128," Wikipedia, April 26, 2020, *https://en.wikipedia.org/wiki/Massachu-setts_Route_128.*

7 Life Sciences Initiative, accessed June 22, 2020, *https://budget.digital.mass.gov/bb/h1/fy10h1/prnt10/exec10/pbudbrief23.htm.*

8 Damien Garde, "Get to Know Kendall Square, Biotech's Booming Epicenter," STAT, June 6, 2016, *https://www.statnews.com/2016/05/05/kendall-beating-heart-biotech.*

at the Innovation Institute at the Massachusetts Technology Collaborative, or MassTech. Her job was to connect people from different backgrounds and have them collaborate in high-impact projects to grow the Massachusetts **innovation economy**.

Definition

Innovation economy: The economy made of knowledge workers, educational institutions, and entrepreneurs, who continually innovate through technological change. Whereas the traditional economy simply generates profits for shareholders,[9] the innovation economy creates "good for all," by generating faster economic growth and making better lives for its citizens.[10]

In practical terms, MassTech is the tech and innovation arm of the Massachusetts government, focused on supporting emerging tech sectors in the state's economy. Among its many responsibilities, MassTech invests public resources to support new and emerging technologies to grow the economy—as well as technology infrastructure projects like statewide broadband access and incubation hubs for entrepreneurs.

"We are looking toward the next five years to support key technology sectors," Jasmijn told John over a soup and salad. "My job is to research a number of new technologies—artificial intelligence, quantum computing, fintech—to see where Massachusetts is strongest, and where we might be able to lead."

The discussion turned to blockchain. John had become a board member of the Boston Blockchain Association, an industry group of blockchain professionals. He invited Jasmijn to attend one of their meetups, which she did several times over the next few years. This started a process of awareness and education that benefited both sides: Jasmijn and her organization learned more about the technology; John and his organization learned more about how government worked.

We partnered with Eric Roux, a fellow board member of the Boston Blockchain Association. As a partner at firms like KPMG and Ernst & Young, Eric had served as an international technology consultant in London, Switzerland, and

---

9 Milton Friedman, "A Friedman Doctrine: The Social Responsibility of Business Is to Increase Its Profits," *New York Times*, September 13, 1970, *https://www.nytimes.com/1970/09/13/archives/a-friedman-doctrine-the-social-responsibility-of-business-is-to.html*.

10 David Ahlstrom, "Innovation and Growth: How Business Contributes to Society," *Academy of Management Perspectives* 24, no. 3 (2010): 11–24, *https://doi.org/10.5465/amp.24.3.11*.

Luxembourg. His work had recently brought him back to the US, where he had been responsible for building partnerships between governments, companies, and academia.

Jasmijn brought in her boss, Pat Larkin, who had a distinguished government career including 15 years as the director of the Innovation Institute division of MassTech. Throughout his career at MassTech, Larkin had overseen some of the Commonwealth's biggest technology-based economic development initiatives, including the Renewable Energy Trust, Mass Life Sciences Collaborative, and initiatives in robotics and big data.

Over several meetings and several months, both groups learned that the biggest need was *blockchain education*. As in the early days of the internet, it was hard for people to understand what this new technology was all about, much less why they needed it. As with our Chamber of Digital Commerce case study (see Chapter 10), building relationships and building awareness comes first; building blockchain projects comes later.

As the group grew, so did the government's interest. Fast-forward to early 2020, when the Baker-Polito administration officially introduced a new Economic Development Bill, which called for investments in the development of technologies to build the industries of tomorrow. Victory at last: blockchain was on the list!

MassTech launched a blockchain education program for government leaders across Massachusetts. John and Eric teamed up with their colleague Evan Karnoupakis, a Wharton MBA with an expertise in blockchain and a career split between the consulting world and the classroom, to put together a blockchain education and discovery program for government employees.

Over the next several months, we met with leaders from all levels of government, explaining how blockchain technology worked and sharing use cases from other governments around the world. Then we listened to the leaders' needs and collaboratively discussed how blockchain solutions might meet those needs.

This process of teaching, listening, and learning provided a valuable feedback loop, just like our initial work with MassTech. The plan was to use this feedback to recommend a beginning blockchain project that would most benefit the Massachusetts government...and then the virus hit.

The Pandemic Pivot

While blockchain is sometimes criticized as a "solution in search of a problem,"[11] the team saw the opposite: the coronavirus crisis was rapidly creating problems for which blockchain was a natural solution. We began to apply the lessons of this book—what we had learned from these success stories—to the biggest problems we saw unfolding around us.

The first such problem was the *supply chain*. In the early months of the pandemic, there were supply chain problems around personal protective equipment (PPE) like masks and gowns, as well as vital medical equipment like ventilators and respirators used to treat COVID-19 patients. As the pandemic wore on, many other supply chains began to break down, in unpredictable and surprising ways. (There were tofu shortages.[12])

The second problem was *tracking who was healthy*. This took several forms: getting adequate testing programs in place, setting up contact tracing programs to notify people who may have been exposed to a sick person, and on-site testing to see who was safe to enter a building.

The third problem was *keeping the economy running*. Most governments jumped into action very quickly by "printing money," but we saw this as a short-term solution—with long-term consequences. Also, it worked at only the federal level: local governments (such as state governments in the US) could not print their own money. Or could they?

It seemed to us that blockchain offered solutions to all three problems. During the first wave of quarantine, we worked diligently to build out three solutions that we could present to the Massachusetts state government and the world.

Inspired by the open-standard framework of Helium (Chapter 4) and the open source philosophy of the Chamber of Digital Commerce (Chapter 10), we made these solutions open to the public. We explained them in user-friendly whitepapers that could be downloaded and distributed, free of charge (Figure 13-1).

---

11 André Schweizer et al., "A Solution in Search of a Problem: A Method for the Development of Blockchain Use Cases," ResearchGate, 2018, *https://www.researchgate.net/publication/324603293_A_Solution_in_Search_of_a_Problem_A_Method_for_the_Development_of_Blockchain_Use_Cases.*

12 Mark Van Streefkerk, "Solving the Great Capitol Hill COVID-19 Tofu Shortage of 2020," CHS Capitol Hill Seattle, April 6, 2020, *https://www.capitolhillseattle.com/2020/04/solving-the-great-capitol-hill-covid-19-tofu-shortage-of-2020.*

Figure 13-1. The next generation of blockchain whitepapers

SOLUTION 1: BLOCKCHAIN-BASED SUPPLY CHAINS

One of the many strange details of the pandemic was the lack of toilet paper.

Common sense said that people weren't using any more toilet paper than usual. Sure, some people were panic-buying essential items, and panic breeds panic: if you see the shelves stripped bare of toilet paper, you're going to start panic-buying toilet paper too.

But the more important and less obvious reason was the supply chain. Toilet paper is sold in two types: residential and commercial. The residential stuff is sold in small rolls and is generally comfortable. The commercial stuff, as we all know from our time in workplace bathrooms, is sold in huge rolls and is generally terrible.

During the pandemic, there was a huge demand for residential toilet paper (most people were home), and very little for commercial (few people were at work). As demand shifted, the supply couldn't keep up: there was plenty of toilet paper, just the wrong kind.

Worse were the supply chain issues with the critical medical equipment needed to protect frontline workers or treat patients with COVID-19. In the US, some states took to duct-taping their own supply chains. In New York, Governor Andrew Cuomo encouraged competing hospitals to work together by using a "surge and flex" strategy: move critical equipment to where the virus was surging, flexing supply chains daily.[13]

The challenge was that no nationally shared database existed. No master list indicated where all the critical healthcare supplies were located; instead, we had a patchwork quilt of Google Sheets, Excel files, and legacy inventory systems. When you moved 12 respirators from upstate New York to Manhattan, how did those hospitals keep track? How did other hospitals know who had extra respirators?

But the real supply chain challenge would be the vaccine. If and when we developed a vaccine against the coronavirus, we'd need to get it quickly produced and delivered around the globe. And it wasn't just the vaccine: the limiting factor might be the syringes, or the vials, or the rubber stoppers for the vials.[14]

Blockchain, we knew, was an excellent solution to these problems. As we discussed in our Everledger case study (see Chapter 11), a shared ledger would allow us to track and trace every vial of the vaccine—not to mention masks, respirators, and toilet paper. (Maybe not all on the same chain.)

How to describe this technology to government decision-makers was our biggest challenge, without getting "caught in the weeds" of how blockchain works. We used three simple talking points to clearly explain the problem and the solution:

The toilet paper example
> It wasn't the most pleasant image, but it stuck. By showing a public health example that everyone was experiencing firsthand—a lack of toilet paper on grocery shelves—we could make the point that our public health supply chains had to be a priority.

13 "Amid Ongoing COVID-19 Pandemic, Governor Cuomo Announces Federal Government Is Deploying Approximately 1,000 Personnel to New York State," Governor Andrew M. Cuomo, April 5, 2020, *https://www.governor.ny.gov/news/amid-ongoing-covid-19-pandemic-governor-cuomo-announces-federal-government-deploying.*

14 Knvul Sheikh, "Find a Vaccine. Next: Produce 300 Million Vials of It," *New York Times*, May 1, 2020, *https://www.nytimes.com/2020/05/01/health/coronavirus-vaccine-supplies.html.*

The Google Sheet example

We often described blockchain like a "giant shared Google Sheet," before showing that Google Sheets usually devolve into chaos. (See Figures 13-2 and 13-3.) This idea of a shared spreadsheet of healthcare supplies was a simple way of explaining blockchain.

The eBay example

We also talked about the opportunity to create a marketplace of goods, where states could begin manufacturing high-demand items and selling them to other states. Blockchain would provide a higher level of trust in the quality of these suppliers and their goods: "like eBay, but better."

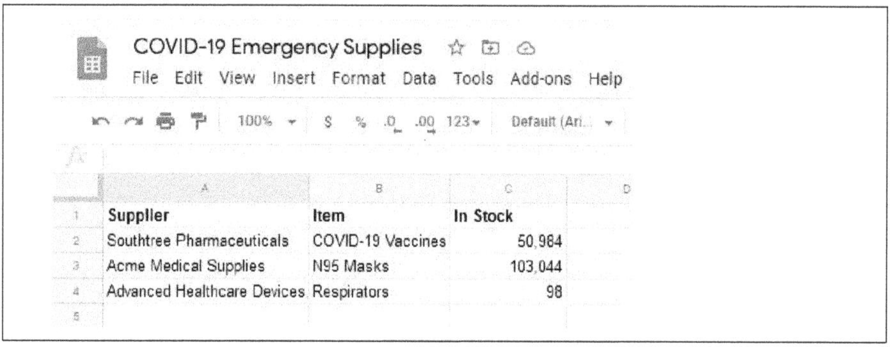

Figure 13-2. Explaining blockchain by using the Google Sheet example[15]

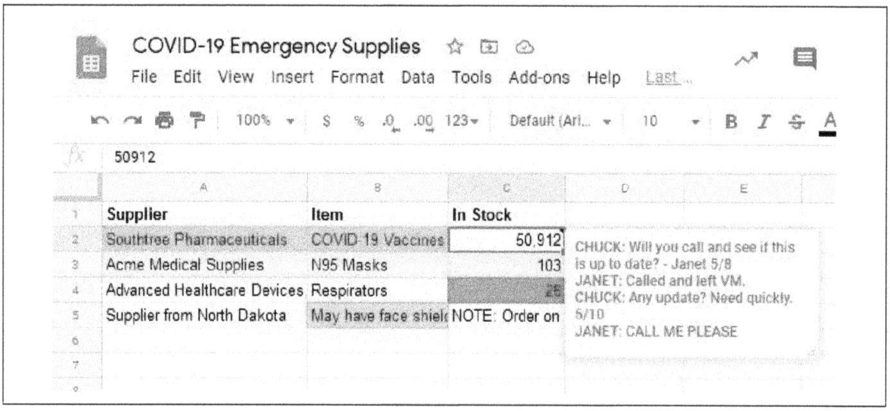

Figure 13-3. All Google Sheets eventually devolve into chaos

---

15 John Hargrave, "Blockchain and the Supply Chain: They Even Sound the Same," Media Shower, May 12, 2020, *https://mediashower.com/blog/blockchain-supply-chain*.

How would supply chains be managed in the age of COVID-19? we asked ourselves. Most governments would use existing procurement systems to track the new inventory. Could these be upgraded to blockchain?

SOLUTION 2: BLOCKCHAIN-BASED HEALTH TRACKERS

Another public health issue boiled down to one simple question: how do you know the people around you are safe?

Anywhere people gathered in groups was a potential viral hotspot. There were massive implications for businesses, schools, daycare centers, hospitals, prisons, and houses of worship. How could you reopen the state in a way that kept people safe?

Early on, China introduced the Alipay Health Code, a QR code that residents were required to scan at city checkpoints. Integrated with Alipay, the popular mobile phone payment system, the app used statistical modeling of recent outbreaks to assign each citizen a color code, along with propaganda-style messaging: "Green, travel freely. Red or yellow, report immediately."[16]

However, this solution had problems: the artificial intelligence wasn't so intelligent, often flagging false positives for people who were healthy. More worrying was this personal data being shared with the Chinese government, which could further open the door for mass surveillance of Chinese citizens.

In the US, discussion around this kind of "immunity passport" was a nonstarter. America has a cultural distrust of government, dating back to its war of independence from British rule. Americans have a strong belief in liberty, usually interpreted to mean the freedom to do as they please.

In America, then, we had opposing forces. Citizens wanted to move about freely, without being tracked by the government—but they also wanted the government to look after their safety. Framed another way, the challenge was balancing privacy (no government snooping) with security (good government safety). See Figure 13-4.

---

16 Paul Mozur, Raymond Zhong, and Aaron Krolik, "In Coronavirus Fight, China Gives Citizens a Color Code, with Red Flags," *New York Times*, March 2, 2020, *https://www.nytimes.com/2020/03/01/business/china-coronavirus-surveillance.html*.

Figure 13-4. Balancing safety and privacy[17]

We saw blockchain as the solution to balance these two forces. A blockchain-based health tracker could function like China's QR code, ensuring that a citizen was healthy by querying an encrypted blockchain that would give an "all clear" while still protecting personal privacy.

We were inspired by Learning Machine's Blockcerts solution (see Chapter 12), where the certification (like a college degree) was issued by a trusted institution (like a university), then stored on a blockchain. Remember that the graduate's personal information was never shared: rather, it was a cryptographically signed hash of the credential that could be verified by, say, a potential employer.

This was a mouthful to explain to the government. So again we leaned on a few simple analogies to describe this concept:

TSA PreCheck

In the US, frequent travelers can sign up for TSA PreCheck, which gives you expedited screening at airport security by storing your credentials in a national database. We pointed out that TSA PreCheck is a huge violation of citizen privacy—the government literally *takes your fingerprints* when you apply—and blockchain could do it better.

17 John Hargrave, "Introducing FastYes: The Blockchain-Based Immunity Passport," Media Shower, May 19, 2020, *https://mediashower.com/blog/blockchain-immunity-passport.*

Disney FastPass+

At Disney theme parks, guests can sign up for FastPass+, which allows you to reserve specific times for rides and attractions. Like TSA PreCheck, it's optional, and it costs extra—but it cuts down on wait times, so you get more out of your day. Like TSA PreCheck, it also comes at the expense of privacy—but hey, Disney is already watching you.[18]

Immunization records

The US already requires immunizations to allow children to go to school.[19] We framed our blockchain idea as an opportunity to upgrade this largely paper-based system to the digital age, while also paving the way for the coronavirus vaccine.

Much of our work was pitching the idea whenever we could—on phone calls, during business meetings, in casual conversation—and then listening to how people responded. "Imagine a smartphone app, where you scan a QR code that shares your latest COVID-19 test results. If it's green, you're clean." (We never mentioned blockchain, just the user experience.)

As we heard feedback, we refined the pitch, compiling a list of frequently asked questions (Table 13-1).

Table 13-1. Common questions and answers

Question	Answer
How do I know the app is private?	Your personal info is never stored online. It's just a verification between you and your doctor.
How does it actually check my test results?	Your doctor or testing center gives you a certificate that you're healthy (like a key). You also have a copy of the certificate (a matching key). When they scan your QR code, it's checking that the two keys match.
Why should I have to use this app?	You don't. It's 100% opt-in.

---

18 Austin Carr, "Disneyland Makes Surveillance Palatable—and Profitable," *Bloomberg*, July 15, 2019, *https://www.bloomberg.com/news/articles/2019-07-15/disneyland-is-tracking-guests-and-generating-big-profits-doing-it-jy49hb9t*.

19 "Required Vaccines for Child Care and School," Centers for Disease Control and Prevention, May 17, 2019, *https://www.cdc.gov/vaccines/parents/records/schools.html*. Thanks to Mary Strain of Hyland Credentials, who opened our eyes to upgrading existing healthcare systems.

Question	Answer
Why do you think people will use the app?	Because they'll want to know that their coworkers, their kids' teachers, and other people at the gym are healthy.
What if businesses don't want to use the app?	They don't have to. It's a free country.
Why do you think governments will support this?	Because the economy will never completely recover until people feel safe to leave the house.

One big problem remained: the name. *Immunity passport* was terrible. It was misleading, because without a vaccine, the health tracker didn't guarantee immunity—just that you recently had a test. And *passport* had all the wrong connotations: border control, police, surveillance.

Building on America's love of speed and efficiency, we called this idea *FastYes*. Like Disney FastPass+, the benefit of the app was expedited access into areas where the virus could easily spread: schools, workplaces, shopping malls. Like TSA PreCheck, FastYes was 100% opt-in: if you wanted to go to a restaurant or health club without FastYes screening, you were free to take the gamble (so was the business). And like school immunization records, the app would eventually provide a digital record of who had the vaccine (Figure 13-5).

Figure 13-5. When explaining blockchain, hide the complexity

As the pandemic continued its relentless march forward, businesses began taking people's temperatures at the door using infrared thermometers—a crude health check that technically proved nothing, except that you were not yet feverish. We felt that a health-checking smartphone app was inevitable; we just wanted to see it designed in a way that protected citizen privacy.

Beyond the public health benefit, the app had a simple and powerful economic motivator: the economy couldn't recover until people felt safe to leave the house. Citizens had to feel safe to work, safe to shop, safe to spend. Only a trusted technology, backed by rigorous testing and vaccination, could provide that safety, that confidence.

And as citizen confidence returned, we predicted, so would consumer confidence. People would once again start making money and spending money; slowly the great wheels of the economy would begin to turn. When we developed and distributed the vaccine—when we could verify who had immunity—*then* confidence would be fully restored. Then the Great Recovery could begin.

SOLUTION 3: BLOCKCHAIN BONDS

It was common to hear people calling the coronavirus crisis an "unprecedented time," but we've had many historical precedents: most recently, the Flu Pandemic of 1918.

This pandemic came at an even worse time: on the heels of World War I. The US was mired in debt and needed to quickly raise money. Raising taxes was a tough sell for Americans, who were already worn down from the merciless grind of war, while even more frightened for their personal health; that particular strain of influenza was far deadlier and more terrifying than COVID-19.[20]

The government's solution was to create a new kind of bond—the so-called *Liberty Bond*—to help finance the war effort. Today, most people understand how bonds work: you loan money to an institution, they pay you back interest on a fixed timetable, then they pay back your loan at the end of the period. Back then, bonds were new and unusual, and the public had to be educated and convinced.

To help raise funds, the government launched an enormous PR campaign around Liberty Bonds. It was a multiyear, nationwide advertising blitz (or propaganda campaign, depending on your view) involving visual artists, journalists, and the biggest celebrities of the day. Americans were reminded, over and over again, that they *could* invest, and in fact they *should* invest, in Liberty Bonds, as their patriotic duty. See Figures 13-6 and 13-7.

---

20 Liz Mineo, "Harvard Expert Compares 1918 Flu, COVID-19," *Harvard Gazette*, May 20, 2020, *https:// news.harvard.edu/gazette/story/2020/05/harvard-expert-compares-1918-flu-covid-19.*

Figure 13-6. Some of the more family-friendly Liberty Bond posters[21]

Figure 13-7. Movie star Douglas Fairbanks headlines a Liberty Bond rally[22]

---

21 "Liberty Bond," Wikipedia, July 3, 2020, *https://en.wikipedia.org/wiki/Liberty_bond*.

22 "Liberty Bond," Wikipedia.

It worked. In four Liberty Bond offerings, issued between 1917 and 1918, the US government raised $16.7 billion, *from its citizens*. More important, it galvanized public support for the war. Now Americans had skin in the game. They pulled together for the Allied cause, because their own money was on the line.

This financial trick of issuing war bonds, wrapped in patriotic slogans, was used again and again by countries around the world, effectively financing both world wars. Eventually, government-backed bonds became a fact of life: they're no longer considered unusual, and are now considered to be one of the safest investments you can buy. War bonds introduced a new generation to a new way of investing.

The coronavirus crisis, then, was not "unprecedented times"; it was very much precedented. We began to think about how governments might raise money—particularly local governments, which were facing a looming economic crisis. In the US, most state government money comes from income tax and sales tax: since so many people weren't working and weren't spending, it created a negative feedback loop.

The problem was how states were going to raise money. Without the ability to generate new revenue, they would be waiting for handouts from the federal government, like everyone else. Fortunately, a framework was already in place, called the **municipal bond**.

Definition

Municipal bond: A government bond issued by a local authority (like a city or state). Like other bonds, investors loan money to local governments to spend on new projects (like a school or subway system), in return for a regular series of interest payments, with the full amount repaid at the end of the period.

The municipal bond issuing process, however, was bloated and complex, with a gang of advisers, attorneys, and underwriters who all took fees out of the offering. Then there was the problem of recordkeeping: keeping track of all the bondholders, which got more complicated once the bonds entered the secondary market (i.e., when original investors began reselling bonds to other investors).

Blockchain would simplify everything.

Here we had another precedent: two years earlier, the World Bank and the Commonwealth Bank of Australia, that country's largest bank, had jointly issued a public bond using blockchain technology.[23] Called *Bond-i*, short for *Blockchain Operated New Debt Instrument*, these were two-year bonds that raised A$100 million, priced with a 2.25% return.

A private blockchain consisting of two nodes at the World Bank and two nodes at Commonwealth Bank, Bond-i provided a real-time ledger that could be instantly accessed by investors, with all the related "paperwork" carried out by smart contracts.[24] In other words, it simplified bond issuance, a complicated and costly process, into something that happened online, instantaneously.

We had the surfboard, and we saw the wave coming. Just as Circle introduced a blockchain bank (see Chapter 5), we just had to introduce a *blockchain bond*. We started a massive PR effort, bringing Liberty Bond ad campaigns into the digital age (Figure 13-8).

Figure 13-8. Everything old is new again

As we began to hammer home this message across social media, newsletters, and blog posts, we saw an encouraging development from across the world:

23 Marie Huillet, "World Bank and Australia's Largest Bank Issue Bond Exclusively Through Blockchain," Cointelegraph, August 23, 2018, *https://cointelegraph.com/news/world-bank-and-australias-largest-bank-issue-bond-exclusively-through-blockchain.*

24 "Project Bond-i: Bonds on Blockchain," CommBank, accessed June 27, 2020, *https://www.commbank.com.au/business/business-insights/project-bondi.html.*

Thailand's Ministry of Finance announced plans to issue a blockchain bond offering worth 200 million baht (about $6 million).[25] The government pointed out that, in addition to blockchain's efficiency, blockchain allowed more citizens to participate: whereas most government bonds had a minimum buy-in of 1000 baht, blockchain bonds could be bought for as little as 1 baht (about 32 cents).

To get through the COVID crisis, we anticipated that tremendous funding would be needed. This was not a war effort—you couldn't fight germs with guns —but it would require wartime levels of financing. Blockchain bonds, we thought, would be a way to unify public support while raising public funds.

Next Steps

John, Eric, and Evan had made much progress in the spring of 2020, defining three blockchain solutions, identifying partners and developers who could help build prototypes, and developing education and awareness campaigns that were picking up steam on the internet.

The challenge was getting funding to prototype one or more of these projects. It was difficult to even get on the calendar of critical decision-makers, given the unpredictable nature of the virus and the constant demands on their time. When you're faced with a crisis that changes by the day, how do you think about next year?

If you were in the team's position, several months after the coronavirus outbreak, where would you focus your efforts next?

- *Developing a blockchain supply-chain solution.* What kind of supply chain would you focus on first?

- *Developing a blockchain health-tracking solution* (like FastYes). How would you get government buy-in, and where would you introduce it first?

- *Developing a blockchain fundraising solution* (like blockchain bonds). Who would you pull together to make this happen?

How would you work for the common good of the Commonwealth...and the world?

---

25 Jaspreet Kalra, "Thailand to Raise $6.4M with Sale of Blockchain-Based Bonds," CoinDesk, June 17, 2020, *https://www.coindesk.com/thailand-to-raise-6-4m-with-sale-of-blockchain-based-bonds.*

14

Lessons Learned: Blockchain Best Practices

What a journey we've taken together! You've learned practical, real-world insights into how successful blockchain projects are built. You've taken the difficult, messy paths of these early pioneers and distilled their valuable lessons into stories that will stick.

By reading (and rereading) these lessons, you'll save countless hours and millions of dollars in creating your own blockchain success story. Now, let's lock in that learning by summarizing the blockchain best practices seen throughout these success stories.

Blockchain Best Practice 1: Have a Great Origin Story

Draw inspiration from bitcoin and its mysterious founder Satoshi Nakamoto, who created a world-changing invention, accumulated a fortune, and then vanished without a trace. The human brain is hardwired for stories, so whether you are pitching a blockchain business or launching a new token, strive for a great origin story:

- Remember, for example, how Nimit Sawhney's childhood experience with voter coercion in India led him to start Voatz, the blockchain-based voting system.

- Or Helium, where Sean Fanning's background from Napster and Amir Haleem's background in gaming led them to ask, "What if we could get these network hotspots to mine bitcoin?"

- In CryptoKitties, that great quote from Mack Flavelle: "We're going to put cats on the blockchain. Why cats? The question you should be asking is, 'Why *not* cats?'"
- With the Binance Charity Foundation, recall Helen Hai's childhood trip to Beijing, which led to her vision of helping the "bottom billion."
- Nathan Kaiser, the self-described "lawyer geek," bought a bitcoin ATM, started solving crypto legal problems, and then ended up running the Cardano Foundation.
- With Learning Machine, remember MIT's dean of admissions falsifying her resume, which led to a partnership between MIT and Learning Machine to create blockchain-based credentials.
- At Circle, think back to Jeremy Allaire's three aha moments, in which open protocols led to three successful businesses: decentralized information, decentralized video, and decentralized money.
- The Chamber of Digital Commerce came about when Perianne Boring, a financial services reporter in the right place at the right time, saw that the US needed a trade association for the emerging blockchain industry.
- Everledger started when Leanne Kemp read the bitcoin whitepaper, and then saw an opportunity for using the technology to track and trace diamonds and other high-value items.
- In our concluding case study, as the authors finish up this book (this gets meta), the COVID-19 pandemic hits the world, calling them to rapidly figure out blockchain solutions.

Blockchain Best Practice 2: Open It Up

Be as decentralized, open source, and permissionless as possible. Remember our sweet spot diagram (Figure 3-2): your blockchain doesn't need to be 100% open source, but favoring open standards will make it easier to build your blockchain network, and thus create valuable network effects. For example:

- The Helium Hotspot, sensors, and software are all open source; Helium even calls it *The People's Network* to show it's owned by users, not owned by Helium.

- Remember how the developers of CryptoKitties invented the ERC-721 open source standard for non-fungible tokens, creating a new kind of asset (the *crypto collectible*) for anyone to use.

- At Learning Machine, not only was Blockcerts an open source project, but it was blockchain agnostic, meaning it worked with any blockchain.

- Circle spent years creating an open and decentralized financial system, using open protocols and the open source USDC.

- Meanwhile, the Chamber of Digital Commerce released the Legislator's Toolkit as an open source, non-copyrighted document that politicians could cut and paste to draft new laws.

Blockchain Best Practice 3: Collaboration, Communities, Consortia

Don't try to go it alone. It is better to have a seat at the big table than to sit at the kiddie table all by yourself. Take advantage of opportunities to pool resources and promote common goals, even with competitors. When you make the pie bigger, everyone gets a bigger slice of pie. For example:

- When CryptoKitties bogged down the Ethereum blockchain, the team collaborated with Ethereum, MetaMask, and Grid+ to quickly handle its system crash and save the kitties.

- To improve the lives of the bottom billion, the Binance Charity Foundation partnered with a host of institutions—from local charities to the United Nations.

- Circle formed the Centre Consortium with Coinbase—another industry leader and would-be competitor—to support the growth of the USDC stablecoin, aligning everyone's incentives.

- Cardano used its Cardano Ambassadors to collaborate with its community at scale, receiving input on future improvements without getting stuck in the weeds.

- The essence of the three Cs—collaboration, communities, consortia—is the Chamber of Digital Commerce, which brought together competitors to make decisions in the best interest of the industry.

- Finally, Everledger was part of the collaborative Hyperledger project, itself a consortium of competitors that collaborate.

Blockchain Best Practice 4: Stick to Your Vision

While everyone's journey takes twists and turns, remembering the original "seed of the idea" helped these founders keep focus:

- Voatz had a vision of secure voting from home on a mobile phone.
- Helium floated a wireless network for the low-cost, low-power Internet of Things.
- CryptoKitties created digital collectibles that users could buy, sell, and breed.
- The Binance Charity Foundation helped the world with a charity that accepts digital assets for donations.
- Learning Machine launched digital credentials, owned by the people who earned them.
- Circle built a bitcoin bank.
- Cardano Foundation developed a platform for developing blockchains, governed well.
- The Chamber of Digital Commerce lobbied for smart regulation around digital assets.
- Everledger launched a trusted ledger for diamonds and other high-value items.
- In our concluding case study, we presented blockchain as the antivirus for the citizens of Massachusetts.

Blockchain Best Practice 5: Work Within the System

Revolution, or evolution? The *revolutionary* approach of ignoring laws has resulted in legal crackdowns; the *evolutionary* approach of working within existing frameworks has generally had better success. When the frameworks are not built for blockchain, see if they can be upgraded, as in the following:

- Voatz worked out issues in small, low-stakes elections before making the jump to high-stakes federal elections.
- Remember how the Binance Charity Foundation worked closely with local relief agencies, to determine which solutions would maximize social impact (such as with the floods in Bududa).

- In one of the best examples of evolution over revolution, Circle went state to state to become the most licensed company in the industry, overcoming the industry's skepticism about bitcoin.

- The Chamber of Digital Commerce worked within the system to earn a seat at every table, including the three biggest tables: the Federal Reserve, the International Monetary Fund (IMF), and the World Bank.

- In our concluding case study, we worked alongside government agencies to build blockchain awareness and education, before building blockchain solutions.

Blockchain Best Practice 6: Hide the Complexity

Make products that people can actually use. Create fun and friendly interfaces, and then test them out on your grandmother. In order to gain mass adoption, adopt a mass mindset. For example:

- Voatz hired marketing and communications professionals to develop a beautiful mobile app that was user-friendly for voters of all ages.

- Helium's experienced product developers created seamless, user-friendly experiences for both setting up Hotspots and monitoring usage statistics.

- The cross-functional product team at CryptoKitties hid the complexity of blockchain technology behind adorable artwork in a game that was simple, intuitive, and fun.

- Remember how Learning Machine created a simple, user-friendly interface for both issuing and verifying credentials like a college degree.

- And through publications like "Chamber Reports" and "Legislator's Toolkit," the Chamber of Digital Commerce simplified the complexity around blockchain regulation.

Blockchain Best Practice 7: Eliminate Intermediaries

Buying direct has always been a way to save money; blockchain makes this possible in new ways, using smart contracts to streamline a whole swath of the supply chain. You've seen this throughout these stories:

- The Voatz solution, for example, provided a better paper trail for voting, since each vote comes with triple verification.

- At Helium, no central server is necessary to set up new Helium Hotspots, and as more Hotspots are added, the cost to use the network actually goes down.

- With the Binance Charity Foundation, donations go directly to recipients, and each transaction is viewable on the ledger.

- Circle eliminated the need for third-party compliance checks, or for banks to provide traditional custody services, by enabling customers to work directly with USDC.

- Everledger's one-time authentication verifies the quality of the diamond, eliminating the need for future appraisals.

Blockchain Best Practice 8: Automate Transactions

Smart contracts work best with routine transactions, where they can eliminate mountains of paperwork. Although smart contracts struggle with more complex transactions (they're not *that* smart), they'll get smarter in the future. We've covered many examples of these routine transactions:

- The process for the absentee vote on the Voatz mobile app is the same, regardless of who is voting or where the election is being held.

- Remember the Binance Charity Foundation's Pink Care Token, which lets all women access the same feminine products; these "crypto coupons" can't be bought, sold, or traded for anything else.

- With Learning Machine, graduates have to download their digital credential only once. They are then free to share their degree with anyone, anytime, thus eliminating the need for transcripts.

- Circle simplified financial transactions by using stablecoins, eliminating the need for currency conversion.

- FastYes, the health-checking app proposed in the concluding case study, makes routine and predictable calls to a blockchain to check whether citizens are healthy.

Blockchain Best Practice 9: Build for Scale

By understanding the chicken-or-egg problem of two-sided marketplaces, block-chain leaders can design tokenomics that quickly build up both the supply and demand side. This builds network effects, which can quickly go into hyper-growth. Keep only the bare minimum on blockchain; be ready to scale!

- Remember how Helium outsourced the infrastructure by paying users to manage their own Hotspots and open sourced the Hotspot design so other companies could build the hardware, allowing them to rapidly scale.

- Think back to how CryptoKitties added a simple button to its user interface as a quick fix, while moving nonessential transactions off the blockchain for long-term scalability.

- Learning Machine also made its product scalable by storing only the hash on the blockchain.

- Through the growth of its Ambassador Program, Cardano scaled commu-nity responsiveness. Remember that hub-and-spokes model of a central-ized team and the decentralized Ambassadors.

- Attracting enough members to fund a full-time staff enabled the Chamber of Digital Commerce to attract even more members, creating a virtuous circle of participation and support.

- Finally, the blockchain supply-chain solution proposed in the concluding case study allows scalable distribution of the coronavirus vaccine, instead of managing everything using Google Sheets.

Blockchain Best Practice 10: Educate, Educate, Educate

In the early days of any technology, the challenge is explaining *what it is* and *what it does*. Like the original internet, this new Internet of Value needs some explaining.

Show, don't tell. As we've done throughout this book, show working proto-types. Send digital assets. Slide them a little bitcoin. If a picture is worth a thou-sand words, a demo is worth a thousand pictures.

If you must tell, then *tell stories*. You'll remember these lessons because you'll remember these stories. You'll be better equipped to deal with problems, because you'll recognize the patterns: "That's just like the story of..."

Most of all, we hope you'll be inspired to start your own story. We want you to be a part of this great human story, this new Internet of Value. We want you to become one of the great heroes and luminaries that used this time and this technology to change the world.

It's time to start your story.

Teacher's Guide

When we do guest lectures on blockchain at schools and universities, professors often tell us the same thing: by the time they've developed a curriculum to teach a class about blockchain, the technology has totally changed. We designed *Blockchain Success Stories* to be enduring examples that you can teach using the case study method.

If you're new to case studies, we can do no better than pointing you to Harvard Business School's excellent website, "Teaching by the Case Method."[1] HBS case studies are the gold standard, and we worked hard to make the case studies in this book meet that level of rigor and quality, while adding our own special sauce.

Here are a few blockchain-specific tips that we've found helpful from observing other instructors teach about this technology:

Be a fellow learner
> The most successful blockchain professors are also blockchain students. Consider opening the session by asking a student to summarize the case in front of the class, while the instructor literally sits in a student's seat. Blockchain technology evolves so quickly that no one has all the answers. Approach it as a lifelong learner.

---

1 "Teaching by the Case Method," Christensen Center for Teaching & Learning, Harvard Business School, *www.hbs.edu/teaching/case-method*.

Prepare thoroughly

In addition to reading the case, study up on where the blockchain project is today, thinking deeply about larger principles from these stories that can be applied to other companies and blockchains. The chicken-or-egg problem from Helium (Chapter 4), for example, could be used to discuss any number of two-sided internet marketplaces.

Structure the discussion

Think in terms of discussion segments, perhaps five segments to a class, where you discuss pieces of the story. For example, the Binance Charity Foundation study (Chapter 8) might have segments around the following:

- The value of making charitable donations in cryptocurrency
- The concept of a crypto coupon
- The benefits and drawbacks of a transparent ledger
- The challenge of cryptocurrency price stability
- Where Binance Charity Foundation should go next

Allow for spontaneity

In the case study method, the teacher provides the framework, but the students drive the discussion. There are no wrong answers; students should come up with ideas from analysis as well as their own experience. Encourage dialogue and debate among different points of view. Plan, but don't overplan; adopt an attitude of "we're in this together."

The big reveal

Be sure to end the class with a "where are they now" moment, showing the blockchain project's current website or a promotional video. This can spark a final round of questions: do you agree with the direction they ultimately took the project? Why or why not?

We hope these stories engage and inspire your students to learn more about blockchain—and perhaps to create blockchain success stories of their own.

Acknowledgments

The authors wish to thank our terrific team at O'Reilly Media, including Amelia Blevins, Michelle Smith, Michele Cronin, Kristen Brown, Sharon Wilkey, Scarlett Lindsay, Ellen Troutman-Zaig, and Suzanne Huston. Thank you to our incredible bestselling audiobook producer Maywood!

Evan wishes to thank his family: Katie Karnoupakis, Milena de Avila, Cecilia Karnoupakis, and Andrew Karnoupakis, and his parents, John and Tommie Karnoupakis, for supporting the completion of our book during these challenging times.

John wishes to thank his family: Jade Hargrave, Isaac Hargrave, Luke Hargrave, and his parents, Pat and John Hargrave, for their endless support and good humor.

Thank you to our early readers: Scott Allen, Brian Ray, Michael Rinzler, Stephen Sautel, and Gregg Spiridellis.

From Helium, thank you to Amir Haleem and Dal Gemmell.

From Circle, thanks to Jared Favole, Josh Hawkins, and Jeremy Allaire.

From CryptoKitties, thanks to Mack Flavelle and Jordan Castro.

From Voatz, thank you to Nimit Sawhney and Hilary Braseth.

From Binance Charity Foundation, thank you to Helen Hai, Jill Ni, and Simone Wu.

From Cardano, thanks to Nathan Kaiser and Clara Jian.

From the Chamber of Digital Commerce, thanks to Perianne Boring, Patrick South, Jennifer Chontos, and Jackie Price.

From Everledger, thanks to Leanne Kemp, Patrick Degenhardt, and Natalie King.

From Learning Machine, thanks to Chris Jagers, Natalie Smolenski, and Mary Strain. Thanks also to Alexa Marinos from Hyland.

From our concluding case study, thanks to Jasmijn van der Horst-Rompa, Patrick Larkin, and Brian Noyes.

Thanks to our O'Reilly tech reviewers: Aaron Caswell, Karen Kilroy, and Jorge Lesmes.

If you enjoyed reading *Blockchain Success Stories*, you'll love our companion book, *Blockchain for Everyone*, available at *blockchainforeveryone.com*.

You can follow our latest adventures at our blockchain company, Media Shower: *www.mediashower.com*.

Index

About the Authors

Sir John Hargrave is the CEO of Media Shower (*http://www.mediashower.com*), the leading blockchain media company. His company publishes the blockchain investor website, Bitcoin Market Journal (*http://www.bitcoinmarketjournal.com*), which reaches 100,000 blockchain investors monthly. He holds an MBA from Babson College, and is the author of the bestselling *Blockchain for Everyone* (Simon & Schuster, 2019). Sir John is a high-energy speaker and leader of the blockchain revolution.

Evan Karnoupakis is a blockchain consultant who has authored works on blockchain industry disruption, the legality of smart contracts, crypto market making, blockchain governance, China's lead in blockchain, and the relationship between bitcoin and the blockchain industry. He holds an MAT in Integrated Mathematics from Kent State University, and an MBA in Strategic Management and Entrepreneurial Management from the Wharton School.

The two have coauthored two companion reports called *What Is Blockchain?* (*https://oreil.ly/HId4P*) and *State of Blockchain* (*https://oreil.ly/W-SZ5*).

Colophon

The image on the cover of *Blockchain Success Stories* is a photograph by Lori Eanes.

The cover fonts are Balboa and Bebas Neue Pro. The text font is Scala Pro and the heading font is Benton Sans.

Lightning Source UK Ltd.
Milton Keynes UK
UKHW022219211020
371991UK00008B/27